5·Minute
APOLOGETICS
for TODAY

Ron Rhodes

HARVEST HOUSE PUBLISHERS
EUGENE, OREGON

Cover by Dugan Design Group, Bloomington, Minnesota

5-MINUTE APOLOGETICS FOR TODAY
Copyright © 2010 by Ron Rhodes
Published by Harvest House Publishers
Eugene, Oregon 97408
www.harvesthousepublishers.com

Library of Congress Cataloging-in-Publication Data
Rhodes, Ron.
5-minute apologetics for today / Ron Rhodes.
  p. cm.
ISBN 978-0-7369-2457-3 (pbk.)
ISBN 978-0-7369-3758-0 (eBook)
1. Apologetics—Miscellanea. I. Title.
BT1103.R56 2010
239'.7—dc22

2009017210

Printed in the United States of America

21 22 23 24 / BP-SK / 10 9 8 7 6

To Kerri

ACKNOWLEDGMENTS

———

Kerri, David, and Kylie—
Words are inadequate to express my gratitude
for your enduring love and support.
I am truly blessed!

All my friends at Harvest House Publishers—
Thanks for your collective hard work.
You are *hugely* appreciated!
It is always a delight to partner with you.

Introduction

Would you like to gain more Christian wisdom, biblical discernment, and doctrinal expertise over the next year, all in just five minutes a day?

If so, then this book has been designed especially for you. You are my target audience. If you'll commit just five minutes a day—not just to read the brief material, but to ponder it, meditate on it, and perhaps look up some of the verses I cite—then over the next year, you will learn a lot. I can promise you that.

This does not mean you will learn virtually everything there is to know about the Bible or Christianity or doctrine or ethics over the next year. But it does mean that by the time the year is through, your Christian wisdom and biblical discernment skills will be significantly more than they are today! And you'll be better off for it.

If you feel you already have a good level of Christian wisdom and biblical discernment, then consider this book a review. Who among us couldn't use a little tune-up from time to time? You may even learn something new!

I have been motivated to write this book because of the strange times in which we are living. Our country has become a virtual cafeteria of different religions, cults, and non-Christian worldviews that are all vying for supremacy on America's religious landscape. Our country is also currently confronted by many tough domestic and global issues. We need Christian wisdom and biblical discernment as never before.

In this book, I devote a single page—one page for each of the 365 days of the year—to an issue that is related in some way to Christian apologetics, such as these:

truth (such as the distinction between absolute truth and relative truth)

hermeneutics (principles of Bible interpretation)

Christian doctrine (including such issues as the Trinity, the absolute deity of Christ, and the personality of the Holy Spirit)

Christian ethics (including such issues as abortion, suicide, capital punishment, homosexuality, different views on war, and divorce)

alleged Bible contradictions

difficult Bible verses

philosophies of Bible translation

archaeological discoveries that support the Bible

extrabiblical literature that supports the truth of Christianity

atheistic arguments

the problem of evil

creationism and evolution

cults and false religions

end-times prophecy

I even address some controversial issues, including whether life exists on other planets and whether Ezekiel saw a UFO. All in all, this book will expose you to a wide variety of topics and issues that will sharpen your apologetics acumen.

You will notice that in some cases, several consecutive days deal with loosely related topics. In other cases, a new day brings a completely new and unrelated topic. I hope this arrangement will help to keep things interesting!

May the Lord be pleased to use this book to strengthen your spiritual convictions. That is my hope and prayer!

Absolute Truth

As we begin our 365-day journey together, let's start with the recognition that absolute truth is real. In fact, Christianity rests on a foundation of absolute truth, and that foundation is as sturdy as a rock. (See 1 Kings 17:24; Psalm 25:5; John 8:44; 2 Corinthians 6:7; Ephesians 4:15; 2 Timothy 2:15; 1 John 3:19.)

Biblical Christians believe that moral absolutes—such as "You shall have no other gods before me" and "You shall not murder" (Exodus 20:3,13)—are grounded in the absolutely moral God of Scripture (Matthew 5:48). God stands against the moral relativist, whose behavior is based on whatever is right in his own eyes (Deuteronomy 12:8; Judges 17:6; 21:25). The absolutely moral Creator-God (Isaiah 44:24) has communicated precisely what moral behavior He expects of us (Exodus 20:1-17), so we, His creatures, are responsible to render obedience (Deuteronomy 11:13,27-28).

This is an important issue because moral relativism leaves no way to distinguish between truth and error, right and wrong. The road of moral relativity has no center stripe of absolute truth. Consequently, this highway is littered with casualties (see Proverbs 5:23).

Pearl of Wisdom: *You can be absolutely sure that absolute truth is real and that each of us will one day face the absolutely moral God of the universe to give an account for the way we responded to His absolute truth.*

Be Reasonable

God is a God of reason (Isaiah 1:18), and He has created us as rational creatures in His image (Genesis 1:27; Colossians 3:10), so surely He intends for us to utilize the gift of reason. God wants us to take an intelligent step of faith in the light of good evidence, not a blind leap of faith into the dark (see John 20:27).

The Bible is filled with exhortations to use reason. Jesus commanded His followers, "Love the Lord your God...with all your mind" (Matthew 22:37). The apostle Paul taught, "Whatever is true...think about these things" (Philippians 4:8), and he reasoned with Jews and philosophers (Acts 17:17,22-31). Church elders are instructed to refute those who contradict sound doctrine (Titus 1:9). Paul says he was appointed for "the defense of the gospel" (Philippians 1:16). Jude urged, "Contend for the faith that was once for all delivered to the saints" (Jude 3). Peter commanded us to be "prepared to make a defense to anyone who asks you for a reason for the hope that is in you" (1 Peter 3:15). All these activities involve the use of God-given reason.

Pearl of Wisdom: *We were designed by a reasoning God to be reasoning people. It is in our own best interests to use that reason to test the competing truth claims that daily confront us.*

Philosophy Can Be Helpful

Many Christians today seem to misunderstand the apostle Paul's warning in Colossians 2:8: "See to it that no one takes you captive by philosophy and empty deceit, according to human tradition." The truth is, the Bible—interpreted rightly—is no more against philosophy than it is against religion. The Bible is against *vain* philosophy. Likewise, the Bible is not opposed to religion per se, but only against *vain* religion (James 1:26-27).

In Colossians 2:8, Paul is not speaking about philosophy in general, but about a particular philosophy that was apparently influencing the church at Colossae, which is usually understood as an early form of Gnosticism. This is indicated by Paul's use of a definite article (in the original Greek), which should be translated "the philosophy" or "this philosophy." So Paul was referring to this particular Gnostic-like philosophy that had invaded the church in Colossae—a philosophy that involved legalism, mysticism, and asceticism (all of which are antithetical to Christianity)—and not to *all* philosophy. God places no premium on ignorance or shallow thinking (see Matthew 22:37; Acts 17:17,28,34; Philippians 1:16; Titus 1:12; 1 Peter 3:15). An awareness of the various philosophical disciplines can equip Christians to argue against anti-Christian philosophies (Acts 17:22-31) and use philosophical tools in proving the truth of Christianity. More on this tomorrow!

Pearl of Wisdom: *We shouldn't be reluctant to study philosophy, for it can help us refute error and defend the truth of Christianity.*

Reasonable Faith

Some philosophy can help establish the truth of Christianity. For example, here are some philosophical arguments for the existence of God:

The cosmological argument. Every effect must have an adequate cause. The universe is an effect. Reason demands that whatever caused the universe must be greater than the universe. That cause is God—who Himself is the uncaused First Cause (Hebrews 3:4).

The teleological argument. The universe displays an obvious purposeful design. This perfect design argues for a Designer, and that Designer is God (Psalm 19:1-4).

The moral argument. Every human being has an innate sense of "ought-ness," or moral obligation. Where did this sense of oughtness come from? It must come from God. The existence of a moral law in our hearts demands the existence of a moral Lawgiver (Romans 1:19-32).

The anthropological argument. Human beings have a personality (mind, emotions, and will). Since the personal cannot come from the impersonal, there must be a personal cause—and that personal cause is God (Genesis 1:26-27).

The ontological argument. Most human beings have an innate idea of a perfect being. Where did this idea come from? Not from man, for man is an imperfect being. Some perfect being must have planted the idea there. Thus God must in fact exist.

Pearl of Wisdom: *Some people claim believing in God is unreasonable, but the truth is that not believing in Him is actually unreasonable.*

Christians Can Be Deceived

Truth, reason, and clear thinking are important because Christians can be doctrinally deceived—that is, they can succumb to false doctrine. Ezekiel 34:1-7 clearly affirms that God's sheep can be abused and led astray by wicked shepherds. Moreover, Jesus warned His followers to beware of false prophets who may appear to be good on the outside but are dangerous on the inside (Matthew 7:15-16). Why would Jesus warn His followers to beware if they could not possibly be deceived?

Jesus also warned His followers, "Watch out that no one deceives you. For many will come in my name, claiming, 'I am the Christ,' and will deceive many...Many false prophets will appear and deceive many people" (Matthew 24:4,11). Why would Jesus warn His followers of such deception if they could not possibly be deceived and end up believing a lie?

Likewise, in 2 Corinthians 11:2-3, the apostle Paul warned the Christians in Corinth about the possibility of being led astray from a sincere and pure devotion to Christ. Paul clearly saw the possibility of Christians being deceived and led astray by false doctrine.

In Acts 20:28-30, Paul warned the Ephesian elders to keep a close watch on the congregation and especially to watch out for false teachers, who speak "twisted things, to draw away the disciples after them" (see Ephesians 4:14; 2 Timothy 4:3-4).

———

Pearl of Wisdom: *Christians who are ungrounded in biblical truth are especially vulnerable to succumbing to false doctrine. Christians therefore need to stay thoroughly—indeed, daily—grounded in the Scriptures.*

False Doctrine

T hose who doubt that Christ is set against false doctrine should peruse Revelation 2–3, where we read Christ's words to the seven churches of Asia Minor. In these chapters, Christ chastises those who tolerate false doctrine and commends those who take a stand against it.

For example, Christ commends the church at Ephesus because it has "tested those who call themselves apostles and are not, and found them to be false" (Revelation 2:2). He commends the church at Pergamum: "You hold fast My name, and did not deny My faith even in the days of Antipas, My witness...who was killed among you, where Satan dwells" (2:13 NASB). But He also chastens this church, saying, "I have a few things against you: you have some there who hold the teaching of Balaam," and "you have some who hold the teaching of the Nicolaitans" (2:14-15). He also chastened the church at Thyatira: "You tolerate that woman Jezebel, who calls herself a prophetess and is teaching and seducing my servants to practice sexual immorality" (2:20). Christ observes and evaluates our own stand against false doctrines in the church as well as our positive stand for the truth. Let us not be found wanting!

Pearl of Wisdom: *Our sternest attention ought to be on the Word of God: "Let the word of Christ dwell in you richly" (Colossians 3:16). Only the Word of God is a lamp to our feet and a light to our path (Psalm 119:105). Never cease defending the Word (Jude 3).*

All Religions Are Not the Same

S ome people claim that all religions are essentially the same and only superficially different. The truth is, all religions are essentially different and only superficially the same.

Some say all religions are similar because they all teach ethics. The truth is that the other world religions fundamentally seek to help bad people become better by choosing better personal ethics. Christianity, on the other hand, invites spiritually dead people to become spiritually alive (John 3:5).

This is accomplished solely through Jesus' sacrificial death (2 Corinthians 5:21). Jesus claimed that what He said took precedence over all other people's teaching. He said He is humanity's only means of salvation (John 14:6). Those who followed Him confirmed this (Acts 4:12; 1 Timothy 2:5). Jesus also warned about those who would try to set forth a different Christ (Matthew 24:4-5).

The various religions also teach different views of God. Jesus taught about a triune God (Matthew 28:19). Muhammad (the founder of Islam) taught that the one God is *not* a Trinity. Hinduism refers to many gods that are extensions of the one impersonal Brahman. Buddhism teaches that the concept of God is essentially irrelevant. Obviously, these religions are not pointing to the same God. If one is right, the others are wrong. If Jesus was right (as Christians believe), the others are wrong.

Pearl of Wisdom: *A person's commitment to the idea that all religions are essentially the same is based on his or her ignorance of those religions.*

Faulty Doctrine Can Hurt

People can twist Scripture and cause their own destruction (see 2 Peter 3:16). We see multiple modern examples of this.

The Watchtower Society has long prohibited blood transfusions—even when doctors say death is inevitable without one. Jehovah's Witnesses fallaciously believe that the scriptural prohibition against the pagan practice of eating blood applies to transfusions (Leviticus 7:26-27; 17:11-12). For this reason, many Jehovah's Witnesses carry a signed card stating that they are not to receive blood transfusions if they are found unconscious. Many—including children and even babies—have died in this cult as a result.

Here's another example. Larry Parker—under the influence of a teacher who took Scripture verses on faith out of context—stopped giving his diabetic son insulin, and the boy died. In remorse, Parker later wrote the heartbreaking book *We Let Our Son Die*.

The Jong Mal Ron ("end-time theory") movement flourished in Korea in the 1990s. Based on misinterpretations of 1 Thessalonians 4:13-17 and other verses, followers set a specific date for the rapture. They also believed that if a person was too heavy, he or she would not be caught up in the rapture. A number of pregnant women in the group got abortions.

Pearl of Wisdom: *Bad hermeneutics can lead to human suffering. We need to imitate the Bereans by carefully and thoroughly testing all truth claims against the Scriptures (Acts 17:11).*

Marginalizing God's Word

Some church services feature multisensory worship—using skits, story-telling, and various forms of media—but Jesus emphasized the Word of God in making disciples: "If you abide in my word, you are truly my disciples" (John 8:31). Some church leaders say we can no longer look to the Bible alone as a guide for spiritual living, but Scripture says church leaders are to preach God's Word "for building up the body of Christ" (Ephesians 4:12). Some church leaders say we should merely "love" people into the church, but biblical Christians are called to always be "prepared to make a defense to anyone who asks you for a reason for the hope that is in you" (1 Peter 3:15).

Paul sternly instructed Timothy, a young pastor, "Keep a close watch on yourself and on the teaching. Persist in this, for by so doing you will save both yourself and your hearers" (1 Timothy 4:16). He also affirmed to Timothy, "From childhood you have been acquainted with the sacred writings, which are able to make you wise for salvation through faith in Christ Jesus. All Scripture is breathed out by God and profitable for teaching, for reproof, for correction, and for training in righteousness, that the man of God may be competent, equipped for every good work" (2 Timothy 3:15-17).

Pearl of Wisdom: *A Christianity without the Bible is much like a doctor who misdiagnoses a patient and then prescribes the wrong treatment. The patient doesn't get well, and he has a false sense of security, blindly trusting that what he has been told is the truth.*

Contend for the Faith

Every Christian should follow Jude's example and "contend for the faith that was once for all delivered to the saints" (Jude 3). The definite article (*the*) preceding *faith* in this verse points to the one and only faith; there is no other faith. "The faith" refers to the apostolic body of truth God gave the church through divine revelation (see Galatians 1:23; 1 Timothy 4:1).

The Greek word translated *once for all* (*apax*) in this verse refers to something that has been done for all time, something that never needs repeating. The revelatory process was over and done with after this faith had been once for all delivered.

The word translated *delivered* in this verse is what Greek grammarians call an aorist passive participle, indicating an act that was completed in the past with no continuing element. It leaves no room for a new faith or body of truth communicated through psychics or channelers or cultists!

How can you and I contend for Christian truth? The word translated *contend* (Greek: *agonia*) was often used in New Testament times to refer to competition in athletic contests. The English word *agony* comes from the noun form. The idea behind the word is of an intense and vigorous struggle to defeat the opposition. Believers are to engage in an intense and vigorous struggle in defending Christianity.

Pearl of Wisdom: *As "athletes" for God, let's train and become equipped in God's Word (2 Timothy 3:17), always being ready with an answer (1 Peter 3:15; see also Acts 17:2,17; 18:4,19).*

Non-Rock-a-Boatus

M any Christians today seem to be secret-agent Christians who are afraid of blowing their cover before an unregenerate world. Such Christians apparently have a hideous disease called non-rock-a-boatus. This disease has so effectively neutralized Christians that the cancer of false religion has spread at an incredible, unprecedented pace in this country.

Many Christians are so fearful of rocking the boat that they clam up and keep their Christianity to themselves. They think that if they speak out for Christ and for Christian values in this predominantly anti-Christian culture, they may offend someone or perhaps be ridiculed and embarrassed.

If this disease continues unchecked, we can count on the continued spiritual deterioration of our country. If Christians do not act, the followers of false religions will. The war is on—and we Christians will be soldiers in the midst of the conflict or casualties left behind.

The task cannot be left in the hands of the professional clergy. The challenge is too massive for church leaders alone. The involvement of every Christian is necessary if the growth of false ideas in this country is to be turned back (1 Peter 3:15; Jude 3). The task begins with a single person—*you*. If you really want to see things get better in our country, why not take the first step—*you*, without waiting for others to act—and commit to being an agent of change (see Matthew 28:19; Acts 1:8)?

Pearl of Wisdom: *The entire ocean is affected by a single pebble.*

Flex Some Apologetic Muscle

The word *apologetics* comes from the Greek work *apologia* (defense). Apologetics—which focuses on the defense of Christianity—is seemingly a lost art in the modern church. Today the prevailing emphasis seems to be something like this: "God is a God of love. Let's just love everyone. We shouldn't challenge other people's beliefs because that is unloving." Contrary to such misguided notions, Jesus—love incarnate—constantly challenged (sometimes forcefully) the beliefs of those He encountered (see Matthew 23). We must follow His example.

Scripture provides us with role models in apologetics. Paul, for example, acted as an apologist when he gave reasons for the faith to both the Jews and Gentiles (Acts 17:15-34; 18:4). Apollos is another great example, for in Achaia he earnestly contended for the faith, refuting unbelievers in public debate and proving from the Scriptures that Jesus truly is the Christ (Acts 18:24-28).

Apologetics provides well-reasoned evidences that empower nonbelievers to choose Christianity rather than any other religion. Apologetics can be used to show the unbeliever that all the other options in the smorgasbord of world religions are not really options at all because they are false. Apologetics can remove mental roadblocks that prevent nonbelievers from responding to the gospel.

Apologetics not only provides a defense for the faith but also provides security to Christians. Believers can be sure their faith is not a blind leap into a dark chasm, but rather an intelligent decision founded on fact. Apologetics does not replace our faith; it grounds our faith.

Pearl of Wisdom: *Apologetics demonstrates why we believe what we believe.*

Salt and Light

Y ou are the salt of the earth, but if salt has lost its taste, how shall its saltiness be restored? It is no longer good for anything except to be thrown out and trampled under people's feet" (Matthew 5:13). Salt is known for its preservative effect. Christians are to have that effect on the world by influencing the world for Christ.

To accomplish this, however, Christians must first make sure they are fully committed to the Savior and preserved in personal purity and righteousness. Only then can they act as preservatives in society. Christians must be cautious, ever guarding against becoming tainted. The danger is that instead of raising the morality of the world, the world may lower the morality of the Christian (Romans 12:2). Beware of compromise (1 Thessalonians 2:3-4)!

"You are the light of the world. A city set on a hill cannot be hidden" (Matthew 5:14). Jesus did not call us to be secret-agent Christians. Spiritual darkness is hovering over Western culture as never before, so each individual Christian's light is needed now more than ever. We can let our light shine at church, at home, in our own neighborhoods, at the workplace, and at social events, reflecting Christ in our actions and speech.

———

Pearl of Wisdom: *Diamonds sparkle best against a black velvet cloth. Let's resolve to shine brightly in our dark world.*

Living Ethically

S alvation is by faith in Christ alone (Acts 16:31) with no works in view (Romans 3:28), but God desires the believer to live a life of high ethics and good behavior. As Christians depend on the Holy Spirit, they are empowered to live the kind of lives that are pleasing to God (Galatians 5:16-24).

Scripture admonishes us, "Keep your conduct among the Gentiles honorable, so that when they speak against you as evildoers, they may see your good deeds and glorify God on the day of visitation" (1 Peter 2:12). Our walk is to be blameless (Psalm 15:2), and our obedience to God should be obvious to all (Romans 16:19).

We are to be "without blemish in the midst of a crooked and twisted generation," in which we "shine as lights in the world" (Philippians 2:15). We are to "renounce ungodliness and worldly passions, and to live self-controlled, upright, and godly lives in the present age" (Titus 2:11-12).

God calls us to rid ourselves of such things as "anger, wrath, malice, slander, and obscene talk" (Colossians 3:8), as well as "deceit and hypocrisy and envy" (1 Peter 2:1). And we must keep a clear conscience (1 Peter 3:16), ever remembering that just as God is holy, so we are called to be holy in all we do (1 Peter 1:15). We are to take on the family likeness (that is, God's family)!

Pearl of Wisdom: *Ethical living can be contagious. Your example can motivate change in others.*

A Desire for More

Being wealthy is not a sin! Some very godly people in the Bible—Abraham and Job, for example—were quite wealthy. But God does condemn a love of possessions or riches (Luke 16:13; 1 Timothy 6:10; Hebrews 13:5). A love of material things is a sure sign that a person is living according to a temporal perspective, not an eternal one.

Paul stated that "those who desire to be rich fall into temptation, into a snare, into many senseless and harmful desires that plunge people into ruin and destruction" (1 Timothy 6:9). Jesus warned His followers, "Take care, and be on your guard against all covetousness, for one's life does not consist in the abundance of his possessions" (Luke 12:15). He then urged His followers to have an eternal perspective: "Do not lay up for yourselves treasures on earth, where moth and rust destroy and where thieves break in and steal, but lay up for yourselves treasures in heaven, where neither moth nor rust destroys and where thieves do not break in and steal" (Matthew 6:19-20).

Whether we are rich or poor, we are stewards of what God has provided us. We should mirror Paul, who said, "I know how to be brought low, and I know how to abound. In any and every circumstance, I have learned the secret of facing plenty and hunger, abundance and need. I can do all things through him who strengthens me" (Philippians 4:12-13).

Pearl of Wisdom: *How you handle your wallet says a lot about the state of your heart.*

Charity

In Old Testament times, the Mosaic law encouraged charity among people. Leviticus 25:35 offers this instruction: "If your brother becomes poor and cannot maintain himself with you, you shall support him as though he were a stranger and a sojourner, and he shall live with you." Old Testament law also stipulated that farmers should not harvest the corners of their fields so that poor people who walked by could pick some food to eat (Leviticus 19:9-10).

The New Testament is replete with admonitions to freely give to others. Hebrews 13:16 instructs us to do good and share with others. We are admonished to give to the poor (Matthew 19:21; Luke 11:41; 12:33; 1 John 3:17) and to those who ask (Matthew 5:42). We are called to share food with the hungry (Isaiah 58:7,10), to share money generously (Romans 12:8), and to use money for good (1 Timothy 6:17-18). The early church certainly showed charity as an evidence of Christian love (Acts 9:36; 10:2,4; Romans 12:13; Ephesians 4:28; 1 Timothy 6:18; Hebrews 13:16; 1 John 3:17-19). Jesus advises us to give to others secretly, not openly to win the praise of men (Matthew 6:1-2).

The New Testament often describes such generous activities as *almsgiving*. The word *alms* derives from the Greek word *eleos* (mercy). *Almsgiving* thus means "mercy-giving." We are called to show mercy and kindness to others whenever the opportunity arises.

Pearl of Wisdom: *Our attitude toward God shows itself in the charity we show to others.*

Permissible but Not Necessarily Beneficial

Drunkenness, of course, is forbidden by God. It is simply not an option for the Christian. In Ephesians 5:18, the apostle Paul explicitly instructed, "Do not get drunk with wine, for that is debauchery, but be filled with the Spirit."

Drinking wine in moderation, however, is permissible (see John 2:9; 1 Timothy 3:3,8). I should note, though, that in biblical times wine was typically diluted by a ratio of 20 parts water to one part wine—essentially wine-flavored water. Sometimes in the ancient world, hosts would go as strong as one part water and one part wine, and this was considered strong wine. Anyone who drank wine unmixed was looked upon by the Greeks as a Scythian, a barbarian.

We must all ask ourselves, though drinking may be permissible, is it beneficial? The following verses speak to this issue:

- "'All things are lawful for me,' but not all things are helpful. 'All things are lawful for me,' but I will not be enslaved by anything" (1 Corinthians 6:12).

- "It is good not to eat meat or drink wine or do anything that causes your brother to stumble" (Romans 14:21).

- "Whether you eat or drink, or whatever you do, do all to the glory of God" (1 Corinthians 10:31).

Pearl of Wisdom: *Being other-centered instead of self-centered brings a smile to the face of God.*

Lying

Some critics allege that God condoned lying in Old Testament times. This is a false accusation.

Scripture forbids lying (Exodus 20:16; Leviticus 19:11), passing along false reports (Exodus 23:1), and testifying falsely (Exodus 20:16; Deuteronomy 5:20). We are assured that liars will not go unpunished (Proverbs 19:9; 21:28). Lying is viewed as a sin (Psalm 59:12) and is considered an abomination to God (Proverbs 12:22), for God abhors falsehood (Psalm 119:163). Scripture also affirms what, to many, is obvious: "God is not man, that he should lie" (Numbers 23:19).

But some people point to 2 Chronicles 18:20-21, where we are told that God permitted the activity of a "lying spirit." Of course, what God *causes* and what He *allows* are two different things. God allowed Adam and Eve's sin in the Garden of Eden, but He did not cause it. God allowed Lucifer's rebellion against Him, but He did not cause it. God allowed Ananias and Sapphira to lie to Peter, but He did not cause them to do so.

Likewise, 2 Chronicles 18:20-21 reveals that God permitted the activity of a lying spirit, but He did not cause the spirit to engage in this activity. As boggling as it is to the human mind, God is able to bring good even out of the freewill, evil acts of others (Romans 8:28).

Pearl of Wisdom: *The triune God is full of truth—the Father (Psalm 31:5), the Son (John 14:16), and the Holy Spirit (John 14:17).*

Oaths

An oath is a solemn promise. Oaths were taken quite seriously in biblical times (Exodus 20:7; Leviticus 19:12), for lying about an oath could result in death (Ezekiel 17:16-18).

Oaths are sprinkled throughout both the Old Testament (Leviticus 5:1; 19:12; Numbers 30:2-15; Deuteronomy 23:21-23; Exodus 20:7) and New Testament (Acts 2:30; Hebrews 6:16-18; 7:20-22). Paul once said, "I call God to witness..." (2 Corinthians 1:23). So we see a biblical precedent for taking oaths.

Some dispute this, citing Jesus' words in Matthew 5:33-37 and particularly His main point: "Let what you say be simply 'Yes' or 'No.'" However, Jesus was dealing with Pharisees. The Pharisees used oaths to affirm that they were telling the truth, and the oath included a self-invoked curse if the word was not true or the promise was not fulfilled. Eventually, people assumed someone was not telling the truth unless an oath was attached to the statement.

Jesus was against this use of oaths. In Matthew 5:33-37, He was telling His followers that their character, their reputation for honesty, and the words they speak should be so consistently true and without duplicity that no one would ever think it necessary to make them swear an oath, for no one would suspect them of deception.

———

Pearl of Wisdom: *Your reputation as an honest person will be a key component in all your future successes in life.*

Civil Disobedience

This issue calls for caution and balance. The Bible encourages us to obey the government unless the government requires us to disobey God's laws. Let's look at a few details.

Paul commanded believers to be submissive to the government because authority is ordained of God (Romans 13:1-7). Paul said resistance to government is resistance against God (verse 2). Government, Paul indicated, resists evil (verse 4). Even after the Roman government imprisoned him several times, Paul taught believers to obey the government.

Despite this, Scripture also indicates that when the government commands believers to go against God's commands, they must obey God rather than the government. After being commanded by the Sanhedrin not to preach any further, "Peter and the apostles answered, 'We must obey God rather than men'" (Acts 5:29).

This is also illustrated in the book of Daniel. Shadrach, Meshach, and Abednego righteously disobeyed the king when they were commanded to worship the golden image (Daniel 3). Daniel also righteously disobeyed the government when it commanded him to stop praying to God (Daniel 6). In both cases, God confirmed that they had made the right choice by delivering them from their punishment.

Pearl of Wisdom: *Always obey God. No exceptions. Always obey government. One exception—when obeying government causes you to disobey God.*

Capital Punishment

In Genesis 9:6, capital punishment is instituted in view of the sanctity of human life. The basis for this severe punishment is the fact that human beings are created in the image of God (Genesis 1:26). The idea in Genesis 9:6 seems to be that human beings are so valuable as individuals that anyone who tampers with their sacred right to live must face the consequences of losing his or her own life. Moreover, murdering a human being is an outrage against the sovereign God who created humanity.

The death penalty was incorporated into the Mosaic code (Exodus 21:12; Numbers 35:16-31). As well, in Romans 13:1-7 the apostle Paul taught that human government has a God-given right to use force in its resistance of evil. Romans 13:4 specifically indicates that the government has the right to take the life of a criminal. Second Peter 2:13 indicates that the government is authorized to punish those who do evil, and capital punishment is evidently one of the means of accomplishing this. This threat of capital punishment constitutes a deterrent to crime.

The Ten Commandments include a prohibition against murder (Exodus 20:13). However, murder by a citizen and execution by a government are two different things in Scripture. One is a premeditated crime; the other is a deserved punishment.

Pearl of Wisdom: *Government is set up by God (Romans 13:1-7), so capital punishment is the enacting of divine judgment through the instrumentality of government.*

Suicide

Issues of life and death lie in the sovereign hands of God alone. Job acknowledged to God, "[man's] days are determined, and the number of his months is with you, and you have appointed his limits that he cannot pass" (Job 14:5). David likewise acknowledged to God, "All the days ordained for me were written in your book before one of them came to be" (Psalm 139:16 NIV).

Suicide certainly violates God's commandments. The sixth commandment instructs, "You shall not murder" (Exodus 20:13). This command is based on the fact that human beings were created in the image of God (Genesis 1:26). Moreover, the command itself has no direct object. It doesn't say, "You shall not murder someone else." It simply says, "You shall not murder." The prohibition thus includes not only murdering someone else but also murdering oneself.

The lives of certain biblical saints are instructive on the issue of suicide. Paul, for example, went through extremely tough times: "We do not want you to be ignorant, brothers, of the affliction we experienced in Asia. For we were so utterly burdened beyond our strength that we despaired of life itself" (2 Corinthians 1:8; see also 1 Kings 19:4). Nevertheless, Paul did not succumb to breaking God's commandment against murder and commit suicide. He depended on God, and God came through and sustained him. We must follow Paul's example.

Pearl of Wisdom: *You have probably heard people say that God helps those who help themselves. The truth is, God helps the helpless. Trust Him when life throws you a punch.*

Divorce

D ivorce is a very difficult issue. Scripture is clear that God Himself created the institution of marriage, and He intended it to be permanent (Genesis 2:18-25; Matthew 19:4-6). Divorce was never a part of God's original plan. In fact, God hates divorce (Malachi 2:16). The marriage relationship was intended to be dissolved only when one of the marriage partners died (Romans 7:1-4; 1 Corinthians 7:8-9; 1 Timothy 5:14).

When sin entered the world, it affected God's ideal in marriage and many other things. Scripture tells us that even though divorce was not God's ideal, He nevertheless allowed it because of man's sinfulness (Deuteronomy 24:1-4; Matthew 19:7-8).

From a biblical perspective, divorce is allowable only under two circumstances: when one of the marriage partners is unfaithful (Matthew 19:9), and when the unbelieving partner deserts the believing partner (1 Corinthians 7:15-16). Divorce for any other reason is a violation of God's ideal.

Even in cases in which a person has biblical grounds for divorce, God's desire is that the innocent person, if at all possible, forgive the offending spouse and be reconciled to him or her. This follows from God's command to forgive others of their wrongs toward us (Ephesians 4:32; Colossians 3:13).

Pearl of Wisdom: *God forgives us of all our sins—including the sin of divorce (Colossians 2:13). However, we may still experience the painful consequences of our actions. Violating God's ideal brings a heavy price.*

Slavery

Some critics claim that Paul seemed to favor slavery when he sent a runaway slave, Onesimus, back to his owner (Philemon 16). Such is not the case.

From the very beginning, God declared that all humans are created in His image (Genesis 1:27). Paul reaffirmed this, declaring that all humans are God's offspring (Acts 17:29) and that God "made from one man every nation of mankind" (Acts 17:26).

Moreover, even though the Semitic cultures of the day practiced slavery, the Mosaic law demanded that slaves eventually be set free (Exodus 21:2). Likewise, servants had to be treated with respect (Exodus 21:20,26).

Paul declared that in Christianity "there is neither slave nor free...for you are all one in Christ Jesus" (Galatians 3:28). All social classes are broken down in Christ; we are all equal before God.

When Paul urged slaves to obey their earthly masters (Ephesians 6:5), he was not approving of slavery; he was simply alluding to the situation of his day. In doing so, he was not commending slavery. Paul also instructed believers to be obedient to de facto oppressive governments for the Lord's sake (1 Peter 2:13). But this doesn't condone oppression and tyranny, which the Bible condemns (Exodus 2:23-25).

A closer look at Philemon reveals that Paul did not perpetuate slavery. In reality, he undermined it, for he urged Philemon—Onesimus's owner—to treat him as "a beloved brother" (verse 16).

Pearl of Wisdom: *The more we focus on God, the less we see ourselves as superior to others.*

An Activist View of War

Activism is the view that Christians should participate in all wars in obedience to their government. This is based on the belief that all government is ordained by God. "Let every person be subject to the governing authorities. For there is no authority except from God, and those that exist have been instituted by God" (Romans 13:1; see also Titus 3:1; 1 Peter 2:13-14).

In view of such verses, activists see a connection between obedience to government and obedience to God. Whoever resists government is resisting God. As a duty to God, Christians are duty bound to obey their government. If a government issues the command to go to war, Christians must obey the government as an expression of obedience to God.

Other Christians cite problems with activism: (1) This view does not adequately deal with Scripture verses that call for peace and nonresistance (such as Matthew 5:38-48), and (2) this view does not account for the fact that a government might engage in an unjust war.

Christian activists say that even if one's country is in the wrong in a war, a citizen should nevertheless obey the government in going to war, for the evil of war is lesser than the evil of anarchy or revolution. Maintaining order by obeying a misguided government is better than participating in societal disorder.

Pearl of Wisdom: *On volatile issues where Christians do not see eye to eye (such as war), we can agree to disagree in an agreeable way.*

A Pacifist View of War

Some Christians espouse pacifism—the idea that it is always wrong to injure or kill other humans regardless of the circumstances. This view is usually based on the exemplary life and teachings of Jesus.

Jesus set forth a biblical mandate to turn the other cheek when encountering evil and violence (Matthew 5:38-42). He instructed, "Do not resist the one who is evil" (Matthew 5:39). He urged, "Love your enemies" (Luke 6:35). He said the kingdom was not to be advanced by physical force (John 18:36).

One of the Ten Commandments instructs, "You shall not murder" (Exodus 20:13). Proponents of this view believe that war is mass murder. Murder is prohibited because human beings are created in God's image (Genesis 1:26-27). Vengeance belongs to God (Deuteronomy 32:35), so Christians should never retaliate (Romans 12:19-21).

We are instructed to not be overcome by evil but rather overcome evil by good (Romans 12:19-21). Paul urged, "If possible, so far as it depends on you, live peaceably with all" (Romans 12:18).

Other Christians criticize pacifism as not reflecting the whole of Scripture. For example, the New Testament commends Old Testament warriors for their military acts of faith (Hebrews 11:30-40). None of the New Testament saints—not even Jesus—ever instructed a military convert to resign from his commission. Jesus instructed the disciples to sell their outer garments in order to purchase a sword for self-defense (Luke 22:36-38).

Pearl of Wisdom: *A Christian can respect another Christian's view even if he or she strongly disagrees with it.*

A Selectivist View of War

Selectivism is the view that Christians should participate in just wars but not unjust wars. Paul urged Christians to be at peace with all men if possible (Romans 12:18), but such peace is not always possible, especially in circumstances where an evil bully—or evil nation, like Nazi Germany—attacks others. Paul said Christians are not to be overcome by evil but are to overcome evil with good (Romans 12:19-21). Sometimes overcoming evil with good necessitates good people justly using force against terrorists.

Selectivists emphasize that nonresistance is not the essential point of Christ's teaching in Matthew 5:38-42 to "turn the other cheek." Jesus was saying only that Christians should not retaliate when insulted (Romans 12:17-21).

Selectivists do not always equate killing with murder (Exodus 20:13). When God instituted human government during Noah's time, He delegated authority to the government to take human life—capital punishment (Genesis 9:6). This was not considered murder. Paul mentions capital punishment in Romans 13.

The selectivist acknowledges cases in which a war sponsored by his government may be unjust. In this situation, the selectivist declines participation. Scripture teaches that obedience to the government is not always appropriate—especially when the government issues a command that violates a higher command from God (Exodus 1:17-21; Daniel 3:6; Acts 4:5). The selectivist thus feels justified in declining participating in a war if it is unjust in the light of Scripture.

Pearl of Wisdom: *God must forever remain the highest authority in the life of a Christian.*

Just War

War is justifiable only under certain circumstances. Seven principles have been suggested to guide our thinking. Augustine of Hippo (AD 354–430) enunciated many of these early in the fifth century.

- *Just cause.* Defensive wars are just; unprovoked aggression and attempts to plunder are not.

- *Just intention.* Revenge, conquest, economic gain, or mere ideological supremacy do not justify war. Just wars protect or rescue people from a hostile attack.

- *Last resort.* War is an alternative only after all nonviolent methods of solving disputes have been exhausted.

- *Formal declaration of war by a nation.* Terrorists, militias, and mercenaries cannot declare war.

- *Limited objectives.* The goal of a just war is never the complete destruction of the opposing nation. Hostilities must cease as soon as the objectives have been reached.

- *Proportionate means.* Only the level of force necessary to secure victory over opposing combatants should be utilized. Annihilation is out of the question.

- *Safety of noncombatants.* Every effort must be made to protect civilians.

Pearl of Wisdom: *Just-war principles help minimize the death and devastation of war.*

Self-Defense

S elf-defense may result in one of the greatest examples of human love. Jesus said, "Greater love has no one than this, that someone lays down his life for his friends" (John 15:13). When protecting one's family or neighbor, a Christian is unselfishly risking life for the sake of others.

To *not* engage in self-defense (or defense of others) is morally wrong. To allow murder to take place when one could have prevented it is immoral. To permit a young girl to be raped when one could have hindered it is an evil. To watch a child be treated with cruelty without intervening is morally reprehensible. Not resisting evil is an evil of omission (see James 4:17).

The basis for self-defense is similar to just-war theory and selectivism. To not respond to a bully nation seeking to destroy or injure a less powerful nation or group of people is to fail morally. This principle is illustrated in Abraham's battle against the kings of Genesis 14, in which Abraham sought to rescue Lot from these unjust aggressors. (For another example, see 1 Samuel 23:1-5.)

When Paul's life was in great danger of being unjustly taken, he engaged in self-defense by appealing to his Roman citizenship. He appealed to the military might and protection of the Roman army (Acts 22:25-29). Nothing in the text indicates that Paul thought anything was wrong with such military defense.

Pearl of Wisdom: *The Bible defends the concept of self-defense.*

Laziness

The Bible has much to say about work versus laziness. Solomon, the wisest man who ever lived, points out in Proverbs that the lazy person's home and lawn are practically in ruins because he never works and sleeps most of the time (Proverbs 24:30-34). Lazy hands truly make a man poor (10:4), so he ends up with nothing (20:4).

Such a person has a tough life and suffers the consequences of his laziness (15:19). Yet he continually makes excuses to get out of work instead of working to make a better life (22:13; 26:13). He also acts like a know-it-all, not listening to the wisdom of others (26:16). This kind of person is a continual pain to employers (10:26). He is always chasing fantasies instead of doing real work (28:19). He may say he intends to do a good job, but mere talk leads only to poverty (14:23).

Solomon thus warns against loving sleep too much—it will inevitably lead to poverty (Proverbs 20:13). Drowsiness clothes a person in rags (23:21). A wise person works whenever work needs to be done (10:5).

Solomon recommends that we learn a lesson from the ant: "Go to the ant, you sluggard; consider its ways and be wise! It has no commander, no overseer or ruler, yet it stores its provisions in summer and gathers its food at harvest. How long will you lie there, you sluggard? When will you get up from your sleep?" (6:6-9 NIV).

—————

Pearl of Wisdom: *Work hard, doing all things as if you were working for the Lord (Colossians 3:23).*

Human Life Begins at Conception

Scripture asserts that everything God has created reproduces after its own kind (Genesis 1:21,24). This means that following the moment of human conception, what is in the womb is truly human (see Psalm 139:13-15; Jeremiah 1:5; Exodus 21:22-24).

Some babies are born months before their due date, and even though they may need medical life support to survive, they are obviously human beings. Some babies born as early as the fourth month have survived! Does a simple change in location—from inside the womb to outside it—render the baby a human being? Such an idea is absurd.

Abortionists sometimes rebut that abortion is certainly acceptable if the child will have birth defects. However, this is not the issue. If the unborn fetus is a human being, no one has the right to take its life, regardless of whether it has birth defects.

Consider a child who is already born and has birth defects. Should we execute this child simply because of a missing limb? Of course not! If the unborn baby is a human person, then to kill the unborn baby is really no different from killing a young child.

Pearl of Wisdom: *Human life is precious because humans are created in the image of God (Genesis 1:26).*

Abortion

A baby in the womb is not part of the mother's body. The baby's body belongs to the baby while it is in the mother's womb (see Psalm 139:13-15). The mother's body sustains the baby's body with nutrients and a protective environment, but the two bodies are nevertheless distinct. An abortion is not only an operation on the mother's body but also the killing of another human being whose body is within her body.

Abortionists sometimes rebut that the unborn baby is not conscious, and therefore abortion is acceptable. However, brain-wave activity has been detected one and a half months following conception. Moreover, the very argument of consciousness is flawed. Killing a sleeping or comatose person is wrong; killing a baby in the womb is no different.

What about cases of rape? Of course, rape is a terrible indignity, but two wrongs never make a right. Christian ethicists agree that the sin of a mother murdering an unborn baby is ultimately greater than the sin of the rapist violating a woman. Having an abortion in this situation amounts to punishing an innocent party. The rapist deserves punishment, not the unborn child.

Pearl of Wisdom: *We must ever be on guard against the human mind's capability of rationalization.*

Fornication and Adultery

Scripture has a lot to say about human sexuality.

A sexual relationship is appropriate only within the confines of marriage (between a man and woman) (1 Corinthians 7:2). Sex within marriage is good (Genesis 2:24; Matthew 19:5; 1 Corinthians 6:16; Ephesians 5:31). Sex was a part of God's good creation. Indeed, God created sex, and everything created by God is good (1 Timothy 4:4). But again, sex is good only within the confines of marriage (see Hebrews 13:4).

Sexual intercourse actually fulfills one of God's first commands to Adam and Eve: "Be fruitful and multiply and fill the earth" (Genesis 1:28). Sex is so important in the marriage relationship, the apostle Paul said, that husbands and wives should always be available to each other (1 Corinthians 7:1-5).

The apostles urged all Christians to abstain from fornication (Acts 15:20). Paul said that the body is not for fornication and that a man should flee it (1 Corinthians 6:13,18). We must not forget that the body is the temple of the Holy Spirit (1 Corinthians 6:19). Paul told the Ephesians that no one should have any reason to talk about fornication among them (Ephesians 5:3).

Adultery is condemned in Scripture (Exodus 20:14). In the Old Testament, adulterers were to be put to death (Leviticus 20:10). Jesus broadened adultery to include improper thoughts (Matthew 5:27-28). Paul called adultery an evil work of the flesh (Galatians 5:19). John envisioned those who practiced adultery suffering in the lake of fire (Revelation 21:8).

Pearl of Wisdom: *Blessed are the pure in heart!*

Polygamy

Just about every month I receive e-mails from people who argue that polygamy is okay for today and that Scripture allows it. Amazingly, polygamy is still alive and well in America—particularly in Utah. But monogamy is God's standard for the human race.

- God set the pattern of a monogamous marriage with one man and one woman (Genesis 1:27; 2:21-25).

- Monogamy was the general practice of the human race (Genesis 4:1) until it was interrupted by sin (Genesis 4:23).

- The law of Moses clearly commands people not to multiply wives (Deuteronomy 17:17).

- Our Lord affirmed that God created one "male and [one] female" and joined them in marriage (Matthew 19:4).

- The New Testament stresses, "Each man should have his own wife, and each woman her own husband" (1 Corinthians 7:2). Paul insisted that a church leader should be "the husband of one wife" (1 Timothy 3:2,12).

- Monogamous marriage prefigures Christ's relationship with His bride, the church (Ephesians 5:31-32).

- God never instituted polygamy for any people under any circumstances.

Pearl of Wisdom: *God's original creation—including one woman for one man—was "very good" (Genesis 1:31).*

Homosexuality

When Paul said homosexuals will not inherit God's kingdom, he was not simply stating his private opinion (1 Corinthians 7:25). All of Paul's writings are divinely authoritative (Galatians 1:12; 2 Corinthians 2:13; 12:12). Moreover, his primary condemnation of homosexuality is in Romans 1:26-27, and the divine authority of this passage is undisputed.

The Levitical law against homosexuality (Leviticus 18:22) has *not* been abolished (Acts 10:15) along with the Levitical law against eating pork and shrimp (Leviticus 11:2-3,10). God's law against homosexuality is a part of His moral law, not ceremonial law, and God's moral law is still binding (see Romans 1:26-27; 1 Corinthians 6:9).

If God's law against homosexuality was merely ceremonial (and thus abolished in New Testament times), we would have to conclude that rape, incest, and bestiality are not morally wrong either, because they are condemned together with homosexual sins (Leviticus 18:6-14,22-23).

Homosexual acts connected with idolatry are condemned (1 Kings 14:24), but Scripture also condemns homosexuality apart from idolatry (Leviticus 18:22). Moreover, homosexuality is condemned alongside other forms of sexual sin, such as adultery and incest. Are we to conclude that adultery and incest are wrong only when associated with idolatry, and that all other forms of these practices are okay? Such reasoning is warped.

———

Pearl of Wisdom: *Only by twisting Scripture can a person allege that the Bible sanctions homosexuality.*

Liberation from Homosexuality

Paul speaks of complete liberation from homosexual sin in 1 Corinthians 6:9-11: "Neither the sexually immoral...nor men who practice homosexuality...will inherit the kingdom of God. And such were some of you. But you were washed, you were sanctified, you were justified in the name of the Lord Jesus Christ and by the Spirit of our God."

Liberation requires an unwavering commitment, knowing that complete wholeness may require several years of hard work (see Luke 14:28). A key component of liberation is a commitment to complete obedience to God.

The heart of liberation is stated in 2 Corinthians 5:17: "If anyone is in Christ, he is a new creation. The old has passed away; behold, the new has come!"

Personal counseling plays a key role. The goal is to discover gender-identity disorders in early childhood, difficulties in relating to parents as a child, and other such issues.

Repentant homosexuals need the support of a good Bible-believing church. A small group that can provide encouragement and accountability is especially beneficial (James 5:16).

Temptations will still come. However, "God is faithful, and he will not let you be tempted beyond your ability, but with the temptation he will also provide the way of escape, that you may be able to endure it" (1 Corinthians 10:13).

To help minimize temptations, one should get rid of all homosexual literature, pornography, and vestiges of one's former lifestyle.

Pearl of Wisdom: *With God all things are possible!*

Skepticism

The word *skepticism* comes from the Latin word *scepticus* (inquiring, reflective, doubting). This Latin word, in turn, comes from the Greek word *scepsis* (inquiry, hesitation, doubt). Regarding the question of God's existence, skeptics are tentative in their beliefs, neither denying nor affirming God's existence. They are hesitant, doubtful, and unsure whether God exists. And if He does, skeptics are unsure whether people can know Him.

An obvious philosophical problem with this viewpoint is that skeptics are not skeptical that their skepticism is correct. They are not doubtful that their worldview of doubt is accurate. In fact, skeptics seem certain that their viewpoint of uncertainty is true. They don't hesitate to affirm that their worldview of hesitation is correct.

I love to ask skeptics questions like these: How do you explain the incredible evidence for intelligent design in our universe? What do you make of the 25,000 archaeological discoveries—many by non-Christian archaeologists—that confirm people, places, and events in the Bible? How to you explain the direct fulfillment of hundreds of Old Testament messianic prophecies in the person of Jesus Christ? Why do you suppose the New Testament writers were willing to suffer and die in defense of what they believed?

Pearl of Wisdom: *Without a doubt, the worldview of doubt philosophically collapses.*

Agnosticism

The word *agnosticism* comes from two Greek words: *a* (no, without) and *gnosis* (knowledge). Agnosticism literally means "no knowledge" or "without knowledge." Regarding the question of God's existence, agnostics claim they are unsure—having no knowledge—about the existence of God. Questions about God are allegedly inherently impossible to prove or disprove.

We see two forms of agnosticism. Soft agnosticism, or weak agnosticism, says a person does not know if God exists. Hard agnosticism, or strong agnosticism, says a person cannot know if God exists.

Logically, agnosticism is a self-defeating belief system. To say "one cannot know about reality" is a statement that presumes knowledge about reality. The statement is therefore self-falsifying. In other words, the statement amounts to saying, "We know enough about reality to affirm that we cannot know anything about reality." Ultimately, one must possess knowledge of reality in order to deny knowledge of reality. Put another way, to say that we cannot know anything about God is, in fact, to say something about God. Agnosticism is thus not a logically satisfying position to take.

Pearl of Wisdom: *Logic has a thorny way of poking holes in false worldviews.*

Denying God's Existence Is Not Logical

Atheists often categorically state that God does not exist. This assertion is logically indefensible. Only someone who is capable of being in all places at the same time—with a perfect knowledge of all that is in the universe—can make such a statement based on the facts. One would have to search every portion of the universe thoroughly and simultaneously—in essence, having infinite knowledge of the universe—in order to make this assertion based on the facts.

This view amounts to saying, "I have infinite knowledge that no being exists with infinite knowledge." To put it another way, a person would have to be God in order to say God cannot exist.

Some atheists have realized they cannot prove God does not exist from their own pool of knowledge, and they refrain from arguing against the existence of God. Instead, they affirm, "I lack a belief in God." They turn the tables and hold that Christians must prove that God does exist, rather than accepting the burden of proof that He does not exist. Of course, the fatal flaw with this line of argumentation is that once you say "I lack a belief in God," you have in fact affirmed a religious belief and are therefore now required to prove it.

———

Pearl of Wisdom: *My friend Norman Geisler says, "I don't have enough faith to be an atheist."*

Miracles

God has provided overt proof of His existence, especially in historical seasons when miracles were clustered—during the times of Moses, Elijah and Elisha, Daniel, and Jesus and the apostles. All such miraculous events were reliably recorded in Scripture for the benefit of future generations (1 Corinthians 10:11).

Interestingly, however, in each of these seasons, some people still refused to turn to God. For example, during the wilderness wanderings, many Israelites who had witnessed God's mighty miracles in Egypt nonetheless rebelled against God. Jesus' ministry was filled with miracles, yet many still refused to turn to Him for salvation. This indicates that some people will not turn to God even if God's miraculous evidence punches them in the nose. Such is the hardness of some people's hearts.

I believe God has a reason for not continually knocking us on the head with miracles. God, in His sovereign plan, has chosen to work through human intermediaries. God's prophets shared the good news about God to people in Old Testament times (Exodus 4:22) just as God's apostles did in New Testament times (Acts 4:33). All Christians since New Testament times are commissioned by Christ as His representatives to share the good news with people around the world (Matthew 28:19; Acts 1:8).

Pearl of Wisdom: *God has chosen to work through people in making Himself known to people. That is His chosen modus operandi.*

Empirical Observation

E mpirical observation is essential for scientific endeavors. Science would be impossible without it. Empirical observation, however, is not the all-determining factor as to what is real and what is not real.

Philosophers have pointed out that plenty of things in the world are real—things that are rational to accept—but cannot be scientifically proven. For example, love, beauty, and loyalty are intangible but real traits.

Consequently, atheists ought to consider the possibility that they have a limited worldview—a worldview that excludes God—precisely because they utilize a limited, insufficient methodology that requires empirical evidence for belief. Wrong methodology will always yield wrong conclusions.

Pearl of Wisdom: *The fatal flaw in the statement, "I only believe in what can be observed empirically," is that it cannot itself be derived from empirical observation.*

A Cause and a Beginning

Something does not come from nothing. Scientists and philosophers have long agreed that "from nothing, nothing comes." To conclude otherwise is to violate one of the foundational principles of the scientific enterprise: causality. To claim that the universe is uncaused is ultimately absurd.

To claim that the universe is *self*-caused would likewise be absurd. The big problem is that if the universe created itself, it would have had to exist and not exist at the same time.

Let's look at it philosophically. An eternal universe would include an infinite series of causes and effects that would never lead to a first cause or starting point. This is known as an infinite regress, which is philosophically impossible. One cannot assert that this finite thing caused this finite thing, and another finite thing caused the first one, and on and on into eternity past, because this merely puts off the explanation indefinitely. Regardless of how many finite causes are in the past, eventually one of them would have to both cause its own existence and be an effect of that cause at the same moment. This is absurd!

If the universe is not uncaused, if it is not self-caused, if it is not eternal, the atheist is in a real dilemma to explain where the universe came from. Atheism cannot explain why there is something rather than nothing.

Pearl of Wisdom: *Out of nothing, nothing comes. But something exists. Where did it come from?*

Christian Atrocities

A brief historical survey leads to the sad but true observation that Christians have been guilty of committing some atrocities. The proper response is not to deny this but to confess it. What occurred during the Crusades and Inquisition, in particular, went against the "love your enemy" philosophy of the one whom Christians claim to serve—Jesus Christ.

This violence in church history, however, must be considered in the light of other factors. For one thing, these isolated occurrences of violence are not a pattern of church history. They were the exception and not the rule. Much of church history has been characterized by God-honoring love, benevolence, compassion, and generosity.

Further, in the interest of fairness, not all who call themselves Christian are Christian (Matthew 7:22-23). Some are authentic Christians; others are cultural Christians. In like manner, we must distinguish between the true church (composed of only true believers) and institutional churches (including state churches). Lumping these together is neither fair nor accurate.

Despite this distinction, assuming that even some authentic Christians are guilty of atrocities, this illustrates a primary plank of Christianity—that all human beings are deeply engulfed in sin (Romans 3:23). When people become Christians, they are forgiven, but they still retain the sin nature and will continue to commit sinful acts (Romans 7:18).

Pearl of Wisdom: *God never intended that the truth of Christianity be measured by Christians' behavior. One is better served in examining the identity, life, and teachings of Christianity's founder: Jesus Christ.*

Extermination

G od commanded His people, the Israelites, to exterminate "whole peoples"—the Canaanites in particular. God issued this command not because He is cruel and vindictive, but because the Canaanites were so horribly evil, oppressive, and cancerous to society that—as with a human cancer—the only option was complete removal. To not "excise" the gangrenous Canaanites would amount to dooming Israel and all the righteous of the earth to suffer a slow death (see Deuteronomy 20:16-18). The Canaanites regularly burned their children in worship of false gods, engaged in sex with animals, and practiced all kinds of loathsome vices (see Leviticus 18:21,23-24; 20:3).

The Canaanites had had plenty of time to repent. The biblical pattern—indeed, God's promise—is that when nations repent, God withholds judgment (see Jeremiah 18:7-8). This principle is clearly illustrated for us in the case of Nineveh (Jonah 3).

The Canaanites were not acting blindly. They had heard of the God of the Israelites and knew what was expected of them, but they defied Him and continued in their sinful ways. They were ripe for judgment. God, as the absolutely sovereign Ruler over affairs of life and death, maintains the right to take life when circumstances call for it.

Pearl of Wisdom: *God is absolutely loving (Psalm 33:5; 86:5; Jeremiah 31:3; 1 John 4:8) but has no choice but to respond in wrath (Revelation 20:11-15) when people callously violate His holiness (Leviticus 11:4; Psalm 99:9; Isaiah 6:3).*

Hypocrisy

Regrettably, Christians are sometimes hypocritical. However, a Christian's success or failure to live up to Christ's ethical principles is not the decisive factor in evaluating whether Christianity is true. The more important issue is whether the historical, factual, and theological claims of Christianity are true. Important questions include these: Does historical evidence suggest that the Bible is, in fact, the trustworthy Word of God? Does evidence suggest that Jesus was a historical person? That He was God in human flesh? That He was crucified and resurrected from the dead? The answers to questions like these ought to guide our evaluation of Christianity.

The fact that some Christians are hypocritical is actually a proof of one of the primary doctrinal planks of Christianity: All human beings are fallen in sin (Isaiah 53:6; Romans 3:23; 5:12). When people become Christians, their sin nature does not vanish. They become redeemed, but they are still sinners (Romans 7:18).

Thankfully, many Christians in the world are not hypocritical and are strong witnesses for the truth of Christianity. Again, however, the more important point is whether the historical, factual, and theological claims of Christianity are true. I believe the evidence presented in this book establishes that Christianity is indeed true.

Pearl of Wisdom: *C.S. Lewis commented that Christians are at once the best argument* for *and the best argument* against *Christianity.*

Jesus Is the Messiah

In the first century, many Jews expected that when the Messiah came, He would deliver them from Roman domination (see John 6:15). The people were expecting a political Messiah-Deliverer. Circulating too soon the news that Jesus was the Messiah would have excited people's preconceived ideas about what He was supposed to do.

Seeking to avoid an erroneous popular response to His words and deeds, Jesus—especially early in His ministry—was cautious about revealing too much about Himself. As time passed, however, Christ's identity became increasingly clear to those who encountered Him (see, for example, Matthew 16:16; John 1:41).

Jesus had another reason to be cautious about revealing His identity too quickly. By the time He came on the scene, the doctrine of the Trinity had only been glimpsed in Old Testament times (for example, Isaiah 48:16). For Jesus to come right out and say, "I am the divine Messiah" would have caused incredible confusion, for people would not have understood His claim to be the second person of the Trinity. So Jesus slowly revealed all He needed to about Himself and His relationship with the Father and the Holy Spirit. To do otherwise would have caused a huge distraction for people and thus would have been counterproductive to His ministry.

Pearl of Wisdom: *Jesus always kept His audience in mind when communicating truth to them.*

Jesus and Pagan Myths

Some critics claim the virgin birth is rooted in pagan mythology. However, Greek mythology taught that male gods came down to have sex with human women, who gave birth to hybrid beings. This bears no resemblance to the virgin birth. When the Holy Spirit overshadowed Mary (Luke 1:35), He produced a human nature within her womb for the eternal Son of God to step into, after which He was born nine months later.

Many alleged similarities between Christianity and the Greek pagan religions are either greatly exaggerated or fabricated. For example, some critics often describe pagan rituals in language they borrowed from Christianity, thereby making them falsely appear to be parallel doctrines.

Furthermore, the chronology for such claims is all wrong. To uncritically assume that the pagan religions always influenced Christianity is to forget that the influence often probably moved in the opposite direction. Leaders of pagan cults that were challenged by Christianity would logically seek to counter the challenge by offering a pagan substitute.

Unlike mythical accounts, the New Testament accounts are based on eyewitness testimony. In 2 Peter 1:16 we read, "We did not follow cleverly devised myths when we made known to you the power and coming of our Lord Jesus Christ, but we were eyewitnesses of his majesty."

Pearl of Wisdom: *The New Testament eyewitnesses gave up their lives defending what they knew to be the truth about Jesus Christ. No one makes the ultimate sacrifice in defense of a myth.*

Jesus and Simple Legends

The claims about Jesus in the New Testament could not be legends. Only a very brief time elapsed between Jesus' miraculous public ministry and the publication of the Gospels—not enough time for the development of miracle legends. Countless eyewitnesses to Jesus' miracles were still alive when the Gospels were written, and those witnesses could have refuted any untrue miracle accounts (see 1 Corinthians 15:6).

Also, consider the noble character of the men who witnessed these miracles—Peter, James, and John, for example. Such men were not prone to misrepresentation, having been schooled from early childhood in the Ten Commandments—including God's commandment against bearing false witness (Exodus 20:16). These men were willing to be tortured and give up their lives rather than deny what they knew to be true about Jesus.

Jesus' enemies also witnessed His miracles. When Jesus raised Lazarus from the dead, for example, none of the chief priests or Pharisees disputed the miracle. They gathered at a council and asked, "What are we to do? For this man performs many signs" (John 11:45-48). Clearly, if these individuals could have disputed Jesus' miracles or signs, they would have. Scripture reveals that their primary goal was simply to stop Jesus (verses 47-48). These hostile witnesses who observed and scrutinized Christ would have prevented the Gospel writers from fabricating the miracle stories.

———

Pearl of Wisdom: *Nothing dispels the legend myth like reliable eyewitness testimony!*

Is Fulfilled Prophecy a Hoax?

This allegation does not fit the facts. First, the biblical writers were God-fearing Jews who demonstrated the highest moral character, each having been raised to obey the Ten Commandments—including the commandment against bearing false witness (Exodus 20:16). To say these men sought to fool people into believing Jesus was the Messiah when He really was not breaches credulity. To argue that these men chose to give up their lives in defense of a lie is ridiculous.

Jesus fulfilled many prophecies that the biblical writers could not have manipulated, such as His birthplace in Bethlehem (Micah 5:2), His descent from David (2 Samuel 7:12-16) and Abraham (Genesis 12:2), His virgin birth (Isaiah 7:14), the identity of His forerunner, John the Baptist (Malachi 3:1), the Sanhedrin's gift of 30 pieces of silver to Judas (Zechariah 11:12), the soldiers gambling for His clothing (Psalm 22:18), and His legs remaining unbroken (Psalm 22:17).

Finally, the biblical writers would not be likely to steal the body to give the appearance of a prophecy-fulfilling resurrection (Psalm 16:10; 22:22). The tomb was sealed with a stone that weighed tons, it had a seal of the Roman government, and it was guarded by Roman guards. To say Jesus' small band of Jewish followers overcame these guards, moved the stone, and stole the body is impossibly naive.

Pearl of Wisdom: *The odds of one person fulfilling the hundreds of Old Testament messianic prophecies are astronomical.*

Theological Bias

Some people imagine that when people give an account of something they passionately believe in, they will always distort history. This is simply not true. Some of the most reliable reports of the Holocaust were written by Jews who were passionately committed to making sure such genocide never happens again.

If the Gospel writers fabricated stories because of their theological motives, why would they have included embarrassing details about themselves? Peter denies Christ, the disciples scatter like cowards at Jesus' arrest, Thomas doubts Jesus' resurrection, and on and on. Surely if the biblical documents were influenced by biases, the writers would have removed such unflattering elements.

The truth is that the biblical writers were historically accurate. Consider Luke as an example. Modern archaeologists who have studied the Gospel of Luke have concluded that he was extremely accurate in his writings and wrote in an erudite and eloquent way with excellent Greek. At the very outset of his Gospel, Luke is careful to emphasize that he based his account on reliable, firsthand sources (Luke 1:1-4). He wanted to present the truth about Jesus in an ordered and accurate way. Top-rate scholars have studied Luke and have concluded that he was an amazingly accurate historian.

Pearl of Wisdom: *Only people who are biased against Christianity try to claim that the Gospel writers were biased.*

The Problem of Evil

The problem of evil is a conflict of three realities: God's power, God's goodness, and the presence of evil in the world. Common sense seems to tell us that all three cannot be true at the same time. Solutions to the problem typically involve modifying one or more of these three concepts: limit God's power, limit God's goodness, or call evil an illusion. (Some people deny God's existence. More on this later.)

If God made no claims to being good, the existence of evil would be easier to explain. But God does claim to be good (1 Chronicles 16:34; Psalm 118:29). If God were limited in power and too weak to withstand evil, the existence of evil would be easier to explain. But God does claim to be all-powerful (Psalm 147:5; 2 Chronicles 20:6; Ephesians 1:19-20). If evil were just an illusion, the problem would not exist in the first place. But evil is not an illusion, and we have plenty of evidence for its reality.

Today we face the reality of moral evil committed by free moral agents (war, crime, cruelty, class struggles, discrimination, slavery, and so on) and of natural evil (hurricanes, floods, earthquakes, and the like).

God is good, God is all-powerful, and yet evil exists. This is the problem of evil in its most basic form.

Pearl of Wisdom: *Never assume that the unexplained is unexplainable. (We'll gain some keen biblical insights on this issue over the next few days.)*

God Does Not Create Moral Evil

Some people suggest that the Bible itself indicates that God creates evil or is involved in evil in some way. For example, they cite Isaiah 45:7: "I form light and create darkness, I make well-being and create calamity, I am the Lord, who does all these things." Exodus 4:21 says that God hardened Pharaoh's heart. Let's consider these verses.

Isaiah 45:7. Hebrew linguists tell us that the word for *calamity* need not have any moral connotations at all. This word would be perfectly fitting for the plagues that God inflicted on the Egyptians through Moses. God, the Judge of the earth, can righteously inflict such plagues on sinful human beings.

Exodus 4:21. Exodus contains ten references to Pharaoh hardening his own heart (Exodus 7:13,14,22; 8:15,19,32; 9:7,34-35; 13:15) and ten references to God hardening Pharaoh's heart (4:21; 7:3; 9:12; 10:1,20,27; 11:10; 14:4,8,17). Pharaoh hardened his own heart seven times before God first hardened it, though the prediction that God would do it preceded all. The whole of Scripture seems to indicate that God hardens for the same reason He shows mercy. If men will accept mercy, He will give it to them. If they will not, thus hardening themselves, He is only just and righteous in judging them. Mercy is the effect of a right attitude; hardening is the effect of stubbornness or a wrong attitude toward God.

———

Pearl of Wisdom: *God's actions are always in perfect harmony with His holy, righteous, and just nature.*

Evil and Free Will

The original creation was "very good" (Genesis 1:31). It included no sin, no evil, and no death. Yet today, the world is permeated with sin, evil, and death. Scripture indicates that the turn downward came the moment Adam and Eve used their God-given free wills and volitionally chose to disobey God (3:1-7).

Some people wonder why God could not have created man in such a way that he would never sin, thus avoiding evil altogether. But this would mean that man could not make choices and freely love. God would have created robots that acted only in programmed ways—like a chatty doll that says "I love you" when you pull a string on its back. But true love cannot be programmed.

God's plan had the potential for evil when He gave man the freedom of choice, but evil originated on the earth when man directed his will away from God and toward his own selfish desires. Ever since Adam and Eve made evil actual, a sin nature has been passed on to every man and woman (Romans 5:12), and that sin nature causes us to misuse our free wills (Mark 7:20-23).

Even natural evils—earthquakes, tornados, floods, and the like—are rooted in man's wrong use of free choice. Earth suffered no natural disasters or death until Adam and Eve sinned (Genesis 1–3; Romans 8:20-22).

Pearl of Wisdom: *Choosing wrongly always has consequences.*

Evil and Intelligent Design

An intelligent design of the universe does not preclude the existence of evil. Evil is a corruption of something good that already exists. For example, tooth decay is the corruption of a good tooth. Blindness is the corruption of a good eye. Deafness is the corruption of a good ear.

God's original creation was "very good" (Genesis 1:31). Today, however, we see sin, evil, pain, and death. This good earth became corrupted the moment Adam and Eve used their God-given free wills to choose to disobey Him (Genesis 3). At that moment, an environment that was once painless and deathless became painful and deadly. God's good earth became a place of evil, pain, and suffering.

Look at it this way: If a person purchases a gadget, it generally works so long as it is operated according to the instructions. If a person ignores the instructions, the gadget will likely not function as it was designed to. Adam and Eve ignored God's instructions. Not surprisingly, things no longer operate in our world as they were designed to. Things are running down and dying.

Today we rest our faith on these truths: God is all-good, so He plans to defeat evil. God is all-powerful, so He is able to defeat evil. This has not happened yet, but God can and will one day defeat evil (Revelation 21:1-4).

Pearl of Wisdom: *We've not yet arrived at the last chapter in God's redemptive story. Stay tuned for a rousing finale, in which God defeats all evil.*

Evil and an All-Powerful God

S ome churchgoers claim that the existence of evil in our world proves that God is not all-powerful. They agree that He may be completely good, but they allege that He is not powerful enough to bring about His good desires.

But Scripture reveals that God *is* all-powerful. Scripture declares 56 times that God is almighty (for example, Revelation 19:6). God is abundant in strength (Psalm 147:5) and has incomparably great power (2 Chronicles 20:6; Ephesians 1:19-21). Nothing is too difficult for Him (Genesis 18:14; Jeremiah 32:17,27).

Christian philosophers suggest that this may not be the best possible world as it now exists, but it is the best way *to* the best possible world. In other words, when it's all over, a body of Christians who have freely chosen to follow Christ for all eternity will be in heaven.

Christian theologians and philosophers emphasize that God's timing is not human timing. The fact that God has not defeated evil today does not mean He is not eliminating it in the future (see 2 Peter 3:7-12; Revelation 21–22). Let's not be shortsighted and conclude that because something evil has happened today, God therefore must be limited in power. God may have reasons we know nothing about for allowing something evil to happen today, and He will surely use it to bring about some greater good in the future.

Pearl of Wisdom: *When we get to heaven, we will likely say, "Ah, I get it now," and we will understand why God allowed certain things to happen.*

Good out of Evil

God has the unique, sovereign ability to bring good out of evil. This is illustrated in the life of Joseph, whose own brothers sold him into slavery (Genesis 38–39). This situation was painful at the time, but God used it to bring Joseph to Egypt, where He elevated Joseph to a position of great authority (Genesis 41).

Of course, during the time of suffering itself, Joseph had no idea what God's intentions were. He did not know that God was using these dire circumstances—spread out over several years—to bring him to a position of prominence. That is why trusting God regardless of the circumstances is so important. God truly did bring about a greater good through the pain Joseph suffered. Joseph summarized the matter when he later told his brothers, "You meant evil against me, but God meant it for good" (Genesis 50:20).

We also see this in the life of Paul, who trusted God as few others have. Paul was thrown into prison repeatedly during his ministry (see Acts 16:23-37; Ephesians 3:1; Philippians 1:7; Colossians 4:10; Philemon 9). This was certainly painful at the time, but we know that Paul wrote Ephesians, Philippians, Colossians, and Philemon (four very important New Testament books) while he was in prison. God brought about a greater good through Paul's suffering.

Pearl of Wisdom: *"We know that for those who love God all things work together for good" (Romans 8:28).*

The Boundaries of Evil

God's ultimate solution to the problem of evil awaits the future, but He has already taken providential steps to ensure that evil does not run amok in our world.

God instituted human government to withstand lawlessness. Romans 13:4 says this about the one in authority: "He is God's servant for your good. But if you do wrong, be afraid, for he does not bear the sword in vain. For he is the servant of God, an avenger who carries out God's wrath on the wrongdoer." God has clearly given government the option of capital punishment in fighting crime.

God founded the church to be a light in the midst of the darkness, to strengthen God's people, and to help restrain the growth of wickedness in the world through the power of the Holy Spirit (see, for example, Acts 16:5; 1 Timothy 3:15).

God has given us the family unit to bring stability to society (Proverbs 22:15; 23:13). The healthier families are, the healthier society will be.

God has provided a moral standard to guide us and keep us on the right path—His Word (Psalm 119). As we live according to God's Word, others around us are affected as well.

God has promised a future day of accounting in which all human beings will face the divine Judge (Hebrews 9:27). This promise serves (especially for Christians) as a deterrent to committing evil acts.

Pearl of Wisdom: *God has built checks and balances into human society so that evil does not have total free rein.*

Evolution

Here are six of the biggest problems with the theory of evolution:

1. Scientists today generally agree that the universe had a beginning. This implies the existence of a Beginner or Creator (see Hebrews 3:4).

2. The universe is so perfectly fine-tuned for life on earth, it must have come from the hands of an intelligent Designer (God) (see Romans 1:20; Psalm 19:1-4).

3. If evolution were true, the fossil records would reveal progressively complex evolutionary forms with transitions. However, no transitional links (with species forming into different species) have been discovered in the fossil records.

4. Evolution assumes a long series of positive and upward mutations. In almost all known cases, however, mutations are not beneficial but are harmful to living beings. This is a huge problem for evolution.

5. The second law of thermodynamics, which has never been contradicted in observable nature, says that in an isolated system (like our universe), the natural course of things is to degenerate. The universe is running down, not evolving upward.

6. Evolutionists often make false claims. Some have claimed that scientific evidence confirms that evolution is true. They generally appeal to the fact that mutations do occur within species (microevolution). But an incredible leap of logic is required to say that mutations within species prove that mutations can yield entirely new species (macroevolution). Two dogs cannot produce a cat!

Pearl of Wisdom: *Believing evolution requires more faith than believing creationism.*

Microevolution and Macroevolution

M**icroevolution** refers to changes that occur within a species; *macro-evolution* refers to the evolution of one species into another. We see microevolution in all the different races of human beings that have descended from a single common human ancestor (Adam). Likewise, all kinds of dogs have "microevolved" from the original dog species God created. In no case, however, have scientists observed macroevolution. In truth, the genetic pool of DNA in each species sets parameters beyond which the species simply cannot evolve—that is, dogs can take on new characteristics, but they cannot evolve into cats.

Scripture indicates that God created the initial kinds of animals, and each species reproduced, generation by generation, "according to its kind" (Genesis 1:21,24). This type of evolution is micro in the sense that small changes have taken place in the various species. So, for example, human DNA allows humans to have different eye, hair, and skin colors, different heights, a bulky frame or a scrawny frame, and so forth. The possibility for all kinds of variations such as these is encoded into the DNA of the human species.

Evolutionists tend to speak of evolution as a single process—merging micro- and macroevolution into one basic category, as if a proof of microevolution is as also a proof of macroevolution. Such a conclusion is utterly unwarranted.

Pearl of Wisdom: *Proof for microevolution is not proof for macroevolution.*

Mutations

Contrary to the theory of evolution, the great majority of mutations—more than 99 percent—are detrimental to the organism. Most mutations cause deterioration and breakdown. Such changes tend to make organisms less well suited for their environment, thereby threatening their survival. If most mutations are destructive to organisms, then any series of multiple mutations will, on average, have a significantly higher chance of harming those organisms. This fact greatly undermines evolutionary theory.

Even if mutations were positive, they could not bring about new species because tremendous amounts of new information would have to be added to the DNA (which carries genetic information). However, numerous studies have demonstrated that mutations not only fail to produce new information, they actually delete information and thus bring harm to the organism.

Mutations generally involve copying errors in the DNA, like typing mistakes, and they are incapable of increasing information. Even over a long period of time, not nearly enough information could be added to cause single-celled organisms to evolve into complex human beings.

So individual complex organs could not conceivably develop through mutations. Even more absurd is the idea that these multiple complex organs evolved in a single species so as to function synergistically with each other as an interrelated whole through positive mutations. How could these parts evolve in unison with the other parts?

Pearl of Wisdom: *Mutation studies deal a hard blow to evolutionary theory.*

Natural Selection

According to evolutionary theory, the process of natural selection is blind and unguided. It cannot intelligently direct mutations. And therein lies a huge problem.

Mutations cause only one small change at a time, and the development of a complex organ—an eye, for example—would require thousands of positive mutations. How would natural selection, at each minimal step along the way over innumerable generations, know whether to keep each small mutational change or breed that small mutational change out of the species? How would natural selection know that a small flap of skin on the side of the body would in many generations be a wing, and thus decide to keep that flap of skin? At each step along the way, the individual small mutational changes have no obvious immediate benefit, so why wouldn't natural selection breed that change out of the species? I have never heard a good answer to this problem.

The problem is compounded by the fact that the eye is only one among many complex organs in a human being. What about the ear? What about the nose? What about the brain, the heart, the liver, the kidney, the nervous system? Supposedly, again and again, natural selection blindly and mindlessly brought about complex organs by means of a step-by-step, generation-by-generation process over an incomprehensibly long period of time.

Pearl of Wisdom: *Darwin had good reason for expressing some doubts about evolutionary theory.*

The Meaning of Miracles

Scripture uses four primary Greek words for *miracle*. The first is *dunamis* (strength, inherent power, or power for performing miracles). In the New Testament the word can be translated *miracles* or *mighty works*.

A second Greek word is *semeion* (a sign, mark, or token, or that by which a person or a thing is distinguished from others and is known). A sign is a miracle with a meaning. It always points beyond itself to attest God and His messengers.

The third Greek word is *terata* (a wonder). It refers to something that evokes astonishment or amazement in the beholder.

And last is the Greek word *erga* (works). Jesus used the word to describe His distinctive works that no one else has done or can do (Matthew 11:2-3).

On the basis of these four Greek words, we might concisely define a miracle as a unique and extraordinary event that awakes wonder (*terata*), is wrought by divine power (*dunamis*), accomplishes some practical and benevolent work (*erga*), and points beyond itself to God and His messengers (*semeion*).

Scripture identifies several purposes for miracles. For example, miracles accredit God's messengers (Hebrews 2:3-4), bring glory to God and Jesus (John 2:11), demonstrate the presence of God's kingdom (Matthew 12:28), promote faith among God's people (Exodus 14:31; John 20:30-31), demonstrate God's sovereignty (Exodus 7:5; Deuteronomy 29:5-6), and help people in need (for example, Matthew 14:14; 20:30,34).

Pearl of Wisdom: *If God exists (He does!) and can act (He can!), we should not be surprised to see acts of God.*

Miracles Can Happen

Some atheists claim miracles are not possible because they violate the laws of nature. However, when God miraculously intervenes in His creation, He does not violate the laws of nature but rather supersedes them with a higher, supernatural manifestation of His will. The forces of nature are not obliterated or suspended; they are only counteracted at a particular point by a force superior to the powers of nature.

The laws of nature are merely observations of uniformity or constancy in nature. They are not forces that initiate action. They simply describe the way nature behaves when its course is not affected by a superior power. God, however, is not prohibited from taking action in the world if He so desires.

David Hume, a famous atheist, argued that because all of one's knowledge is derived from experience, and because this experience conveys the absolute regularity of nature, any report of a miracle is much more likely to be a false report than a true interruption in the uniform course of nature. However, Hume's experience was greatly limited. All possible experience could not confirm his naturalistic viewpoint unless he had access to all possible experiences in the universe, including those of the past and the future. Hume did not have access to this nearly infinite body of knowledge, so his conclusion is baseless.

———

Pearl of Wisdom: *A person who is biased against all things supernatural will never believe in anything beyond the natural.*

Miracles and Deity

J esus' deity is clearly revealed not only by His divine names and attributes but also by His many miracles. The New Testament often refers to Jesus' miracles as *signs* (John 2:11). Signs always signify something—in this case, that Jesus is the divine Messiah.

According to the New Testament, Jesus changed water into wine (John 2:7-8), healed the nobleman's son (John 4:50), healed Peter's mother-in-law (Matthew 8:15), caused the disciples to catch a great number of fish (Luke 5:5-6), healed a leper (Matthew 8:3), healed a paralytic (Matthew 9:2), healed a centurion's servant (Matthew 8:13), and raised a widow's son (Luke 7:14).

He also calmed a stormy sea (Matthew 8:26), healed the Gadarene demoniac (Matthew 8:32), healed a woman with internal bleeding (Matthew 9:22), healed two blind men (Matthew 9:29), fed huge crowds with almost nothing (Matthew 14:19; 15:36), and walked on the sea (Matthew 14:25).

Still further, He healed a demoniac boy (Matthew 17:18; Mark 9:25; Luke 9:42), caused Peter to catch a fish with a coin in its mouth (Matthew 17:27), healed a woman with an 18-year infirmity (Luke 13:10-17), healed a man with dropsy (Luke 14:4), healed ten lepers (Luke 17:11-19), raised Lazarus from the dead (John 11:43-44), and restored (healed) a severed ear (Matthew 26:51).

Pearl of Wisdom: *Never doubt Jesus' identity, for He was thoroughly attested by "mighty works and wonders and signs" (Acts 2:22).*

Miracles in Jesus' Hometown

In Mark 6:4-5, Jesus affirmed that a prophet is without honor in his hometown. Consequently, He could not perform any miracles in Nazareth except for healing a few sick people. The people of Nazareth were apparently plagued by unbelief and hardness of heart, and they paid little attention to His claims.

At first glance, one might get the impression that Jesus depended on people's faith for His miraculous power to work. That's not the correct meaning of this passage, however. Jesus was not incapacitated in Nazareth. Rather, He could not do miracles there in the sense that He would not do so in view of the pervasive unbelief in that city.

Miracles serve a far greater purpose than simply to provide a raw display of power. The people of Nazareth had already made up their minds against Jesus and had provided more than ample evidence of their lack of faith in Him, so Jesus chose not to engage in miraculous acts there except for healing a few sick people. He refused to provide signs of His identity to people who had already decided to reject Him. Because of Nazareth's rejection of the person and message of Jesus Christ, He went on to other cities that did respond to and receive Him.

Pearl of Wisdom: *Unbelief and hardness of heart can exclude people from the dynamic disclosure of God's grace that others may experience.*

More Miracles than Jesus

I n John 14:12, Jesus said, "Truly, truly, I say to you, whoever believes in me will also do the works that I do; and greater works than these will he do, because I am going to the Father." Some have concluded from this that mere humans can do even more amazing and dazzling miracles than Jesus performed while He was on earth. But is that what Jesus meant?

Most Bible expositors believe that in this verse, Jesus was simply saying that His many followers would do things that were greater in extent (all over the world) and greater in effect (multitudes being touched by the power of God). During His short lifetime on earth, Jesus confined His influence to a comparatively small region of Palestine. Following His departure, His followers were able to work in widely scattered places and influence many more people.

Jesus thus refers to "greater works" in terms of the whole scope of the impact of God's people and the church on the entire world throughout all history. In other words, Jesus was speaking quantitatively, not qualitatively. The works are quantitatively greater because Christ's work is multiplied through all His followers.

Pearl of Wisdom: *Christ's followers can do mighty works only as they depend on Christ. Jesus answers the prayers of His followers (see John 14:13-14; 16:23-26), and only those believers who abide in Him as the true vine produce abundant fruit. Christ asserted, "Apart from me you can do nothing" (John 15:5).*

Cultists in Our Houses

Some Christians believe that 2 John 10 prohibits us from allowing cultists into our houses: "If anyone comes to you and does not bring this teaching, do not receive him into your house or give him any greeting." However, this is a misinterpretation of the verse.

This verse actually prohibits us from giving cultists a platform from which to teach false doctrine. The earliest Christians met in small house-churches (Colossians 4:15; Romans 6:15; 1 Corinthians 16:19; Philippians 2), where we see them "breaking bread in their homes" (Acts 2:46; see also 5:42) and gathering to pray (Acts 12:12). The use of specific church buildings did not begin before the end of the second century.

Apparently, John is here warning against allowing a false teacher into the church and giving this false teacher a platform from which to teach. Seen in this way, this prohibition guards the purity of the church. To extend hospitality to false teachers would imply that the church accepted or approved of their teaching. If the church were to extend hospitality to false teachers, the impostors would be encouraged and interpret this action as an acceptance of their doctrine. This should never happen.

Pearl of Wisdom: *Being a good witness for Christ includes showing hospitality when witnessing to cultists.*

Beware of Cults

A cult is a religious group that derives from a parent religion (such as Christianity) but departs from that parent religion by denying some of its essential doctrines. So, for example, the Jehovah's Witnesses are a cult in the sense that they derive from the parent religion of Christianity but deny essential doctrines of historic Christianity.

What are the essentials of Christianity? Five doctrines are especially important:

1. The Bible is the inspired Word of God and is therefore inerrant and authoritative.

2. The one true God is infinite, eternal, and revealed in three persons: Father, Son, and Holy Spirit.

3. Jesus is eternal God as the second person of the Trinity. In the incarnation, He took on a human nature, being born of a virgin. He died for humankind's sins and three days later physically rose from the dead.

4. People are created in God's image and are morally accountable to Him. They are destined to live forever with God in heaven or suffer eternally in hell, depending on whether they have been saved.

5. All human beings are born into the world in sin and estranged from God. They can do nothing to merit salvation before God. Salvation is by grace alone through faith alone, based solely on Christ's atonement.

Denying doctrines such as these catapults people into the cults.

Pearl of Wisdom: *Cults often look good on the outside but are deadly on the inside.*

Characteristics of Cults

Most cults have similar doctrinal characteristics. Not every cult manifests every characteristic below, but these characteristics are quite common.

1. Many cult leaders claim to receive new revelations and have their own holy writings. If the Bible conflicts with the new revelation, the new revelation supersedes the Bible.

2. Cults espouse a distorted view of God. Some deny the Trinity or teach pantheism (everything is God) or polytheism (there are many gods). God is irrelevant in some cults.

3. Cults see Jesus as just a man or a lesser god than the Father.

4. Cults usually deny that Jesus won our salvation on the cross.

5. Cults often deny the Holy Spirit's godhood and personhood.

6. Many cults deny that humans are fallen in sin. Some claim that humans are God or have the potential to become gods.

7. Most cults deny salvation by grace.

8. Cults often use words from the Bible—*God, Jesus, sin, salvation, the cross, resurrection, ascension*—but not the definitions that historic Christianity teaches.

Pearl of Wisdom: *Cultic doctrines are nothing less than doctrines of demons (1 Timothy 4:1).*

Sociology and the Cults

Cults are best defined theologically, but sociology helps us to understand the human dynamics of cultic groups. Here are some sociological characteristics of cults.

- *Authoritarianism.* The word of an authority figure—often an alleged prophet—is considered ultimate and final.

- *Isolationism.* Extreme cults sometimes create fortified boundaries. They sometimes require members to break off past associations with parents and siblings. The cult then functions as a surrogate family for those who have lost their biological families.

- *Exclusivism.* Cults often believe that only they possess the truth of God and are saved.

- *Threats of satanic deception.* Some cults warn new followers that Satan may use friends and relatives to try to dissuade them from remaining with the group.

- *Shunning.* Minor infractions against the cult (such as not obeying the leader on a matter) might lead to shunning, in which members no longer interact with the offender for a time.

- *Disfellowshipping.* Some cults disfellowship (kick out) any member who questions or resists the teachings or instructions of the group.

Pearl of Wisdom: *To the extent that cults manifest such characteristics, cultists will experience varying degrees of emotional damage.*

Cults' Moral Characteristics

Legalism, sexual perversion, and physical abuse are common moral characteristics of cults. Not every cult, however, manifests every one of these traits.

Legalism. Many cults set down a rigid set of rules by which cult devotees must live. These standards are usually extrabiblical. For example, Mormons forbid the use of coffee, tea, or any other drink with caffeine. The Watchtower Society for Jehovah's Witnesses requires followers to distribute literature door-to-door.

Sexual perversion. Along with legalism, the twin vice of moral perversion is often found in the cults. Joseph Smith and other early Mormon leaders had many wives. The fundamentalist Latter-day Saints remain polygamous to this day. David Koresh claimed to own all the women in his group, even the young girls. The Children of God cult—now called The Family—has long used "flirty fishing" techniques to sexually lure people into the cult. Reverend Moon of the Unification Church has engaged in sexual purification rites with female members.

Physical abuse. Tragically, some cults engage in forms of physical abuse. Ex-cult members sometimes accuse their former leaders of engaging in beatings (of adults and children), sleep deprivation, and food deprivation. Jehovah's Witness parents refuse blood transfusions for their children—even if their children will die without it. Christian Science parents won't take their kids to doctors because they believe sickness is an illusion.

Pearl of Wisdom: *People who leave cults often carry baggage that must be dealt with.*

Talking with Cult Members

These ten suggestions will help prepare you to talk with cult members.

1. Know basic Bible teachings. No one can know all the false teachings of all the cults. But you can learn the Bible well enough to recognize false doctrine.

2. Don't assume every cultist believes the same thing. Ask cultists what they believe.

3. Recognize that cultists are trained to answer objections. Don't get frustrated. Keep taking the discussion back to the Bible.

4. Check Scriptures. Cultists often cite Scripture passages out of context. Check it out.

5. Define your terms. Cultists use many of the same terms we do but redefine them.

6. Ask strategic questions. By doing so, you can get them to think critically.

7. Always be loving. No one cares how much you know until they know how much you care.

8. Demonstrate the deity of Jesus Christ. Compare these Old and New Testament verses: Isaiah 44:24 and John 1:3; Isaiah 43:11 and Titus 2:13-14; Isaiah 6:1-5 and John 12:41.

9. Emphasize the gospel of grace. Focus heavily on verses like Ephesians 2:8-9; Hebrews 10:17; Isaiah 1:18; and Psalm 32:1.

10. Give your testimony. Tell them how Jesus has changed your life forever!

Pearl of Wisdom: *Always be willing to be a missionary on the doorstep!*

Reincarnation

Here are five reasons why reincarnation doesn't make sense.

1. Reincarnation is not fair. Why would people be punished for something they cannot remember doing in a previous life?

2. Reincarnation does not work. If karma progressively rids humanity of its selfish desires, why hasn't human nature improved noticeably after all the millennia of reincarnations?

3. Reincarnation makes people socially passive. It teaches that we should not interfere with others' bad karma (or bad circumstances). To interfere with their bad circumstances will bring more bad karma to them and to us.

4. Reincarnation is fatalistic. The law of karma guarantees that whatever we sow in the present life, we will invariably reap in the next life. It works infallibly and inexorably. There is no grace!

5. Reincarnation is unbiblical. Scripture indicates that each human being lives once as a mortal on earth, dies once, and then faces judgment (Hebrews 9:27). A person does not have a second chance by reincarnating into another body. Scripture indicates that at death believers in the Lord Jesus go to heaven (2 Corinthians 5:8), and unbelievers go to a place of punishment (Luke 16:19-31; 2 Peter 2:9). Moreover, Jesus taught that people decide their eternal destiny in a single lifetime (Matthew 25:46). This is precisely why the apostle Paul emphasized that "now is the day of salvation" (2 Corinthians 6:2).

Pearl of Wisdom: *Be wise and follow Christ during your one lifetime.*

Astrology

I saiah 47:15 records a strong denunciation of astrologers and their craft. The book of Daniel confirms that astrologers lack true discernment and that the only source of accurate revelation is God Almighty (Daniel 2:2,10). God says anything bordering on worship of heavenly bodies is strictly forbidden (Deuteronomy 4:19). Also, astrology is a form of occultism, and occultism in all forms is condemned (Deuteronomy 18:9-12; Jeremiah 10:2).

Astrology has other problems besides these biblical warnings:

1. Different astrologers give different interpretations of the same horoscope chart.

2. Astrologers do not agree on the number of signs of the zodiac. Suggestions include twelve, eight, ten, fourteen, twenty-four. The number of signs influences the interpretation of the data.

3. What is the basis of astrological authority? Who determines how many signs of the zodiac there are? How do we know the meanings of the various planets? All this seems arbitrary.

4. How do we explain the different experiences of twins?

5. How do we explain disasters where many people of different zodiac signs experience the same fate, such as a plane crash?

6. Studies show a prediction failure rate of 90 percent or worse for astrologers.

Pearl of Wisdom: *The only true testimony from the stars is that God is a glorious Creator (Psalm 19:1-4).*

Participation in the Occult

Throughout human history, people have desired success—healthy bodies, prosperity, and all the good things life has to offer. Many individuals, not content to seek these things by natural means or according to God's laws, have tried to use magic and occultism to bring them about. Magic was often used in ancient times for selfish purposes. In pagan cultures, it was a popular way to harness the power of various deities (see Ezekiel 13:20; Revelation 21:8,15).

The New Testament records an incident with a magician named Simon Magus, who amazed the Samaritans with his magic. He became a Christian but apparently was still fascinated with such phenomena. When he witnessed Peter's bestowal of the Holy Spirit, he tried to buy this gift from him. Peter immediately condemned and rebuked him (Acts 8:9-24).

Scripture indicates that God condemns all forms of occultism, including magic (Exodus 22:18; Leviticus 19:31; Deuteronomy 18:9-13; Ezekiel 13:18; Acts 19:19-20; Galatians 5:20; Revelation 9:21; 21:8). Magic is not only an affront to God but also a distraction from trust in Him. Furthermore, God is greater than any form of magic. This is evident in Moses' interactions with the magicians of Egypt. The Egyptian sorcerers were not able to duplicate all the miracles Moses performed by the power of God (see Exodus 7–9).

Pearl of Wisdom: *Keep your feet off the devil's turf.*

Mysticism

Mystical practices expose people to notable dangers. First, we cannot build an accurate knowledge of God through mysticism. The Bible stresses the importance of objective, historical revelation. For example, John 1:18 speaks of Jesus being an objective, historical revelation of the Father in the empirical world of ordinary sense perceptions.

Second, those who practice mysticism seem blind to the possibility of spiritual deception. What if that which mystics assume to be genuine god-consciousness is in fact rooted in Satan, the great impersonator of God and the father of lies (John 8:44; 2 Corinthians 11:14)?

Third, mystical altered states of consciousness can be dangerous and can lead to harmful consequences. For example, such states have led to contact with spirits. Moreover, deep meditation has sometimes led to increased anxiety, confusion, and depression. It can hinder logical thought processes.

Fourth, the mystical goal of attaining a sense of oneness with all things—including a sense of oneness with God—lies in direct contradiction to the biblical view of the eternal distinction between God the Creator and His creatures (Isaiah 44:6-8; Hebrews 2:6-8).

Pearl of Wisdom: *Mystical contemplative techniques can actually hinder true contemplation, as defined in the Bible. After all, God gave us our minds and the gift of rational thinking by which we can objectively meditate on God's Word. However, if we numb our brains, how can we objectively contemplate God's Word?*

A Christian Belongs to Christ

Today let's about talk our identity. You and I are Christians. The word *Christian* is used only three times in the New Testament. In Acts 11:26, we are told simply that "in Antioch the disciples were first called Christians." This would have been around AD 42, a decade after Christ died and rose from the dead. (See also Acts 26:28 and 1 Peter 4:16.)

Until this time, Jesus' followers had referred to themselves as brothers (Acts 15:1,23), disciples (Acts 9:26), believers (Acts 5:14), and saints (Romans 8:27).

What does the term *Christian* mean? The answer is found in the *ian* ending, for among the ancients, this ending meant "belonging to the party of." Herodians belonged to the party of Herod. Caesarians belonged to the party of Caesar. Christians belonged to Christ. And Christians were loyal to Christ, just as the Herodians were loyal to Herod and Caesarians were loyal to Caesar (see Matthew 22:16; Mark 3:6; 12:13).

The significance of the name *Christian* was that these followers of Jesus were recognized as a distinct group. They were separate from Judaism and different from all other religions of the ancient world. We might loosely translate the term *Christians* as "those belonging to Christ," "Christ-ones," or perhaps "Christ-people." They are ones who follow Christ.

Pearl of Wisdom: *Live your life in such a way that no one doubts you are a "Christ-one," one who belongs to Christ.*

Knowing God and Knowing About God

Jesus often spoke of the need to have a personal relationship with Him. He once said, "Come to me, all you who are weary and burdened, and I will give you rest" (Matthew 11:28 NIV). This verse does not say, "Come to the church" or "Come to a Bible study" to obtain rest. Certainly, going to church and Bible studies is important. But Jesus is the center of Christianity. We are to go to Him, and in our relationship with Him we will find spiritual rest for our souls. The biblical emphasis is on personally knowing God and Christ on an intimate level (Philippians 3:8; 1 John 1:3; see also Jeremiah 9:23-24). This is what Christianity is all about.

Knowing Christ is much more than just knowing some things about Him. A person could have various theological notions in his head without ever tasting in his heart the reality to which they refer. Jesus once said to some Jews, "You search the Scriptures because you think that in them you have eternal life; and it is they that bear witness about me, yet you refuse to come to me that you may have life" (John 5:39-40). These lost Jews knew the shell of the Bible, but they neglected the kernel within it—Jesus Christ. Such intellectual knowledge did them no good at all.

———

Pearl of Wisdom: *Knowing Christ in the biblical sense involves personal commitment to His desires, interests, concerns, and commands. It includes personally fellowshipping with Him on a daily basis (1 John 1).*

Knowing God Intimately

Yesterday's topic was so important that I want to make a few more points about it. Our relationship with Jesus Christ begins the moment we trust in Him for salvation (Acts 16:31). Coming to know Him, however, is not possible with just a single encounter. Knowing Jesus—knowing God—requires not only commitment but also time (see Psalm 1:2; 63:6; 88:9; 145:2).

Certainly this is true in human relationships. The only way to get to know people is to spend quality time with them.

The more quality time we spend with Jesus Christ, the more intimately we come to know Him, and the more we come to understand His likes and dislikes. We come to understand, for example, that living in sin greatly displeases Him (Acts 17:30; 2 Corinthians 7:10; 2 Peter 3:9), but seeking righteousness greatly pleases Him (Psalm 34:15; 1 Peter 3:12-18).

Relationships also involve communication. Can you imagine a newlywed husband and wife who never speak to one another? The very idea is preposterous. Every intimate relationship requires communication.

We communicate with God in prayer (2 Chronicles 7:14; Psalm 145:18; Matthew 7:7-8; John 14:13-14; 1 Timothy 2:8; James 5:17-18). Through prayer we talk to God, interact with Him, make requests of Him, verbalize our hurts and our joys to Him, and ask for His help (Philippians 4:6). And He hears us. He answers us.

———

Pearl of Wisdom: *A personal relationship involves communion, and communion necessarily involves communication.*

General Revelation

God has revealed Himself in two primary ways: through general revelation and special revelation. General revelation is available to all persons of all times. For example, God reveals Himself in the world of nature.

In Psalm 19:1-4 we read, "The Heavens declare the glory of God, and the sky above proclaims his handiwork. Day to day pours out speech, and night to night reveals knowledge. There is no speech, nor are there words, whose voice is not heard. Their measuring line goes out through all the earth, and their words to the end of the world." By observing the world of nature, we can detect something of God's existence and discern something of His divine power and glory. We cannot open our eyes without being compelled to see God. Indeed, God has engraved unmistakable marks of His glory on His creation.

There are, of course, limitations to how much we can learn from general revelation. It tells us nothing about God's cure for humanity's sin problem, nothing of the gospel message. Things like these require special revelation. But general revelation does give us enough information about God's existence that if we reject it and refuse to turn to God, He is justified in bringing condemnation against us (Romans 1:20).

———

Pearl of Wisdom: *The so-called heathen are without excuse, for God has manifested Himself to all people everywhere through general revelation.*

Special Revelation

G od is a Spirit (John 4:24) and is thus invisible (Colossians 1:15). With our normal senses, we cannot perceive anything about Him except what we can detect in general revelation. Further, humankind is spiritually blind and deaf (1 Corinthians 2:14). Since the fall of man in the Garden of Eden, humankind has lacked true spiritual perception. We needed special revelation from God in the worst way.

Special revelation refers to God's specific and clear revelation. God delivers this kind of revelation in several ways.

- *History.* God has communicated knowledge of Himself through the ebb and flow of human experience in biblical times.

- *Jesus Christ.* The only way for God to be able to fully do and say all He wanted was to leave His eternal residence and enter the arena of humanity. This He did in the person of Jesus (John 1:18). By observing the things Jesus did and said, we learn much about God.

- *The Bible.* In this one book, God has provided everything He wants us to know about Him and how we can have a relationship with Him (2 Timothy 3:15-17).

Pearl of Wisdom: *We should receive the Bible as God's words to us and revere and obey it as such.*

God and the Old Testament Prophets

I sometimes encounter people who have a somewhat lower view of the Old Testament than the New Testament. New Testament revelation is in fact fuller and more complete than Old Testament revelation (something one would expect with progressive revelation), but God has nevertheless clearly spoken through His chosen prophets in Old Testament times, so the Old Testament is just as much God's Word as the New Testament.

David affirmed, "The Spirit of the LORD speaks by me; his word is on my tongue." In Isaiah 59:21, God affirmed to the prophet, "My Spirit...is upon you," and He refers to His revelation as "my words that I have put in your mouth." In Jeremiah 1:9, the prophet says, "The LORD put out his hand and touched my mouth. And the LORD said to me, 'Behold, I have put my words in your mouth.'" Zechariah 7:12 speaks of "the law and the words that the LORD of hosts had sent by his Spirit through the former prophets."

I want you to notice something here. These verses indicate that God's revelation was not merely general, but quite specific and communicated in words. And even though God used people (prophets) in the process of communicating His words to other people, the Holy Spirit was in charge of the process so that no human error or opinion entered into the picture. God was in control of the process of communicating His Word to man, and it is therefore inerrant (see Revelation 21:5; 22:6).

———

Pearl of Wisdom: *God moved, and the prophets mouthed His revelation to humankind.*

The Apostles

The New Testament apostles were specially handpicked by the Lord or the Holy Spirit (Matthew 10:1-4; Acts 1:26). They were the special recipients of God's self-revelation and were aware that God was providing revelation through them (1 Corinthians 2:13; 1 Thessalonians 2:13; 1 John 1:1-3). They were aware of their special divine authority (1 Corinthians 7:10; 11:23). Scripture reveals that Christ promised to guide them into "all the truth" (John 16:13; see also 14:26; 15:27).

Two key factors show the utter uniqueness of the apostles. First, they were all authenticated by miraculous signs. In Acts 2:43 (NASB) we read that "everyone was filled with awe, and many wonders and miraculous signs were done by the apostles" (see also Acts 3:3-11; 5:12; 9:32-42; 20:6-12).

Second, 12 of the apostles were granted an eternal place of honor. In the description of the New Jerusalem in Revelation 21, the description reads, "And the wall of the city had twelve foundation stones, and on them were the twelve names of the twelve apostles of the Lamb" (verse 14 NASB).

There can be no apostles today, for an apostle had to be an eyewitness of the resurrected Christ (1 Corinthians 9:1; 15:7-8). Further, the church was built on the foundation of the apostles and prophets (Ephesians 2:19-20), and once a foundation is built, it does not need to be built again.

***

Pearl of Wisdom: *The apostles were men of God who spoke the Word of God to the people of God to the glory of God.*

Progressive Revelation

God provided revelation to humankind in progressive stages, with basic revelations in Old Testament times and fuller revelations in New Testament times. This is called *progressive revelation*. By the time the New Testament era was over, God had revealed all He had intended to through the prophets and the apostles.

The doctrine of the Trinity is an example. Early in the course of God's self-disclosure to humankind, He first revealed that He is one and that He is the only true God (Deuteronomy 6:4). This was a necessary point for God to start His self-revelation, for throughout history Israel was surrounded by nations deeply engulfed in polytheism (the belief in many gods). Through the prophets, God communicated and affirmed to Israel the truth that there is only one true God.

So God's unity and oneness is the clear emphasis in Old Testament revelation. But this is not to say that it contains no hints or shadows of the doctrine of the Trinity, for indeed it does (see, for example, Isaiah 48:16). But God did not reveal the fullness of this doctrine until New Testament times (see, for example, Matthew 3:16-17; 28:19; 2 Corinthians 13:14). By reading the Old Testament in the greater light of the New Testament, we find supporting evidences for the Trinity there.

Pearl of Wisdom: *The Old Testament revelation of God is not corrected by the fuller revelation of God contained in the New Testament; rather, it is extended, enlarged, and perfected by New Testament revelation.*

False Prophets and Teachers

Scripture often warns against false prophets and false teachers for the simple reason that God's own people can be deceived (Ezekiel 34:1-7; Matthew 7:15-16; 24:4,11). Therefore, the Bible exhorts believers to test those who claim to be prophets (see 1 John 4:1-3).

How can believers recognize a false prophet? Here are some key considerations:

- False prophets make predictions that aren't fulfilled (Deuteronomy 18:21-22).

- False prophets sometimes entice people to follow false gods or idols (see Exodus 20:3-4; Deuteronomy 13:1-3).

- False prophets often deny the deity of Jesus Christ (Colossians 2:8-9).

- False prophets sometimes deny the humanity of Jesus Christ (1 John 4:1-2).

- False prophets sometimes advocate legalism, such as abstaining from certain foods for spiritual reasons (1 Timothy 4:3-4).

- False prophets often encourage asceticism (Colossians 2:16-23).

- False prophets sometimes teach that marriage is bad (1 Timothy 4:3).

- False prophets often promote various forms of immorality (Jude 4-7).

If a so-called prophet says anything that clearly contradicts any part of God's Word, his teachings should be rejected. The Word of God is our barometer of truth—a litmus test that exposes error.

Pearl of Wisdom: *We ought to follow the example of the Bereans by comparing all truth claims with Scripture (Acts 17:11; 1 Thessalonians 5:21).*

New Testament Prophets

Some in recent years have argued for the fallibility of New Testament prophets—a view that excuses fallible prophecies among modern-day Christians who claim to have the gift of prophecy. They note that New Testament believers are urged to judge what is offered as prophecy (1 Corinthians 14:29), thus allegedly implying that a New Testament prophet could be in error.

Actually, this instruction was given to guard against false prophets. If a prophet tries to pawn off some revelation that contradicts the previous prophets, he or she is clearly a false prophet (Deuteronomy 13; 18). We know that New Testament prophets were infallible because...

- New Testament prophets are portrayed as being in continuity with their Old Testament predecessors (Malachi 3:5; Matthew 11:11; Revelation 22:7).

- Old and New Testament prophets join the apostles as the foundation of the church (Ephesians 2:20), and since the apostles' revelations were infallible (1 Corinthians 14:37), we can infer that the New Testament prophets were likewise infallible

- New Testament prophets received revelations from God (1 Corinthians 14:29) and were therefore just as infallible as Old Testament prophets who received revelations from God.

- New Testament prophets gave bona fide predictive prophecies (Acts 11:28; 21:11), just as the Old Testament prophets did (see Deuteronomy 18:22).

Pearl of Wisdom: *You can absolutely trust your Bible, for God's prophets and apostles never erred in their revelations from God.*

Holy Books

Some people believe that the Bible is not unique because it teaches the same kinds of things found in the Muslim Koran and the Hindu Vedas. They suggest these holy books are essentially the same and only superficially different. The truth is that these books are essentially different and only superficially the same.

Consider the doctrine of God—the most fundamental doctrine of any religious system. In the Bible, Jesus presented one personal God who is triune (Mark 12:29; John 4:24; 5:18-19). In the Koran, Muhammad promoted the idea of one God who is not a Trinity. The Hindu Vedas refer to millions of gods, with a single impersonal and monistic deity underlying them all.

We can find other significant differences. The Muslim Koran and Hindu Vedas, for example, promote a works-oriented view of salvation, whereas the Bible says salvation is a gift for those who trust in Christ alone (Ephesians 2:8-9). Moreover, Christianity teaches that Jesus is absolute deity. Islam denies this and portrays Him as a mere prophet to Israel (who is far lesser than Muhammad). Hindus claim Jesus was a mere avatar. These holy books set forth completely contradictory views on central doctrines.

Pearl of Wisdom: *Many radical and irreconcilable differences separate the Bible, the Vedas, and the Koran. If one is right, the others must be wrong. If the Bible is God's Word (as I argue in this book), then the others cannot be God's Word.*

A Library of Inspired Books

The Bible is a library of books of different literary genres. These writings were penned by numerous authors in different centuries, locations, circumstances, and even languages. Yet from Genesis to Revelation, the Bible tells one primary story of the redemption of humankind. It includes the Old Testament, written in Hebrew (with some Aramaic), and the New Testament, written in Koine Greek. The Bible also has these divisions:

- *the Pentateuch:* Genesis, Exodus, Leviticus, Numbers, and Deuteronomy
- *historical books:* Joshua, Judges, Ruth, 1 and 2 Samuel, 1 and 2 Kings, 1 and 2 Chronicles, Ezra, Nehemiah, and Esther
- *wisdom books:* Job, Psalms, Proverbs, Ecclesiastes, and Song of Solomon
- *major prophets:* Isaiah, Jeremiah, Lamentations, Ezekiel, and Daniel
- *minor prophets:* Hosea, Joel, Amos, Obadiah, Jonah, Micah, Nahum, Habakkuk, Zephaniah, Haggai, Zechariah, and Malachi
- *Gospels:* Matthew, Mark, Luke, and John
- *early church history:* Acts
- *Pauline epistles:* Romans, 1 and 2 Corinthians, Galatians, Ephesians, Philippians, Colossians, 1 and 2 Thessalonians, 1 and 2 Timothy, Titus, and Philemon
- *general epistles:* Hebrews; James; 1 and 2 Peter; 1, 2, and 3 John; Jude; and Revelation

Pearl of Wisdom: *This wide variety of literature is in perfect harmony and agreement because of the inspiration of the Holy Spirit (2 Timothy 3:16)!*

The Holy Spirit: The Agent of Inspiration

Second Peter 1:21 tells us that "no prophecy was ever produced by the will of man, but men spoke from God as they were carried along by the Holy Spirit." Though God used people in the process of writing down His Word, they were literally carried along by the Holy Spirit. This means the human wills of the authors were not the originators of God's message. God did not permit the will of sinful man to divert, misdirect, or erroneously record His message. God moved on the prophets who mouthed these truths; God revealed His Word, and man recorded it.

The Greek word for *carried along* in 2 Peter 1:21 is the same word found in Acts 27:15-17. This passage tells us that experienced sailors could not navigate their ship because the wind was so strong. The ship was being driven, directed, and carried along by the wind. This is similar to the Spirit's driving, directing, and carrying along of the human authors of the Bible as He wished. The word is a strong one, indicating the Spirit's complete superintendence of the human authors. Yet, just as the sailors were active on the ship (though the wind, not the sailors, controlled the ship's movement), so the human authors were active in writing as the Spirit directed.

Pearl of Wisdom: *The Holy Spirit, the Spirit of truth (John 16:13), is the true Author of the Bible, the Word of truth (2 Timothy 2:15).*

Scripture Is "God-breathed"

The biblical Greek word for *inspiration* literally means "God-breathed" (2 Timothy 3:16). God superintended the human authors so that, using their own individual personalities and writing styles, they composed and recorded without error His revelation to man in the words of the original autographs (see Jeremiah 36:1-2; Revelation 14:13). Put another way, the original documents of the Bible were written by men who exercised their own personalities and literary talents under the control and guidance of the Holy Spirit (2 Peter 1:21), resulting in a perfect and errorless recording of the exact message God desired to give to man (Psalm 119:151,160; Proverbs 30:5-6; Matthew 5:17-18; 22:41-46; John 10:35; 17:17).

The biblical evidence shows that Isaiah had a powerful literary style, Jeremiah had a mournful tone, Luke's style had medical overtones, and John was very simple in his approach. Yet the Holy Spirit infallibly worked through each of these writers' individual styles to inerrantly communicate His message to humankind.

The essential elements of the doctrine of inspiration teach us that the Bible (1) came from God (2) through human authors (3) who used words. Inspiration includes (4) all of Scripture (5) but only the original documents. Scripture is therefore (6) inerrant, and it alone has (7) final authority.

Pearl of Wisdom: *You can completely trust your Bible as truly being the Word of God!*

God and Human Writers

The New Testament refers to the Holy Spirit as the author of many Old Testament passages even though people spoke the words in the Old Testament. The psalmist spoke in Psalm 95:7-8, but the words are attributed to the Holy Spirit in Hebrews 3:7. The psalmist spoke in Psalm 45:6, but the words are attributed to God in Hebrews 1:8. The psalmist spoke in Psalm 102:25,27, but the words are attributed to God in Hebrews 1:10-12.

Acts 1:16 likewise tells us, "Brothers, the Scripture had to be fulfilled, which the Holy Spirit spoke beforehand by the mouth of David concerning Judas, who became a guide to those who arrested Jesus." We read in Acts 4:24-25, "They lifted their voices together to God and said, 'Sovereign Lord, who made the heaven and the earth and the sea and everything in them, who through the mouth of our father David, your servant, said by the Holy Spirit, "Why did the Gentiles rage, and the peoples plot in vain?"'"

Again, we read in Acts 28:25-26: "Disagreeing among themselves, they departed after Paul had made one statement: 'The Holy Spirit was right in saying to your fathers through Isaiah the prophet: "Go to this people, and say, You will indeed hear but never understand, and you will indeed see but never perceive."'"

Pearl of Wisdom: *The Bible is not man-made, but God-inspired.*

All of Scripture Is Inspired

In 2 Timothy 3:16 we read, "All Scripture is breathed out by God and profitable for teaching, for reproof, for correction, and for training in righteousness." Was Paul referring to just the Old Testament (a common New Testament usage of the word *Scripture*), or did he also have in mind the New Testament books? My studied opinion is that the latter is the case.

Paul had already described a New Testament book as Scripture in his first letter to Timothy. More specifically, he cited Luke 10:7 and Deuteronomy 25:4 and collectively called the verses *Scripture* (1 Timothy 5:18). It therefore makes sense that Paul's use of *Scripture* in 2 Timothy 3:16 included all the New Testament books that had been written up to that time.

Here is an important consideration: By the time 2 Timothy 3:16 had been written, all of the New Testament books had already been written except for 2 Peter, Hebrews, Jude, and the apostle John's writings. So Paul was probably including these books in the phrase "all Scripture is breathed out by God" in 2 Timothy 3:16 (see 2 Peter 3:16 for support of this claim). And since the remaining books were later acknowledged as belonging in the canon of Scripture, we may safely say that this verse says something about all 66 books of the Bible.

Pearl of Wisdom: *We can trust that the entire Bible came from God, not just portions of it.*

What the New Testament Writers Knew

In 1 Corinthians 2:13, Paul said he spoke "in words not taught by human wisdom but taught by the Spirit." In this passage, Paul—who wrote most of the books in the New Testament—affirmed that his words were authoritative because he learned them from the infallible God (the Holy Spirit). The Spirit is the Spirit of truth, who was promised to the apostles to teach and guide them into all the truth (see John 16:13).

In 1 Corinthians 14:37, Paul also asserted, "If anyone thinks that he is a prophet, or spiritual, he should acknowledge that the things I am writing to you are a command of the Lord." Paul's writings are divinely authoritative because they are "a command of the Lord," not the words of fallen man.

Paul said to the Thessalonian Christians, "We also thank God constantly for this, that when you received the word of God, which you heard from us, you accepted it not as the word of men but as what it really is, the word of God, which is at work in you believers" (1 Thessalonians 2:13). Again, Paul's words were authoritative because they were rooted in God, not in man.

Pearl of Wisdom: *The New Testament books are the Word of God to us, just as they were to the first-century recipients.*

Fulfilled prophecy and Inspiration of Scripture

From Genesis to Malachi, the Old Testament abounds with anticipations of the coming Messiah. Numerous predictions—fulfilled to the crossing of the *t* and the dotting of the *i* in the New Testament—predict His birth, life, ministry, death, resurrection, and glory. These fulfilled prophecies constitute a powerful apologetic for the inspiration of Scripture.

The New Testament writers showed that Christ specifically fulfilled Old Testament messianic prophecies. For example, Jesus was to be the seed of woman (Genesis 3:15), virgin born (Isaiah 7:14), born in Bethlehem (Micah 5:2), and preceded by a messenger (Malachi 3:1). He was to have a ministry of miracles (Isaiah 35:5-6), be betrayed and sold for 30 shekels (Zechariah 11:12), have His hands and feet pierced (Psalm 22:16), be crucified with thieves (Isaiah 53:12), have no bones broken (Psalm 22:17), suffer thirst on the cross (Psalm 69:21), and then be gloriously resurrected from the dead (Psalm 16:10; 22:22).

These prophecies were written many hundreds of years before they were fulfilled. Their fulfillment could never have been predicted by natural means, and their fulfillment depended on factors outside human control. And they were all fulfilled precisely. Obviously the Scriptures have a divine origin and are not simply man-made.

Pearl of Wisdom: *Only God has the ability to declare the end from the beginning and engage in predictive prophecy (Isaiah 46:10), so the Bible is clearly God's Word.*

No Inaccurate Prophecies

S ome people claim that Jesus' prophecy in Matthew 24:34 that the end would come in His lifetime was mistaken.

Jesus here affirmed, "Truly, I say to you, this generation will not pass away until all these things take place." Christians have held to one of two interpretations of this verse. One is that those people who witness the signs stated earlier in Matthew 24 (all of which deal with the future tribulation period) will see the coming of Jesus Christ within that very generation. In other words, the generation alive when such events as the abomination of desolation (verse 15) and the great tribulation (verse 21) begin to come to pass will still be alive when these prophetic judgments are completed. The tribulation will last seven years (Daniel 9:27), so Jesus would be saying that the generation alive at the beginning of the tribulation will still be alive at the end of it, at which time the second coming will occur.

Other Christians say the word *generation* in this verse should be taken in its secondary meaning of "race." The verse could mean the Jewish race would not pass away until all things are fulfilled—including God's land promises to Israel (Genesis 12; 14–15; 17) and the fulfillment of the Davidic kingdom (2 Samuel 7; see also Romans 11:11-26). Either way, the verse does not represent a mistaken prophecy.

———

Pearl of Wisdom: *Biblical prophecies have a 100 percent accuracy rate.*

Our Supreme and Final Authority

We have learned that the authority of Scripture cannot be separated from the authority of God. Whatever the Bible affirms, God affirms. And what the Bible affirms (or denies), it affirms (or denies) with God's authority.

Jesus often testified to the absolute authority of the Bible as the Word of God. He affirmed the Bible's divine inspiration (Matthew 22:43), its indestructibility (Matthew 5:17-18), its infallibility (John 10:35), its final authority (Matthew 4:4,7,10), its historicity (Matthew 12:40; 24:37), and its factual inerrancy (John 17:17).

Jesus asserted that Scripture cannot be broken (John 10:35). He also said, "Truly, I say to you, until heaven and earth pass away, not an iota, not a dot, will pass from the Law until all is accomplished" (Matthew 5:18). He said, "It is easier for heaven and earth to pass away than for one dot of the Law to become void" (Luke 16:17). Jesus appealed to Scripture in every matter under dispute. To the Sadducees He said, "You are wrong, because you know neither the Scriptures nor the power of God" (Matthew 22:29). He told some Pharisees that they invalidated the Word of God by their tradition that had been handed down (Mark 7:13). To the devil, Jesus consistently responded, "It is written" (Matthew 4:4-10). For Jesus, the Scriptures were the final court of appeal on all doctrinal and moral matters.

Pearl of Wisdom: *Following Jesus' lead, we must make the Scriptures alone our supreme and final authority.*

The Canon in New Testament Times

The word *canon* comes from a Greek word meaning "measuring stick." The word eventually came to be used metaphorically of books that were "measured" and thereby recognized as being God's Word. The canon of Scripture includes all the biblical books that collectively constitute God's Word.

Many books written during New Testament times were recognized as being the Word of God during the general time they were written. In 1 Timothy 5:18, Paul joined an Old and New Testament verse and called them both (collectively) Scripture (Deuteronomy 25:4 and Luke 10:7). For a New Testament book to be referred to as Scripture so soon after it was written says volumes about Paul's view of the authority of contemporary New Testament books.

To be more specific, only three years had elapsed between the writing of Luke and 1 Timothy (Luke was written around AD 60; 1 Timothy was written around AD 63). Yet Paul—himself a "Hebrew of Hebrews"—does not hesitate to place Luke on the same level of authority as the Old Testament book of Deuteronomy.

Further, Peter referred to Paul's writings as Scripture (2 Peter 3:16; see also 1 Corinthians 14:37; 1 Thessalonians 2:13). Paul, of course, wrote most of the books in the New Testament.

———

Pearl of Wisdom: *Contrary to those who say no one knew what books belonged in the New Testament canon until a council met centuries later, the Bible itself reveals that many of the New Testament books were already being recognized as belonging in the canon.*

Five Tests for Canonicity

When the church formally recognized what books belonged in the canon at the Council of Carthage in AD 397, it applied five primary tests:

1. Was the book written or backed by a prophet or apostle of God? The reasoning here is that the Word of God, which is inspired by the Spirit of God for the people of God, must be communicated through a man of God (see Deuteronomy 18:18; 2 Peter 1:20-21).

2. Is the book authoritative? In other words, does it ring with the sense of, "Thus saith the Lord"?

3. Does the book tell the truth about God as it is already known by previous revelation? The Bereans searched the Old Testament Scriptures to see whether Paul's teaching was true (Acts 17:11). They knew that if Paul's teaching did not agree with the Old Testament canon, it could not be of God. Agreement with all earlier revelation was essential.

4. Does the book give evidence of having the power of God? The reasoning here is that any writing that does not exhibit the transforming power of God in the lives of its readers could not have come from God (Hebrews 4:12).

5. Was the book accepted by the people of God? The majority of God's people (not merely a faction) will initially receive God's Word as such (see Deuteronomy 31:24-26; Joshua 24:26; 1 Thessalonians 2:13).

Pearl of Wisdom: *Though God determines the canon, the church recognizes the canon as providentially guided by God.*

In or Out?

Hebrews' canonicity was doubted for a short time because the book's author was unknown. However, the book eventually came to be viewed as having apostolic authority if not apostolic authorship.

James was doubted because of its apparent conflict with Paul's teaching about salvation by faith alone. The conflict was resolved by seeing the works James speaks of as an outgrowth of real faith.

Second Peter was doubted because its style differs from that of 1 Peter. It seems clear, however, that Peter used a scribe to write 1 Peter (see 1 Peter 5:12).

Second and 3 John were doubted because the author of these books is called *elder*, not *apostle*. However, Peter (an apostle) is also called *elder* in 1 Peter 5:1. The same person can be both an elder and an apostle.

Jude was doubted because it refers to two noncanonical books—the Book of Enoch and the Assumption of Moses. This objection was eventually overcome because even Paul quoted from pagan poets (see Acts 17:28 and Titus 1:12).

Revelation was doubted because it teaches a thousand-year reign of Christ. Since a local contemporary cult taught the same, some people reasoned that Revelation must not be true Scripture. However, because many of the earliest church fathers also believed in a thousand-year reign of Christ, this objection was eventually seen as being without merit.

Pearl of Wisdom: *The same God who supernaturally inspired the Scriptures also providentially guided the selection of the correct books for admission into the scriptural canon.*

The Apocrypha

The Apocrypha contains 14 or 15 books of doubtful authenticity and authority that were written between the time of the Old and New Testaments (including Tobit, Ecclesiasticus, and 1 and 2 Maccabees). Roman Catholics decided these books belonged in the Bible at the Council of Trent (AD 1545–1563), so the Catholic Bible is larger than the Protestant Bible. Protestants believe these books are not canonical for several reasons.

- No New Testament writer quoted from any of these books as Scripture or considered them to be inspired, though they often quoted from Old Testament books.

- Jesus and the disciples virtually ignored these books. They wouldn't have if they had considered them to be God-inspired Scripture.

- The Jewish Council of Jamnia, which met in AD 90, rejected the Apocrypha as Scripture.

- The Apocrypha contains clear historical errors, such as the assumption that Sennacherib was the son of Shalmaneser instead of Sargon II (see Tobit 1:15).

- Unlike many of the biblical books, no Apocryphal book claims divine inspiration.

- Unlike the Old and New Testaments, the Apocrypha contains no predictive prophecy.

- Augustine acknowledged the Apocrypha at first but then rejected it from the canon and considered it inferior to the Hebrew Scriptures.

Pearl of Wisdom: *We can rest assured that the books in the Protestant Bible are inspired and inerrant and that they belong in the canon.*

Papyri and New Testament Studies

Papyrus is a durable writing material manufactured in ancient Egypt from a river plant called *cyperus papyrus*. It does not rot in the dry conditions that prevail south of Cairo. From 1896 to 1906, a large number of papyri manuscripts were discovered at various sites, leading to the science of papyrology.

The papyri fragments that have been discovered, along with some entire scrolls, deal with a variety of different topics relevant in ancient times. Many of the papyri contain portions of the New Testament. These fragments are helpful in at least five ways:

- They confirm the text of other biblical manuscripts.

- They provide information about the historical context of the New Testament.

- They help biblical scholars determine New Testament grammar.

- This, in turn, helps scholars to more accurately date New Testament books.

- They prove that New Testament Greek was the everyday language.

Among the most important papyri discovered are the Bodmer papyrus and the Chester Beatty papyrus. The Chester Beatty papyrus (P46) dates to about AD 200 and contains ten Pauline epistles (all but the Pastorals) and the book of Hebrews. (*P* stands for *papyrus*.) The Bodmer Papyrus (P66) also dates to about AD 200 and contains the Gospel of John.

Pearl of Wisdom: *We have plentiful and convincing evidence in support of the accurate transmission of the New Testament.*

The Dead Sea Scrolls

I n 1947 in Qumran, an Arab shepherd accidentally discovered the first of some long-hidden writings of an Essene community—an ancient Jewish sect. Since then, thousands of fragments belonging to more than 800 manuscripts have been discovered in 11 different caves in Qumran. These include Old Testament books, commentaries on Old Testament books, apocryphal and pseudepigraphal texts, thematic collections of Old Testament passages, hymns, and sectarian writings of the Qumran community.

Though scholars are unclear on the etymology of the word *Essene,* it seems to be related to the Aramaic *hasya* (pious) and the Hebrew *hasidim* (pious ones). The Essenes were apparently ascetic, semimonastic Jews who withdrew from the pagan, materialistic world to pursue a life of righteousness and virtue.

Admission to the Essene community was restricted, the discipline was rigid, and punishment for disobedience was severe. Because of their belief in the detrimental effects of evil, the Essenes engaged in constant purification rituals. By obedience to Old Testament law and mutual love for one another, they attempted to live in an environment of peace and purity.

The Essenes were highly exclusive. They viewed themselves as the final remnant of God's people on earth. They apparently believed they alone interpreted the Scriptures rightly, so they devoted their exile in the wilderness to the constant study of Scripture. Essene life was also communal, with all property held in common.

Pearl of Wisdom: *Archaeological discoveries have taught us a lot about life in Bible times, and this knowledge helps us to interpret Scripture more accurately.*

The Dead Sea Scrolls and Biblical Manuscript Transmission

As we saw yesterday, thousands of fragments belonging to more than 800 manuscripts have been discovered in 11 different caves at Qumran. Approximately 40 percent of the manuscripts are of the Old Testament.

The scrolls verify the accuracy with which biblical manuscripts were copied. They contain Old Testament manuscripts that date about a thousand years earlier (150 BC) than the oldest Old Testament manuscripts we had previously (which date to around AD 980). The two sets of manuscripts are essentially the same, with very few changes.

The manuscripts include a well-preserved copy of the entire book of Isaiah and another fragmentary scroll of Isaiah. These Isaiah scrolls discovered in Qumran Cave 1 have proved to be word-for-word identical with our Hebrew Bible in more than 95 percent of the text. The five percent of variation consists chiefly of obvious slips of the pen and variations in spelling. The Dead Sea Scrolls prove that the copyists who reproduced biblical manuscripts took great care in their work, meticulously checking their work for errors. Because of this, we can have a high level of confidence that our Old Testament Scriptures faithfully represent the words given to Moses, David, Isaiah, Ezekiel, Jeremiah, and all the other prophets of old.

———

Pearl of Wisdom: *Our modern Bible translations can only be as accurate as the manuscript copies—and the evidence reveals that the manuscript copies are extremely accurate!*

New Testament Variants

In the thousands of manuscript copies that we possess of the New Testament, scholars have discovered that there are some 200,000 "variants" (differences among the thousands of manuscripts). This may seem like a staggering figure to the uninformed mind. But to those who study the issue, the numbers are not so damning as they may initially appear. Indeed, a look at the evidence shows that the New Testament manuscripts are amazingly accurate and trustworthy.

Out of these 200,000 variants, more than 99 percent are virtually insignificant. Many of these variants simply involve a missing letter in a word, some involve reversing the order of two words (such as "Christ Jesus" instead of "Jesus Christ"), and some involve the absence of one or more insignificant words. In fact, only about 40 of the variants have any real significance—and even then, no doctrine of the Christian faith or any moral commandment is affected by them.

In more than 99 percent of the cases, the original text can be reconstructed to a practical certainty. By practicing the science of textual criticism—comparing all the available manuscripts with each other—we can be practically certain of what the original document said. The sheer volume of manuscripts we possess greatly narrows the margin of doubt.

Pearl of Wisdom: *There is overwhelmingly more manuscript support for the Bible than for any other ancient document.*

Has the Bible Been Corrupted?

Muslims claim the Bible became corrupted by Jews and Christians soon after Muhammad's time (the seventh century). This is an attempt to reconcile the Islamic claim that the original Bible was the Word of God inspired by Allah with the fact that today's Bible contradicts Muslim beliefs (for example, the New Testament teaches that God is a Trinity).

To claim the Bible became corrupted by Jews and Christians soon after the seventh century is both inaccurate and unreasonable. By that time, hundreds of thousands of manuscript copies of the Bible were dispersed over a large part of the world. To successfully corrupt the Bible, all these copies would have to be meticulously gathered—assuming that Jews and Christians around the world would be willing to surrender them, which is an impossible-to-believe scenario—and then the changes made.

Moreover, hundreds of years before Muhammad was born, the Bible had already been translated into several different languages. These various translations from all over the world could not possibly have been uniformly altered.

Also, if Christians made changes to the biblical manuscripts, why didn't they alter embarrassing details, such as the disciples scattering like a bunch of spineless cowards after Jesus was arrested? The whole scenario is laced with problems.

Pearl of Wisdom: *Alleged holy books like the Koran cannot invalidate the Bible.*

The Preservation of Biblical Manuscripts

Substantial evidence indicates that the God who had the power and sovereign control to inspire the Scriptures in the first place (2 Timothy 3:16; 2 Peter 1:21) also exercised His power and sovereign control in the preservation of the biblical manuscripts (just as He holds the universe together [Colossians 1:17; Hebrews 1:3]). We see this in the text of the Bible.

This is illustrated in the way Christ viewed the Old Testament. Jesus did not have the original manuscripts penned by the Old Testament writers (like Moses, David, Isaiah, Jeremiah, Ezekiel, and others). Rather, He possessed manuscript copies. Yet He had full confidence that the Old Testament Scriptures He used had been faithfully preserved through the centuries, even though the various manuscript copies contained some variants.

Because Christ raised no doubts or questions about the full adequacy of the Scriptures as He and His contemporaries knew them, we are safe in assuming that the first-century text of the Old Testament, as contained in the manuscript copies, was a wholly adequate representation of the divine word. A look at the Gospels indicates that Jesus regarded the extant manuscript copies of His day as so approximate to the original autographs in their message and content that He unhesitatingly appealed to those copies as reliable and authoritative (see, for example, Matthew 4:4,7,10).

Pearl of Wisdom: *The respect that Jesus and His apostles held for the extant Old Testament manuscript copies is an expression of their confidence that God providentially preserved these copies so that they were substantially identical with the inspired originals.*

Extrabiblical Christian Sources and the Bible Books

Plenty of extrabiblical Christian sources lend support to the veracity of Scripture—especially the Gospel accounts of Jesus.

- Clement was a leading elder in the church at Rome. In his epistle to the Corinthians (dated at about AD 95), he cites portions of Matthew, Mark, and Luke, and he introduces them as the actual words of Jesus.

- Papias, bishop of Hierapolis in Phrygia and author of *Exposition of Oracles of the Lord* (dated at about AD 130), cites the Gospels of Matthew, Mark, Luke, and John.

- Justin Martyr, foremost apologist of the second century, considered all four Gospels to be Scripture.

- The Didache, an ancient manual of Christianity from the end of the first century or the beginning of the second, cites portions of the three synoptic Gospels and refers to them as the actual words of Jesus. This manual quotes extensively from Matthew's Gospel.

- Polycarp, a disciple of the apostle John, quotes portions of Matthew, Mark, and Luke, and he refers to them as the words of Jesus.

- Irenaeus, a disciple of Polycarp, quotes from 23 of the 27 New Testament books, omitting only Philemon, James, 2 Peter, and 3 John.

Pearl of Wisdom: *Our confidence in the veracity of the biblical account is enhanced by the extrabiblical Christian sources that approvingly cite various books in the Bible.*

Secular Extrabiblical Sources and the Bible

Noteworthy secular extrabiblical sources mention various aspects of Jesus' life, thus lending support to the Bible.

- Josephus was a Jewish historian born in AD 37. In *The Antiquities* (20:9 and 18:3), he corroborates that Jesus was the leader of Christians, that He did wonderful works, and that He was a martyr (by crucifixion) for the Christian cause.

- The Talmud, a collection of ancient rabbinic writings on Jewish law and tradition, contains some references to Jesus. The Jewish leaders were opposed to Jesus, so the information in the Talmud is naturally unflattering. Keeping Jewish hostility in mind, the Talmudic text indicates that Jesus was born of an adulteress (a Jewish attempt to explain away the virgin birth), that He practiced sorcery (an attempt to explain away His miracles), and that He was crucified "on the eve of the Passover."

- Pliny the Younger (AD 62–113) was a non-Christian Roman governor who, in personal correspondence to his friend Trajan, noted that Christians met for worship on a "certain fixed day," worshipped Jesus as a god, and changed their behavior as a result of their commitment to Christ.

- The Roman historian Tacitus (AD 56–117) indicates that Christians derived their name from a historical person named Jesus Christ ("Christus"). He "suffered the extreme penalty"—a reference to Roman crucifixion.

Pearl of Wisdom: *Our confidence in the veracity of the biblical account is enhanced by the extrabiblical secular sources that refer to Jesus.*

The Gospels' Apparent Contradictions

The four Gospels have unique perspectives but not actual contradictions.

If all four Gospels were virtually the same, critics would say the writers colluded. The differences in the Gospels show that the writers did not collude but rather represented four different but equally inspired accounts of the same events.

A partial account in a Gospel is not a faulty account. In Matthew 27:5, for example, we learn that Judas died by hanging himself. In Acts 1:18, we find that Judas burst open in the middle, and all his entrails gushed out. These are both partial accounts. Neither account gives us the full picture. But taken together we can easily reconstruct how Judas died. He hanged himself, and sometime later, the rope loosened, and Judas fell to the rocks below, thereby causing his intestines to gush out.

Many alleged contradictions are solved by following proper hermeneutics, like these:

- Remember that the Bible typically uses nontechnical, everyday language.

- Interpret the Old Testament in light of the New Testament.

- Interpret the difficult verses in light of the clear verses.

- Remember that the Bible does not approve of everything it records (such as the words of Satan).

Pearl of Wisdom: *A careful probe into alleged contradictions in the Gospel accounts reveals that they are all explainable in a reasonable way.*

The Gospels Are Selective

The Gospels explain that they are selective in their content (see Luke 1:1-4; John 20:30; 21:25). They focus primarily on Jesus' three-year ministry, with the exception of a short discussion of His birth and infancy and one story from His boyhood (Matthew 1–2; Luke 1–2). God the Holy Spirit inspired these Gospels (2 Timothy 3:16; 2 Peter 1:21), so we can assume that they contain everything God wanted us to know about Jesus' life and ministry. However, as John 21:25 notes, "There are also many other things that Jesus did. Were every one of them to be written, I suppose that the world itself could not contain the books that would be written."

The four Gospel writers were seeking to reach different audiences, so they included different emphases. Matthew wrote his Gospel to prove to Jews that Jesus was the promised Messiah. Mark had no such Jewish motivation, but rather sought to portray Jesus in action rather than as a teacher. Luke's Gospel stresses the wonderful blessings of salvation for all people and emphasizes that God's grace is for the undeserving. John's Gospel focuses on Jesus' identity and thoroughly demonstrates His divine origin and deity. Such factors account for the differences among the Gospels.

————

Pearl of Wisdom: *All four Gospels present Jesus' identity and message, and their unique audiences and emphases account for the differences between them.*

Nature and the Bible

Science depends upon observation and replication. Miracles, such as the incarnation and resurrection, are by their very nature unprecedented events. No one can replicate these events in a laboratory. Therefore, science cannot be the judge and jury as to whether these events occurred.

The scientific method is useful for studying nature but not the supernatural. Just as football stars are speaking outside their field of expertise when they appear on television to tell you what razor you should buy, so scientists are speaking outside their field when they address theological issues, like miracles or the resurrection.

God has communicated to humankind both by general revelation (nature, or the observable universe) and special revelation (especially the Bible). Both of these revelations come from God—and God does not contradict Himself—so these two revelations must agree with each other. Interpretations of the observable universe (science) and interpretations of the Bible (theology) may conflict, but nature and the Bible do not contradict each other.

Is science fallible? In *The Structure of Scientific Revolutions,* secular science historian Thomas Kuhn proved that science is in a constant state of change. New discoveries consistently require us to discard old scientific paradigms in favor of newer paradigms.

Pearl of Wisdom: *Nature and Scripture do not conflict. Rather, science (a fallible interpretation of nature) and theology (a fallible interpretation of Scripture) sometimes conflict.*

Archaeology and the Bible

Archaeology comes from two Greek words—*archaios* (ancient things) and *logos* (the study of). Archaeology is the study of ancient things and is beneficial to Bible study in at least four ways:

1. Archaeology can help us to better understand the historical context of the Bible. For example, it sheds much light on the cruelty of the Assyrians in Old Testament times (see Isaiah 20, 36–37; 2 Chronicles 32).

2. Archaeology can provide background information about subjects the Bible tells us little about. For example, archaeologists have discovered that many ancient floors in homes in New Testament times were cobbled. On such a floor, it would be quite easy for someone to lose a small object (such as a coin) between the stones on the floor. This discovery helps us to better understand Jesus' parable of the lost coin in Luke 15:8.

3. Archaeology can illuminate the meaning of some passages of Scripture. For example, Scripture reveals that Christians will one day stand before the judgment seat of Christ. Archaeologists have uncovered a judgment seat in Corinth—a platform from which officials judged athletic contests and handed out rewards (see 2 Corinthians 5:10).

4. Archaeology can verify the accuracy and reliability of biblical teachings about numerous customs, places, peoples, names, and events in biblical times. For example, the existence of Sodom and Gomorrah has been archaeologically verified.

Pearl of Wisdom: *Archaeologists have provided verification of numerous customs, places, peoples, names, and events in biblical times.*

Archaeology and the Old Testament

S ubstantial archaeological evidence verifies information in the Old Testament. For example, archaeological discoveries now conclusively prove that handwriting existed in Moses' lifetime. Drawings have also been discovered in Egypt depicting Hebrew slaves making bricks for the cities of Pithom and Rameses. Excavations throughout Egypt have uncovered much information about the false gods that the Egyptians worshipped during the time of the Exodus.

Overwhelming archaeological evidence regarding David, Solomon, and their respective empires has been discovered. Saul's fortress at Gibeah has been excavated, and researchers have discovered that slingshots were among the most common weapons of the day (see 1 Samuel 17:4,23; 21:9-10).

Evidence that the world once had a single language is growing. Sumerian literature alludes to this several times.

The tablets discovered at Nuzi (east of the Tigris River) indicate that an infertile wife had the prerogative of giving her maidservant to her husband in order to provide him an heir, who could then be adopted by the wife. This sheds light on Abraham and Sarah's circumstances (see Genesis 16).

A portion of the lower city wall in biblical Jericho has been discovered that did not fall as it did everywhere else. This still-standing portion of wall is up to eight feet high, with houses built against it that are still intact (see Joshua 6:17-25).

Pearl of Wisdom: *The more we dig up in biblical lands, the more we find evidence of people, places, and events mentioned in the Old Testament.*

Archaeology and the New Testament

Substantial archaeological evidence corroborates information in the New Testament. For example, archaeologists have discovered a stone slab at the ruins of Caesarea Maritima that bears the name of Pontius Pilate, who participated in the trial of Jesus (Acts 4:27). It reads, "Pontius Pilate, Prefect of Judea."

The ossuary of Caiaphas, the Jewish high priest who officiated at Jesus' trial, has been discovered (see Matthew 26:57). Inscriptions read, "Caiaphas" and "Joseph, son of Caiaphas." It contained the bones of six people, including a 60-year-old (Caiaphas).

A limestone box has been discovered that apparently contains the bones of James, the half-brother of Jesus. It bears the words, "James, son of Joseph, brother of Jesus" (see Mark 6:3).

Nazareth, Jesus' hometown, has been excavated. Among the discoveries are olive oil presses and a large number of diverse artifacts from the time of Christ (see Matthew 2:23; 4:13). Moreover, Jacob's well, where Jesus spoke with a Samaritan woman, has been discovered near Mount Gerizim (John 4:1-42). Two tombs have been discovered in Jerusalem that are excellent candidates for the site from which Jesus rose from the dead (Matthew 27:57-60).

Archaeologists have uncovered a judgment seat in the city of Corinth. This was a platform from which officials judged athletic contests and handed out rewards. Christians will one day face the judgment seat of Christ (2 Corinthians 5:10).

Pearl of Wisdom: *The more we dig up in biblical lands, the more we find evidence of people, places, and events mentioned in the New Testament.*

Formal Equivalence

Translation based on formal equivalence advocates as precise a word-for-word and form-for-form rendering of the original text as is possible.

This approach is an attempt to accurately reproduce the grammar and syntax of the original Hebrew or Greek text. Infinitives in the Greek are translated as infinitives in the English, and prepositional phrases in the Greek are translated as prepositional phrases in the English.

These translations have several benefits. They attempt to retain the writing style of the original writers, preserve the original beauty of Scripture, and retain theological terminology—terms that are necessary for a full-orbed understanding of what God intended to communicate. For example, such translations will utilize the theological word *justification* instead of inserting a simple substitute, like *being made right with God*.

Formal equivalence translations can also be trusted not to mix too much commentary with the text derived from the original Hebrew and Greek manuscripts. Of course, all translation entails some interpretation, but formal equivalence translations keep it to a minimum. This view sees the translator as a steward of what someone else wrote, not as an editor who has the freedom to correct what someone else has written.

———

Pearl of Wisdom: *Formal-equivalence Bibles make excellent study Bibles!*

Dynamic Equivalence

The goal of the dynamic equivalence approach is to provide an easily readable translation that communicates the meaning of the text rather than a word-for-word rendering. It is a thought-for-thought, meaning-driven method that seeks to produce the same dynamic impact on modern readers that the original had on its audience. Translators who subscribe to this philosophy hold that a word-for-word translation does not always adequately capture the meaning of the original text, so a dynamic-equivalent rendering is necessary.

Dynamic-equivalence translations generally use shorter words, shorter sentences, and shorter paragraphs. They use accessible vocabulary instead of technical theological and cultural terminology. They often convert culturally dependent figures of speech into more direct statements. They seek to avoid ambiguity and biblical jargon in favor of a natural vernacular style.

A dynamic-equivalence translation provides contemporary equivalents to phrases that are not common today, such as "Truly, truly, I say unto you" and "Thus saith the Lord." Such translations also clarify cultural customs within the text—for example, rendering "tore his clothes" as "tore his clothes in grief" (Genesis 37:29).

Dynamic-equivalence translations also sometimes diverge from the word order of the original Hebrew and Greek. They do so to produce a natural translation that is more readily understood.

Pearl of Wisdom: *Dynamic-equivalence Bibles make reading the Bible easier, but comparing them with a formal-equivalence Bible is a good idea.*

Gender-Inclusive Language

The original Greek and Hebrew biblical text often uses words like men and brothers to refer to males and females. A tremendous debate has erupted in recent years as to whether translators should use gender-inclusive language. Gender-inclusive language has these advantages:

- It makes Bibles clearer and more accurate in terms of the author's intended meaning.
- Some grammars permit the use of *they* and *them* instead of *he* and *him*.
- Gender-sensitive language does not change the essential meaning of the text.
- The Bible was written for everyone, so *brothers* is better rendered *brothers and sisters*.
- Many female readers of the Bible feel left out by male terminology.

On the other hand...

- Such translations could lose elegance by an overuse of *people* and *persons*.
- Using *they* or *them* could obscure God's personal dealings with individuals.
- Such translations are not word-for-word renderings.
- God chose the words of Scripture, and humans should not change them.

Pearl of Wisdom: *Christians should study this issue and come to their own conclusion on it. My book* The Complete Guide to Bible Translations *may be of help.*

Principles of Bible Interpretation

You'll be likely to interpret the Bible accurately if you follow these principles:

- Seek the author's intended meaning instead of superimposing a meaning onto the text. The meaning of a passage is fixed by the author and is not subject to alteration by readers.

- When the plain sense makes good sense, seek no other sense. A literal hermeneutic is best!

- Pay close attention to the context. Individual verses are not isolated fragments, but parts of a whole. Interpreting them includes discovering their relationship to each other and to the entire passage.

- Make a correct genre judgment. The Bible contains a variety of literary genres (history, drama, poetry, wise sayings, apocalyptic writings…), each of which has certain peculiar characteristics to consider when interpreting the text.

- Consult history and culture. Step out of a contemporary Western mind-set and into a first-century Jewish mind-set. What did the biblical words mean to the original readers?

- Interpret the difficult verses in light of the clear verses.

- Interpret the Old Testament in light of the New Testament.

Pearl of Wisdom: *Depend on the Holy Spirit for illumination, for He who inspired Scripture (2 Timothy 3:16) is also its best interpreter (John 16:13; 1 Corinthians 2:12).*

A Literal Interpretation of the Bible

Here are some examples that show that the Bible encourages a literal interpretation of itself.

- The Bible looks back at its own accounts and interprets them literally, including the creation of the universe (Exodus 20:10-11), the creation of Adam and Eve (Matthew 19:6), Noah's flood (Matthew 24:38), and Jonah's experience (Matthew 12:40-42).

- More than 100 prophecies about the Messiah were fulfilled literally, including His descent from Abraham (Genesis 12:3) and David (Jeremiah 23:5-6), His virgin birth (Isaiah 7:14) in Bethlehem (Micah 5:2), His suffering for our sins (Isaiah 53), and His resurrection (Psalm 2; 16).

- The Bible indicates the presence of parables (see Matthew 13:3) or an allegory (Galatians 4:24), so the ordinary meaning is a literal one.

- Jesus provided the literal interpretations of His parables (Matthew 13:18-23).

- Jesus rebuked those who did not interpret the resurrection literally (Matthew 22:29-32).

Pearl of Wisdom: *Scripture itself sets the precedent, so we should interpret Scripture literally.*

Esoteric Interpretation

An esoteric method of interpreting Scripture seeks hidden or secondary (spiritual) meanings in Bible verses. This type of methodology is illegitimate for many reasons.

- Scripture tells us not to distort its meaning (2 Peter 3:16).

- Each verse of Scripture has only one correct meaning, not multiple pliable meanings.

- The basic authority in esoteric interpretation is not Scripture, but the mind of the interpreter. Consequently, esoteric interpretations have irreconcilable contradictions.

- Esoteric interpretation relies on inner illumination, not the Holy Spirit (1 Corinthians 2:9-11; John 16:12-15).

- Esotericism superimposes meanings on Bible verses instead of objectively seeking the biblical author's intended meaning. But the author's meaning is fixed and is not subject to alteration by readers.

- Esotericism ignores issues of context, grammar, history, and culture.

- Jesus always interpreted the Old Testament Scriptures literally.

Pearl of Wisdom: *An esoteric method of interpreting the Bible will lead you astray!*

The Wisdom Sayings and Bible Promises

The book of Proverbs contains maxims of moral wisdom. The word *proverb* literally means "to be like" or "to be compared with." Proverbs, then, communicate truth by using comparisons or figures of speech. The proverbs, in a memorable way, crystallize the writers' experiences and observations about life and provide principles that are generally (but not always) true. The reward of meditating on these maxims is, of course, wisdom. But they were never intended to be promises.

Consider Proverbs 22:6: "Train up a child in the way he should go; even when he is old he will not depart from it." Some parents have claimed this verse as a promise and have done everything they could to bring their children up rightly. But in some cases, the children have departed from Christianity and gone astray. The parents of these children become disillusioned and wonder what they did wrong.

But Proverbs 22:6 was never intended to be a promise. Like other wisdom sayings in Proverbs, this verse presents a principle that is generally true. But general principles have exceptions. For example, God Himself is a perfect parent, but His children, Adam and Eve, certainly went astray.

Pearl of Wisdom: *If you follow the general wisdom principles laid out in Proverbs, you will generally see positive results in your life, and your life will generally be much more successful!*

Conditional and Unconditional Promises

Christians sometimes fail to recognize this distinction. God fulfills His conditional promises only after we meet certain obligations. If we don't meet the conditions, God is not obligated to fulfill those promises. For example, John 15:7 says, "If you abide in me, and my words abide in you, ask whatever you wish, and it will be done for you." This promise guarantees that God will answer our prayers only if Christ's words remain in us and we remain in Christ.

An unconditional promise, by contrast, depends on no such conditions for its fulfillment. No ifs are attached. God sovereignly fulfills His unconditional promises to those of us in His family regardless of what we do. Many of the promises relating to our positional standing in Christ or our blessings in Him are unconditional. For example, we read in Galatians 4:6-7, "Because you are sons, God has sent the Spirit of his Son into our hearts, crying, 'Abba! Father!' So you are no longer a slave, but a son, and if a son, then an heir through God." We are sons and heirs in God's family not because we met certain conditions. Rather, all Christians benefit from this promise.

Pearl of Wisdom: *Let's be careful interpreters of God's Word, watching for distinctions between conditional promises and unconditional promises.*

Promises to the Israelites—and to Us?

God made numerous promises in the Old Testament specifically to Israel in specific contexts, so modern believers should not claim them for themselves. In Deuteronomy, for example, God through Moses promised great blessings if the theocratic (God-ruled) nation lived in obedience to the covenant God made at Sinai. God also promised that if the nation disobeyed, it would experience punishment—including captivity in exile (Deuteronomy 28:15-68). The Assyrian captivity of 722 BC and Babylonian captivity of 597–581 BC reveal that God is a promise keeper.

Here is a promise God made to Israel: "If my people who are called by my name humble themselves, and pray and seek my face and turn from their wicked ways, then I will hear from heaven and will forgive their sin and heal their land" (2 Chronicles 7:14). God spoke these words specifically to Solomon regarding Israel in particular, yet how often do people today claim this verse as a promise for their own country?

Of course, God generally responds positively to prayer and humility, so He may well answer our prayer when we humble ourselves, seek His face, and turn from our wicked ways. However, we cannot claim this verse as an ironclad promise for our own country.

We are to avoid distorting the Bible (2 Peter 3:16) and should correctly handle the word of truth (2 Timothy 2:15). Surely these directives include not claiming a promise for ourselves that was intended for others.

Pearl of Wisdom: *Accurately interpreting God's Word is always in our best interests.*

Promises in the Old Testament and Today

Yesterday I noted that God made many Old Testament promises to Israel alone. But this is not the case with *all* promises in the Old Testament.

Many promises in the Old Testament are based on God's nature and not on specific circumstances among the Israelites. For example, Isaiah 55:11 says this about God's Word: "It shall not return to me empty, but it shall accomplish that which I purpose, and shall succeed in the thing for which I sent it." This promise is based on God's sovereignty, which does not change, so it is true at all times in all places. We can rest assured that God's Word is still effective today, just as it was in Old Testament times.

Some Old Testament promises are applicable today because of strong parallel promises in the New Testament. This seems to indicate that God issues certain general promises to His people regardless of whether they lived in Old Testament times or New Testament times and beyond. Consider Psalm 34:22: "None of those who take refuge in him will be condemned." This is quite similar to John 3:18, where we read, "Whoever believes in him is not condemned."

Pearl of Wisdom: *Old Testament promises that are based on God's nature or that have strong parallels in the New Testament can be claimed as promises for today.*

Christian Meditation

In the Bible, meditation entails objectively contemplating and reflecting on God's nature (Psalm 48:9; 104:34), His works (Psalm 77:12; 143:5), and His Word (Psalm 1:2; 19:14; 119; Joshua 1:8). This is completely different from subjectively emptying our minds to meditate on nothing (as in Eastern meditation). In Christian meditation, we look upward to God so our minds may be filled with godly wisdom and insight, and our hearts may be filled with comfort, happiness, and joy.

The Hebrew term translated *meditation* has rich nuances of meaning. In different contexts, it can mean to utter, imagine, speak, roar, mutter, meditate, and muse. For example, in Isaiah 31:4, it is used to express the roar of a lion. In Isaiah 38:14 it refers to the sound of doves mourning. Both cases imply that our outward expression flows from our strong inner emotions and thoughts.

This Hebrew term seems to carry the basic idea of murmuring. It portrays a person who is very deep in thought, mumbling as though talking to himself. When David meditated on God's Word, he concentrated so intensely that he no doubt murmured with his lips as he read.

Pearl of Wisdom: *To daily meditate on God's nature, His works, and His Word is good for us.*

Majestic and All-Powerful but Also Personal

God is an eternal, all-powerful, all-knowing Spirit who is everywhere-present and who is the Creator and Sustainer of the universe (Isaiah 44:24). There are no other gods besides Him. God affirmed through Moses, "See now that I, even I, am he, and there is no god beside me" (Deuteronomy 32:39), and through Isaiah, "I am the first and I am the last; besides me there is no god" (Isaiah 44:6).

This majestic God is personal. A person is a conscious being—one who thinks, feels, purposes, and carries these purposes into action. A person engages in active relationships with others. You can talk to a person and get a response. You can share feelings and ideas with him. You can argue with him, love him, and even hate him. Surely by this description, God must be understood as a person. After all, God is a conscious being who thinks, feels, and purposes—and He carries these purposes into action. He engages in relationships with others. You can talk to God and get a response from Him.

The Bible pictures God as a loving personal Father to whom believers may cry, "Abba" (Romans 8:15). *Abba* is an Aramaic term of great intimacy, loosely meaning "daddy." God is the "father of mercies" for all believers (2 Corinthians 1:3). He compassionately responds to the personal requests of His people (see Psalm 81:10; 91:14-15; 2 Corinthians 1:3-4; Philippians 4:6-7).

Pearl of Wisdom: *Because God is personal, let's make every effort to pursue a personal relationship with Him daily.*

God the Father

S ome people today complain that the biblical portrayal of God as male—
a heavenly Father—is sexist. They may prefer to worship a heavenly
Father-Mother or perhaps a mother-goddess.

The biblical God, of course, values men and women equally, for He
created both in His own image (Genesis 1:26). Christian men and women
are also positionally equal before God (Galatians 3:28). The four Gospels
indicate that Jesus defended and exalted women in a very patriarchal Jewish
culture (see John 4). So Christianity cannot be said to be sexist.

The Bible refers to God as Father and never as Mother, but some of His
actions are occasionally described in feminine terms. For example, Jesus
likened God to a loving and saddened mother hen crying over the way-
wardness of her brood (Matthew 23:37-39). God is also said to have "given
birth" to Israel (Deuteronomy 32:18).

Of course, God is not a gender being as humans are. He is not of the
male sex. God is called Father because He is personal. Unlike the dead and
impersonal idols of paganism, the true God is a personal being with whom
we can relate. In fact, we can even call Him "Abba"—an Aramaic word
that loosely means "daddy." That gives us an idea of the intimate relationship He desires to have with us.

Pearl of Wisdom: *Whether you are male or female, your heavenly Father loves
you personally and passionately.*

God's Names

We learn all kinds of inspiring things about God from the names the Bible ascribes to Him. These names are not man-made; God Himself used these names to describe Himself. They describe His character, each one revealing something new about Him.

Yahweh. This name means God is eternally self-existent (see Exodus 3:14-15). He never came into being at a point in time.

Yahweh-Nissi. This can be translated, "the Lord Our Banner." Israel could not defeat its enemies in its own strength. But the battles were the Lord's because He was Israel's banner—its source of victory (Exodus 17:15).

Elohim. This name means "Strong One" or "Mighty One" and indicates fullness of power (Genesis 1:1). It pictures God as the powerful and sovereign Governor of the universe.

El Shaddai. El in Hebrew refers to the Mighty God, but *Shaddai* qualifies this meaning and adds something to it (Genesis 17:1-20). Many scholars believe *Shaddai* is derived from a root word that refers to a mother's breast. This name, then, indicates not only that God is a Mighty God but also that He is full of compassion, grace, and mercy, just like a mother.

Adonai. This name means "Lord" or "Master" and conveys God's absolute authority over man (Genesis 18:27).

Lord of Hosts. This title pictures God as the sovereign commander of a great heavenly army of angels (Psalm 89:6,8; 91:11-12).

Pearl of Wisdom: *Our God is an awesome God!*

Elohim

Some cults claim that the plural ending of *Elohim*, a Hebrew name for God, allows for polytheism instead of belief in a single God. Nothing could be further from the truth!

Where the Bible uses this word of the one true God (which is the majority of cases), the plural is used grammatically. It is called a "plural of majesty" and points to the majesty, dignity, and greatness of God. The plural form gives a fuller, more majestic sense to God's name.

Many Old Testament verses use the term *Elohim* but declare that God is absolutely one. They prove that this plural form is not intended to indicate more than one God. For example, the Shema uses the term *Elohim*: "Hear, O Israel: The LORD our God [*Elohim*], the LORD is one" (Deuteronomy 6:4). The verse points to one and only one God.

Some may wonder about the plural pronouns—*us* and *our*—being used in reference to *Elohim*. In Genesis 1:26, God says: "Let us make man in our image." Hebrew grammarians tell us that the plural pronouns in the passage are a grammatical necessity. The plural pronoun *us* is required by the plural ending of *Elohim*. One demands the other.

Pearl of Wisdom: *Our God is virtually brimming with majesty, dignity, and greatness!*

God's Attributes

Studying God's awesome attributes is a great way to learn about Him. He is...

- *Self-existent.* He is the uncaused First Cause who created the universe (John 1:3).

- *Eternal.* He has always existed, and is beyond time altogether (1 Timothy 1:17; 6:16).

- *Love.* He is the very personification of love (1 John 4:8).

- *Everywhere-present.* His whole being is in every place (Psalm 139:7-8).

- *All-knowing.* He knows all things, both actual and possible (Matthew 11:21-23); past, present, and future (Isaiah 41:22; 46:10; Hebrews 4:13).

- *All-powerful.* He is almighty (Revelation 19:6). No one can reverse Him (Isaiah 43:13) or thwart Him (Isaiah 14:27).

- *Sovereign.* He rules the universe, controls all things, and is Lord over all (Psalm 50:1; 66:7; Isaiah 40:15,17).

- *Unchanging.* His being, nature, and attributes are always the same (Malachi 3:6).

- *Holy.* He is separate from all evil and absolutely pure in every way (Exodus 15:11).

- *Just.* He carries out His righteous standards justly and with equity (Romans 3:26).

Pearl of Wisdom: *The only appropriate response to God's awesomeness is praise and worship.*

God Is Spirit

The Scriptures tell us that God is Spirit (John 4:24). A spirit does not have flesh and bones (Luke 24:39), so we should not think of God as some sort of exalted Man in the Great Beyond. Because God is spirit, He is invisible. First Timothy 1:17 (NASB) refers to God as "the King eternal, immortal, invisible, the only God" (see also Colossians 1:15).

The theological term *transcendence* describes God's otherness or separateness from the created universe and from humanity. The term *immanence* refers to God's active presence within the creation and in human history—though all the while remaining distinct from the creation.

God's transcendence and immanence are evident in many Bible verses. In Deuteronomy 4:39, we read, "Know therefore today, and lay it to your heart, that the LORD is God in heaven above and on the earth beneath." In Isaiah 57:15 God states, "I dwell in the high and holy place, and also with him who is of a contrite and lowly spirit, to revive the spirit of the lowly, and to revive the heart of the contrite." In Jeremiah 23:23-24 God affirms, "'Am I a God at hand,' declares the LORD, 'and not a God far away?...Do I not fill heaven and earth?' declares the LORD."

Pearl of Wisdom: *Our awesome God is above and beyond us but also right next to us!*

Is God Distant?

Some people wonder why God sometimes seems to keep His distance. Theologians suggest that for God to continually intervene in human affairs would interfere with His overall plan of sifting the true inner character of people over a prolonged time. Each person has been given a stewardship of time on earth, and that person's allotment of time reveals his or her true nature.

In Revelation 2:20-21, the sovereign Jesus in heaven refers to a woman named Jezebel. She "calls herself a prophetess and is teaching and seducing my servants to practice sexual immorality...I gave her time to repent, but she refuses to repent of her sexual immorality." Jesus here speaks of a specific period of time that has been allotted for this person to repent, but she has failed to do so. Had Christ appeared to her directly, she likely would have feigned external obedience. (Even criminals behave rightly when a police officer drives by.) By allotting this woman a period of time during which Christ patiently waited and watched from a distance, He sifted out her true character.

God does the same thing with us. He gives each human being an allotment of time on earth, during which He sifts out his true character. He watches from a distance, observing what he does in response to His Word—but only for a time. Once our allotment of time is up, we must face God and give an account (Psalm 62:12; Matthew 16:27).

Pearl of Wisdom: *Take the "long look." One day we'll give an account to God! Live accordingly.*

Pantheism and the Bible

Pantheism is the view that God is all and all is God. The word *pantheism* comes from two Greek words—*pan* (all) and *theos* (God). In pantheism, all reality is viewed as being infused with divinity.

Theologians and philosophers have noted a number of problems with this view of God. First, it contradicts common sense. If all is truly God, then I am no different from anything else in the world.

Second, the distinction between the Creator (who is infinite) and the creation (which is finite) is completely obliterated in this view. Biblically, however, God is eternally distinct from His creation (Hebrews 11:3; see also Genesis 1:1; Psalm 33:8-9).

Third, the pantheistic God is an impersonal force. By contrast, the God of the Bible is a personal being with whom relationships can be established (see Philippians 3:8; 1 John 1:3; see also Jeremiah 9:23-24).

Fourth, pantheism fails to adequately deal with the existence of real evil in the world. If God is the essence of all life forms in creation, then both good and evil must stem from the same essence (God). The Bible, on the other hand, teaches that God is good and not evil. The God of the Bible is light, and "in him is no darkness at all" (1 John 1:5; see also Habakkuk 1:13; Matthew 5:48). God is utterly good (see Psalm 25:8; 34:8; 86:5; 100:5; 106:1).

Pearl of Wisdom: *We can rejoice that the true God is a personal being with whom we can enjoy a personal relationship.*

God's Sovereignty

God is sovereign. That means He is the absolute Ruler of the universe. He may utilize various means to accomplish His ends, including first causes and second causes, but He is always in control.

Psalm 66:7 tells us that God "rules by his might forever." We are assured in Psalm 93:1 that "the Lord reigns." Job wisely affirmed to God, "I know that you can do all things, and that no purpose of yours can be thwarted" (Job 42:2). Isaiah 40:15 tells us that by comparison, "the nations are like a drop from a bucket." Indeed, "all the nations are as nothing before him" (Isaiah 40:17).

God asserts, "My counsel shall stand, and I will accomplish all my purpose" (Isaiah 46:10). He assures us, "As I have planned, so shall it be, and as I have purposed, so shall it stand" (Isaiah 14:24). God is "the blessed and only Sovereign, the King of kings and Lord of lords" (1 Timothy 6:15).

Proverbs 16:9 tells us, "The heart of man plans his way, but the LORD establishes his steps." Proverbs 19:21 says, "Many are the plans in the mind of a man, but it is the purpose of the LORD that will stand." In Proverbs 21:30 we read, "No wisdom, no understanding, no counsel can avail against the LORD."

Ecclesiastes 7:13 thus instructs, "Consider the work of God: who can make straight what he has made crooked?" Lamentations 3:37 affirms, "Who has spoken and it came to pass, unless the Lord has commanded it?"

Pearl of Wisdom: *Our awesome God reigns!*

God, the Almighty Judge

The God of the Bible is a God of judgment. In the Old Testament we see God expelling Adam and Eve from the Garden of Eden (Genesis 3) and judging the corrupt world of Noah's day by sending a flood (Genesis 6–8). In the New Testament, judgment falls on Ananias and Sapphira for lying to God (Acts 5), on Herod for his self-exalting pride (Acts 12:21), and on Christians in Corinth who were afflicted with illness in response to their irreverent behavior at the Lord's Supper (1 Corinthians 11:29-32).

All believers will one day stand before the judgment seat of Christ (Romans 14:8-10). At that time He will examine the deeds each believer performed on earth. Personal motives and intents of the heart will also be weighed (see 1 Corinthians 3:11-15; 2 Corinthians 5:10). Based on how they fare, believers will either receive or lose rewards (1 Corinthians 9:25; 2 Timothy 4:8; James 1:12).

Unlike believers, whose judgment deals only with rewards and loss of rewards, unbelievers face a horrific judgment at the great white throne that leads to their being cast into the lake of fire (Revelation 20:11-15). Christ will be the divine Judge, and He will judge the unsaved dead of all time. Those who face Christ at this judgment will be judged on the basis of their works (Revelation 20:12-13).

Pearl of Wisdom: *None of us is getting away with anything. We will all face judgment! Live accordingly.*

Our Incomparable God

Yahweh is incomparable. No one is like Him.

Moses expressed God's incomparability in two different ways, most commonly by negation—"There is no one like the LORD our God" (Exodus 8:10). The second way was with rhetorical questions, such as, "Who is like you, O LORD, among the gods?" (Exodus 15:11). The implied answer is, no one in all the universe.

In Egyptian religion, the god at the very top of the totem pole was the sun god, *Re*. Next in line was the Pharaoh of Egypt, who was considered to be the son of *Re*. So Pharaoh was considered a god in his own right. Because *Re* was considered superior to all other gods, his son—Pharaoh—was also considered to possess unmatched power as a god. This adds an entirely new dimension to the Exodus account, where a contest occurs between the true God and the false gods of Egypt's mystery religions (see Numbers 33:4).

Pharaoh was unable to turn back the mighty plagues of Yahweh. The Nile River god *Nilus* was unable to respond when Yahweh turned the whole river to blood (Exodus 7:17-21). The sun god *Re* was unable to respond when Yahweh turned the entire land dark (Exodus 10:21-22). The Egyptian pantheon was impotent before Yahweh.

Pearl of Wisdom: *Truly, no one in the universe is like God! He is incomparable.*

The God of Christianity and the God of Islam

Allah and the God of the Bible (Yahweh) share some similarities: Both are one (as opposed to the gods of pantheism or polytheism), transcendent, creators of the universe, sovereign, and omnipotent. Both have communicated through angels and prophets and will eventually judge all humankind. But the differences are so substantive that a common identity is impossible.

(1) Allah is not a Trinity, but Yahweh is—one God eternally manifest in three persons (Matthew 28:19). (2) Allah cannot have a son (an idea that is considered blasphemous). The Christian heavenly Father has an eternal Son (John 3:16). (3) Allah is not spirit. Yahweh is spirit (John 4:24).

(4) Allah is only transcendent. Yahweh is both transcendent and immanent (Deuteronomy 4:39; Isaiah 57:15; Jeremiah 23:23-24). (5) Allah brings about good and evil. Yahweh never engages in evil (1 John 1:5). (6) Allah is not a Father (Sura 19:88-92; 112:3). Yahweh is a heavenly Father (Matthew 6:9).

(7) Allah loves only those who love him and obey him. Yahweh loves all people, including all sinners (see Luke 15:11-24). (8) Allah desires to afflict people for their sins (Sura 5:49). Yahweh is "not wishing that any should perish, but that all should reach repentance" (2 Peter 3:9). (9) Allah reveals only his laws and not himself. Yahweh has revealed Himself from the beginning. (10) Allah has no objective basis for forgiving people. Yahweh does have an objective basis—the death of Jesus Christ on the cross of Calvary.

Pearl of Wisdom: *Allah bears no relation to the one true God of the Bible.*

God Is a Trinity

God is one, but in the unity of the Godhead are three coequal and coeternal persons—the Father, the Son, and the Holy Spirit—who are equal in the divine nature but distinct in personhood. The doctrine of the Trinity is based on three lines of evidence.

Evidence for one God. From Genesis to Revelation, Scripture consistently testifies to the one true God (Isaiah 44:6; John 17:3; Romans 3:29-30; 1 Corinthians 8:4).

Evidence for three persons who are called God. Though Scripture is clear that God is one, Scripture progressively reveals that three distinct persons are called God: The Father is God (1 Peter 1:2), Jesus is God (Hebrews 1:8), and the Holy Spirit is God (Acts 5:3-4).

Evidence for three-in-oneness in the Godhead. Matthew 28:19 reads, "Go therefore and make disciples of all nations, baptizing them in the name of the Father and of the Son and of the Holy Spirit." The word *name* is singular in the Greek, indicating that God is one, but three distinct persons are mentioned—the Father, the Son, and the Holy Spirit. Paul's benediction to the Corinthians is similar: "The grace of the Lord Jesus Christ and the love of God and the fellowship of the Holy Spirit be with you all" (2 Corinthians 13:14).

Pearl of Wisdom: *The one true God—Father, Son, and Holy Spirit—is holy, holy, holy.*

Is the Trinity a Logical Contradiction?

The most fundamental objection to the Trinity is that it violates the law of noncontradiction, which affirms that God cannot be both one and three at the same time. But this is a misunderstanding of this basic principle of logic.

According to the law of noncontradiction, two propositions are contradictory if they both affirm and deny the same thing, at the same time, and in the same sense or in the same relationship. The doctrine of the Trinity, however, does not affirm that God is both one and three in the same sense or relationship. Rather, it affirms that God is one and only one in His essence, but He is three in His persons. Therefore, the Trinity is not contradictory. *Person* and *essence* are different. *Person* reveals who He is, and *essence* refers to what He is. So the Trinity does not refer to three whos in one *who* (which would be a contradiction), but three whos in one *what* (which is not a contradiction).

So even though the Trinity is a mystery that goes *beyond* reason, it is not a contradiction that goes *against* reason. To comprehend how three persons can exist in one nature is beyond our finite ability, but to apprehend the noncontradictory nature of both premises is not beyond our finite ability.

Pearl of Wisdom: *The doctrine of the Trinity may be beyond reason, but it is not against reason.*

The Trinity and Ancient Paganism

Some cults, such as Oneness Pentecostalism, argue that the doctrine of the Trinity emerged out of paganism. Pagan nations such as the Babylonians and Assyrians, however, believed in triads of gods who headed up a pantheon of many other gods. This triad-pantheon religious system constituted polytheism, which is utterly different from the doctrine of the Trinity. The doctrine of the Trinity affirms only one God (monotheism) with three persons within the one Godhead.

The pagans taught the concept of a creator. They also taught the concept of a great flood that killed much of humankind, as well as the idea of a messiah-like figure named Tammuz, who was resurrected. If cultists were consistent in their reasoning, they would have to strip from their beliefs the idea of a creator, the flood, the Messiah, and the resurrection because of loose parallels of these doctrines in pagan religions.

Though Oneness Pentecostals argue that the Trinity is pagan, their concept of modalism is as pagan as can be. Hindus view God as Brahman (the absolute and undivided one) who is revealed in three modes: Brahma (creator), Vishnu (preserver), and Shiva (destroyer). This is quite similar to the Oneness view of one God revealed in three modes—Father, Son, and Holy Spirit.

Pearl of Wisdom: *Christians believe in the Trinity because the concept is clearly taught within the pages of Scripture (Matthew 28:19; 2 Corinthians 13:14).*

Jesus and the Trinity

Modalists, both ancient and modern, have claimed that Jesus is the one God who manifests Himself in three modes—Father, Son, and Holy Spirit. They point to verses that show that God is absolutely one (Deuteronomy 6:4; Isaiah 44:6). They then reason that because God is one, and because the New Testament reveals that Jesus is God (John 8:58; Colossians 2:9), Jesus must therefore be the one true God—Father, Son, and Holy Spirit.

Numerous scriptural facts counteract this viewpoint. Jesus refers to the Father as someone other than Himself more than 200 times in the New Testament. And more than 50 times in the New Testament, the Father and Son are distinct within the same verse (for example, Romans 15:6; Philippians 2:10-11). Scripture teaches the Trinity (Matthew 28:19).

Scripture also reveals that the Father sent the Son (John 3:16-17) and that the Father and Son love each other (John 3:35), speak to each other (John 11:41-42), and know each other (Matthew 11:27). Jesus is our advocate with the Father (1 John 2:1). Moreover, the Holy Spirit descended upon Jesus at His baptism (Luke 3:22). He is another comforter (John 14:16), who was sent by Jesus (John 15:26). The Holy Spirit also seeks to glorify Jesus (John 16:13-14). In view of such facts, it is impossible to argue that Jesus is the Father or the Holy Spirit.

Pearl of Wisdom: *False doctrine can often be avoided by following this simple interpretive principle: Scripture interprets Scripture.*

Divine Sovereignty and Human Freedom

Scripture portrays God as being absolutely sovereign over all things. All forms of existence are within the scope of His absolute dominion. God asserts, "My counsel shall stand, and I will accomplish all my purpose" (Isaiah 46:10). God assures us, "As I have planned, so shall it be, and as I have purposed, so shall it stand" (Isaiah 14:24). God is said to be "the blessed and only Sovereign, the King of kings and Lord of lords" (1 Timothy 6:15). Proverbs 19:21 says, "Many are the plans in the mind of a man, but it is the purpose of the LORD that will stand" (see also Proverbs 21:30; Ecclesiastes 7:13; Lamentations 3:37).

Scripture is equally clear regarding the fact of human freedom. Human beings are responsible for their moral choices as well as their eternal destiny. For example, God commanded Adam and Eve not to eat the forbidden fruit (Genesis 2:16-17), and after they disobeyed, God asked them: "What is this that you have done?" (3:13). Adam acknowledged his personal responsibility in wrongly using his free will by saying, "She gave me fruit of the tree, and I ate" (verse 12), after which God pronounced judgment: "Because you have listened to the voice of your wife and have eaten of the tree...cursed is the ground because of you" (verse 17; see also Joshua 24:15; 1 Kings 18:21; Matthew 23:37; 2 Peter 3:5).

Pearl of Wisdom: *None of us can blame our sovereign God for our wrong choices.*

Three Views of Predetermination

Extreme Calvinism: Predetermination is in spite of foreknowledge. In this view, God operates with such unapproachable sovereignty that He makes choices with no consideration of the choices people make. God sovereignly saves whomever He wishes to save. The big problem with this view is that it denies people's freedom to make choices.

Arminianism: God's predetermination is based on His foreknowledge. In this view, God in His omniscience knows in advance what choices everyone will make, including whether they will accept or reject salvation. On the basis of this foreknowledge, God elects to salvation those whom He foreknows will accept Christ. The problem with this view is that the Bible indicates not only that God knows things in advance but also that He actually determines what will happen (Isaiah 14:24; 46:10; Proverbs 16:9; 19:21; 21:1).

Moderate Calvinism: God's predetermination is in accord with His foreknowledge. According to this view, God's election is based neither on His foreknowledge (Arminianism) nor in spite of His foreknowledge (extreme Calvinism), but rather is "according to the foreknowledge of God" (1 Peter 1:2). In this view, neither election nor foreknowledge have a chronological or logical priority. All aspects of God's eternal purpose are equally timeless (and simultaneous). Both divine sovereignty and human freedom are fully operational in this system.

Pearl of Wisdom: *The most balanced view is probably moderate Calvinism.*

Resting in God's Sovereignty

When bad things happen in our lives, we can rest assured that all our circumstances are subject to God and that nothing can touch us unless God in His wisdom allows it to. And we can be sure that whatever He allows is for our own good (Romans 8:28).

Anyone who doubts that God can sovereignly direct our daily circumstances for our utmost good should read the book of Esther. Here we find God relentlessly and providentially working behind the scenes on behalf of His people. He does the same for us. Usually, though, we do not recognize that God is at work.

We may struggle with fear and anxiety because God does not sit us down and say, "Okay, listen, I'm going to allow some bad stuff to happen this next week, but I'm in control, and I'm using this event to bring about a great good. So don't worry about it. Everything's fine." Certainly God did not sit down and explain to Job why he suffered so terribly (see Job 1–2).

You and I are given the privilege of going behind the scenes in Job's life by reading the book of Job. But we are not able to discern the mysterious ways God works in our lives. That's why we have to trust Him. We can be sure, though, that God has engineered our circumstances for good (Genesis 45:8; 50:20).

Pearl of Wisdom: *You can trust that God is working in your life even when bad things happen.*

Saved *in* Trouble, Not *from* Trouble

God often does not save us from painful circumstances but rather sustains us in our painful circumstances. Consider the case of Shadrach, Meshach, and Abednego in Daniel 3. These three companions of Daniel refused to worship the image of gold set up by King Nebuchadnezzar, so the king threatened to throw them into a blazing fire (Daniel 3:15). They responded by informing him that God was perfectly able to rescue them (verse 17). This made the king so mad that he heated the furnace seven times hotter and had them tossed into the flames (verses 19-20).

As the king observed what should have been an instant incineration, he was suddenly startled by what he saw and exclaimed, "I see four men unbound, walking in the midst of the fire, and they are not hurt; and the appearance of the fourth is like a son of the gods" (Daniel 3:25). The king then commanded the three to come out, and after seeing that they were unharmed, he exclaimed, "Blessed be the God of Shadrach, Meshach, and Abednego, who has sent his angel and delivered his servants, who trusted in him" (verse 28).

If God had wanted to, He could have intervened earlier and prevented the three from being thrown into the furnace. But He chose not to do this. He allowed the three to be mistreated! But He did not allow them to go through this ordeal alone. God sent his angel to sustain them in the midst of the flames.

———

Pearl of Wisdom: *God's children are never alone in their trials.*

Our Intelligently Created Universe

Our universe is literally fine-tuned for the earth to sustain life. Many highly improbable factors have to be precisely in place in a balanced fashion for life to survive on earth. Without any one of these factors, life would not be possible.

For example, if the strength of gravitational attraction were different, life on earth would not be possible. If our moon were significantly larger, its gravitational pull would be greater, and this would cause tidal waves to engulf the land. If the earth had more than one moon, the tides would be unstable. If the earth were significantly closer to the sun, our atmosphere would be too hot for life to survive. The earth has just enough oxygen (21 percent of the atmosphere) for creatures to be able to breathe. In short, everything about our earth and the universe seems tailor-made for living things to exist.

Are these and a host of other similar factors the result of a random cosmic coincidence, or was an intelligent designer involved? Like many others, I believe the universe was indeed intelligently designed—and the intelligent designer was none other than Jesus Christ (John 1:3; Colossians 1:16; see also Psalm 19; Romans 1:20; Hebrews 3:4).

Pearl of Wisdom: *As we reflect on the majesty and splendor of the creation, we sense the greater majesty and splendor of the Creator.*

God's Fingerprints

People have become adept at recognizing signs of intelligence. Sometimes these signs are obvious, such as the four presidents chiseled into the granite cliff at Mount Rushmore, or a message in the sky like "Free Concert in the Park Tonight."

Other times, signs of intelligence must be uncovered. Many professionals seek for clues of "intelligent design" and intentionality—that is, clues that indicate that something happened because someone intentionally engaged in a particular action and not because of a chance occurrence. For example, crime scene investigators determine whether someone intentionally committed a crime, insurance investigators look for clues of intentional fraud, and archaeologists uncover evidence of intentionally designed artifacts.

Here is the point to remember: Just as crime scene investigators, archaeologists, cryptographers, copyright office workers, and people who see skywriting find evidence of intelligent beings' activity, so also we can clearly see evidence of intelligent design in the universe. Substantial evidence indicates that an intelligent being intentionally brought our universe into existence and that the universe was not the result of random chance or a cosmic accident. Such evidence serves as the primary focus of the academic field of intelligent design. As Romans 1:20 says, "His invisible attributes, namely, his eternal power and divine nature, have been clearly perceived, ever since the creation of the world, in the things that have been made."

Pearl of Wisdom: *The more we study the universe, the more we find the fingerprints of God—the intelligent Designer.*

Scientifically Discernible Design

One scientific test of intelligent design is "irreducible complexity." An irreducibly complex mechanism is composed of a number of well-matched, interacting parts that all contribute to the functioning of that mechanism. If any of these well-matched, interacting parts is removed, the mechanism no longer functions.

A mousetrap is a good example. This mechanism has a number of components that are necessary to its functioning. If any component is missing, it no longer functions correctly. If it's missing a spring, a hammer, or platform, for example, it will not work. That is why we call it irreducibly complex.

The eye is also irreducibly complex. It has many well-matched, interacting parts that contribute to the function of sight. If any of these well-matched, interacting parts is removed, the eye will no longer see. Among these parts are the sclera, the cornea, the aqueous humor, the vitreous humor, the choroid, the retina, rods and cones, and the pupil, all of which function together in harmony with the brain to facilitate sight.

Evolution cannot explain this mechanism. A piece-by-piece development of this incredibly complex organ—resulting from infinitesimally small Darwinian improvements over an unimaginably long period of time, requiring untold thousands of random positive mutations—is impossible to fathom. The evidence points to an incredibly knowledgeable engineer (God).

Pearl of Wisdom: *Given the evidence, one must have a great deal of faith to maintain commitment to evolutionism.*

Creationism and Thermodynamics

The first and second laws of thermodynamics are foundational to science and have never been contradicted in observable nature. The first law is the law of energy conservation, which says that energy cannot be created or destroyed; it can only change forms. The second law says that in an isolated system, the natural course of things is to degenerate. The universe is running down, not evolving upward. Although the total amount of energy remains constant and unchanged, it becomes less available for usable work as time goes on.

Based on the first and second laws of thermodynamics, scientists say our universe is headed toward an ultimate "heat death" in which energy conversions will no longer occur. The amount of usable energy will eventually be depleted. Our universe is decaying, eroding. The universe and everything in it, such as our sun, our bodies, the machines we build, and my car, are running down.

If the second law of thermodynamics is true, the universe must not be eternal. Therefore, the universe must have had a beginning. To use the metaphor of a clock, the universe must have once been fully wound up. This implies the existence of a Creator who initiated things in the beginning.

This is where the *kalam* cosmological argument is relevant: (1) Whatever had a beginning had a cause. (2) The universe had a beginning. (3) Therefore, the universe had a cause.

Pearl of Wisdom: *The universe had a cause, and that cause is the uncaused First Cause: God.*

Intelligent Design Is Science

Critics of intelligent design often argue that science must be based on firsthand observation, repetition, and replication. But we cannot observe a Designer in action, and we cannot repeat and replicate various aspects of intelligent design theory in a laboratory, so these critics conclude that the study of intelligent design cannot be true science.

But of course, firsthand observation and repetition are impossible in many areas of scientific study. Many scientists presently believe in the Big Bang theory, but they say this event happened only once some 13 to 15 billion years ago. No one was there to observe it firsthand, no one was there to take measurements, and obviously no one can repeat the event in a laboratory and test it over and over again. Yet no one balks at including the Big Bang theory within the realm of science.

Likewise, we cannot repeat in a laboratory the fossilization process of ancient life forms, but that does not exclude paleontology from the realm of science. We cannot repeat the inscribing of the Rosetta Stone, but that does not exclude archaeology from the realm of science.

My point is that our inability to observe firsthand and then repeat the work of the original intelligent Designer in a laboratory does not exclude intelligent design from science. The same kind of scientific inquiry utilized by CSI teams and insurance fraud investigators is used in intelligent design theory.

Pearl of Wisdom: *The evidence for intelligent design is credible enough that many scientists today have come to faith.*

Intelligent Design and DNA

DNA is a nucleic acid that carries genetic information in the cell that is capable of self-replication. The volume of information contained in DNA staggers the mind. A single human cell has enough information capacity to store the *Encyclopedia Britannica*—all 30 volumes—three or four times over.

Where did this staggering amount of information come from? I once heard a software expert say that DNA is like a computer program but far more advanced than any software we've ever created. And computer programs do not write themselves. A programmer is always involved. Even if a computer program ran for millions of years, it could not write itself. The same is true regarding the information in DNA. Somebody (God) had to program that complex information into DNA.

I may not have seen the computer programmer write the word processing software I am now using to write this book, but I have no doubt such a programmer exists. In the same way, I may not have seen the divine Designer do His work of programming information into DNA, but I cannot doubt that an intelligent mind was involved in the process.

Pearl of Wisdom: *The complex code in DNA requires the involvement of a super-intellect—and only one candidate fits the bill: God!*

Design Flaws?

Apparent design flaws do not indicate that no designer exists. The floor plan of a house may not be perfect, but that does not mean no one designed it. The same is true with the universe. A structure in the universe might have had a better design, but that does not mean the structure did not come from an intelligent designer (Hebrews 3:4).

Often, when we think we have a better design for an item, one conversation with the designer reveals variables we had not previously considered, and we see the design in a more favorable light. For example, I might think a computer encasing would have a better design if it were much smaller. But when I talk to the design engineer, I discover that the larger size better accommodates the internal cooling system for the components that generate heat. This new information adjusts my thinking so that I now know my idea would not necessarily result in a better design.

In the same way, we may think we can come up with better designs for structures in the universe, but we probably don't recognize some variables that the intelligent Designer is fully aware of. Maybe we do not know as much as we think we do.

Pearl of Wisdom: *Only an arrogant lump of clay presumes to correct the potter (Isaiah 29:16).*

Creation and Divine Revelation

No human spectators witnessed the creation, and the first man and woman were placed in an already existing universe, so we must accept whatever God has revealed about the creation by faith. Otherwise we will know nothing with certainty about the origin of the universe. Hebrews 11:3 tells us, "By faith we understand that the universe was created by the word of God, so that what is seen was not made out of things that are visible." Even if a human observer had been present at the creation, he could not have understood fully what he saw apart from God's own interpretation. Therefore, divine revelation would still have been necessary for us to understand the origin of the universe.

God has revealed that He created the universe *ex nihilo* (out of nothing) in an instantaneous fashion. Psalm 33 tells us, "By the word of the LORD the heavens were made, and by the breath of his mouth all their host...For he spoke, and it came to be; he commanded, and it stood firm" (verses 6,9; see also Genesis 1:3,6,9,14,20,24).

What a magnificent display of God's awesome power! As Jeremiah 32:17 says, "Ah, Lord GOD! It is you who have made the heavens and the earth by your great power and by your outstretched arm! Nothing is too hard for you."

Pearl of Wisdom: *Nothing is too hard for our Creator-God, so He is big enough to handle all your problems.*

Foundational Truths in Genesis

Genesis derives its name from the first three words of the book: "In the beginning." Genesis means "beginning." The book contains an account of the beginnings of the world, the universe, and humankind (Genesis 1–2). It also details the fall of man and the consequences of that fall (3).

The book of Genesis constitutes the foundation for the rest of the Bible. Indeed, if a Creator exists, as the book of Genesis indicates, then we are creatures who are responsible to Him. Moreover, if man is fallen in sin, as the book of Genesis indicates, then we are guilty and in need of redemption. If we dismiss the book of Genesis as a myth, much of the rest of the Bible makes little sense, for redemption from the fall is like a thread that runs through every other book in the Bible.

Genesis also introduces many heroes of faith. For example, Abraham's faith was on display when he was willing to sacrifice his own son Isaac in obedience to God's command (Genesis 22:1-19). (God stopped him just in the nick of time.) Joseph too showed great faith, knowing that even though his brothers treated him cruelly, God was with him and was working in his situations (50:20).

Pearl of Wisdom: *Let's follow the lead of Abraham and Joseph, trusting in God regardless of our circumstances.*

Scripture, Time, and Eternity

The book of Hebrews contains hints regarding the relationship between time and eternity. Hebrews 1:2 says the Father appointed Jesus the "heir of all things, through whom also he created the world." This last phrase is rendered more literally from the Greek, "through whom indeed he made the ages." Likewise, Hebrews 11:3 tells us that "by faith we understand that the universe was created by the word of God." This is more literally rendered, "By faith we understand that the ages were formed by a word of God."

Scholars have grappled with the meaning of "the ages." Some conclude this is an indication that time came into being when the creation came into being. The universe was not created in time; rather, time itself was created along with the universe.

God is sovereign over time. When God created the earth and put man on it, He set boundaries for day and night (Job 26:10) and divided the year into seasons (Genesis 1:14). These are markers by which we can orient ourselves as time passes. As the days continually pass, so seasons eventually pass. As seasons pass, so years eventually pass. And as years pass, we eventually die and enter into eternity—either with God in heaven or without Him in hell (see Matthew 25:31-46). The decision we make about Christ during our short time on earth is all-important.

Pearl of Wisdom: *Our times are in God's hands (Psalm 31:15), so we should "trust in him at all times" (Psalm 62:8).*

The Trinity and Creation

God affirmed in Isaiah 44:24, "Thus says the LORD, your Redeemer, who formed you from the womb: 'I am the LORD, who made all things, who alone stretched out the heavens, who spread out the earth by myself.'" Clearly, God is the sole Creator of the universe.

Many Bible passages attribute the creation simply to God rather than to the individual persons of the Father, Son, or Holy Spirit (for example, Genesis 1:1; Isaiah 44:24). Other passages, however, relate the creation specifically to the Father (1 Corinthians 8:6), to the Son (Colossians 1:16), or to the Holy Spirit (Psalm 104:30).

How are we to put all these passages together into a coherent whole? Some people suggest that creation is from the Father, through the Son, and by the Holy Spirit. First Corinthians 8:6 describes the Father as the one "from whom are all things" and the Son as the one "through whom are all things."

Based on this and other verses, many have concluded that the Father is the Creator in a broad, general sense, and the Son is the actual agent or mediating cause of creation. Through the Son, all things came into being. Creation is *in* or *by* the Holy Spirit in the sense that the life of creation is found in the Holy Spirit.

Pearl of Wisdom: *Our Creator-God is an awesome God, and His creation bears eloquent testimony to that greatness!*

The Days of Genesis 1

Here are four interpretations:

1. Some theologians believe the days were simply *revelatory* days—that is, they were days during which God revealed the creation scene to Moses. (Exodus 20:11, however, seems to contradict this view.)

2. Others believe each day represents an age. The Bible sometimes refers to a long period of time as a day (Psalm 90:4; 2 Peter 3:8).

3. Others believe the days were literal solar days, but each day was separated by a huge time gap. This allegedly accounts for the apparent long geological ages that science has discovered.

4. Still other theologians believe the days are literal solar days with no time gap between them. This is my view. In support of this view, the Genesis account makes reference to evening and morning, indicating that literal days are meant (Genesis 1:5). God created the sun to rule the day and the moon to rule the night, thus indicating solar days (verse 16). Further, Exodus 20:11 plainly states that "in six days the LORD made heaven and earth, the sea, and all that is in them, and rested on the seventh day." Moreover, Hebrew scholars tell us that whenever a number is used with the Hebrew word for day (*yom*), it always refers to a literal solar day. God created the universe in "six days," so Genesis must be referring to literal solar days.

Pearl of Wisdom: *As Psalm 19 indicates, the majestic creation points to the greater majesty and power of the Creator!*

The Gap Theory

The gap theory teaches that the universe was created perhaps billions of years ago, and it was perfect and beautiful in every way. This is the creation of Genesis 1:1. As a result of Lucifer's fall (Isaiah 14; Ezekiel 28), the earth—Lucifer's domain—became chaos. The picture of formlessness and emptiness in Genesis 1:2 is allegedly a picture of divine judgment (see Isaiah 24:1; 45:18). According to this view, millions or even billions of years elapsed between verses 1 and 2. But this theory has substantial problems.

- The grammar of Genesis 1:1-2 does not allow for a gap. Verse 1 is an independent clause. Verse 2 contains three circumstantial clauses that explain the condition of the earth when God began to create.

- The Bible never teaches that Satan's fall resulted in the judgment of the earth.

- According to the gap theory, the earth was "formless and void" because of God's judgment. Such a conclusion is unwarranted.

- The suggestion that Genesis 1:2 should be translated "the earth *became* without form and empty" instead of "the earth *was* without form and empty" is unwarranted. The Hebrew word in question should always be translated *was* unless there is compelling evidence to the contrary.

- Scripture plainly states that God created everything in six days (Exodus 20:11). This leaves no room for God to have engaged in a previous creation.

Pearl of Wisdom: *A look at a verse's grammar often helps us determine the best interpretation.*

Intelligent Life on Other Planets

The Bible offers good reasons to doubt that intelligent life exists on other planets. Scripture points to the absolute centrality of the earth and gives us no hint that life exists elsewhere. Admittedly, the earth is but an astronomical atom among the whirling constellations, only a tiny speck of dust among the ocean of stars and planets in the universe. But the earth is nevertheless the center of God's work of salvation in the universe.

On the earth God presents Himself in solemn covenants and divine appearances; on it the Son of God became man; on it stood the cross of the Redeemer of the world; and on it—though indeed on the new earth, yet still on the earth—the throne of God and the Lamb will rest (Revelation 21:1-2; 22:3).

The centrality of the earth is also evident in the creation account, for God created the earth before He created the rest of the planets and stars (see Genesis 1). The rest of the universe exists simply as a testimony of God's greatness (Psalm 19:1-4).

Adam's sin seems to have affected the entire universe (Genesis 3:14-19; Romans 8:19-22). How then could unfallen creatures live on another planet?

Pearl of Wisdom: *The earth is the theological heart and center of God's work of salvation in the universe.*

Progressive Creationism

According to progressive creationism, God engaged in a series of creative acts over a very long period of time. The days of Genesis are viewed as long ages (see Psalm 90:4; 2 Peter 3:8). God created the first member of each species, and from that original, other members of that same species developed by means of microevolution (evolution within species). So, for example, God created the cat, which led to the evolution of lions, tigers, leopards, and so forth. When God created man, however, He created him anew, both physically and spiritually.

Many Christians have criticized progressive creationism and the day-age theory. If Genesis intended to communicate that God created over long periods, the Hebrew word *olam* would have been ideal. But this word is not used. *Yom* (day) is used, and when *yom* is preceded by a number, it always refers to a 24-hour day.

Second Peter 3:8 says that "with the Lord one day is as a thousand years," but the verse does not say that a day for God actually lasts a thousand years. Rather, it indicates that God is above the limitations of time.

Finally, the Genesis account indicates that Adam was created on day six, and he then lived on through day seven (Genesis 1:26-31; 2). If the days of Genesis were long ages, how can these many thousands of years be reconciled with the biblical statement that Adam died at age 930 (Genesis 5:5)?

Pearl of Wisdom: *Here is yet another area where Christians must agree to disagree in an agreeable way.*

Theistic Evolution

Theistic evolutionists believe God initially began creation but then directed and controlled the processes of naturalistic evolution to produce the universe as we know it today. God allegedly entered into the process of time on occasion to modify what was developing. Most theistic evolutionists hold to the day-age theory.

Theistic evolutionists typically deny the historicity of Adam and Eve. They suggest that God took an already existing higher primate (an ape), modified it, put a soul within it, and transformed it into Adam, who bore the image of God. (Likewise with Eve.) This viewpoint does not reconcile with Scripture.

- It makes Genesis 1:1–2:4 an allegory. This is unwarranted.

- Genesis 2:7 indicates that God formed Adam's body from inorganic material and that Adam became a living being at the moment of creation, not before.

- Christ flatly affirms of Adam and Eve that "He who *created them* from the beginning made them male and female" (Matthew 19:4).

- The apostle Paul teaches in 1 Corinthians 15:39 that "not all flesh is the same, but there is one kind for humans, another for animals." Man was therefore not created from an ape.

- The idea that the woman came from a female higher primate is certainly unbiblical. Paul affirms in 1 Corinthians 11:8,12 that woman was made from man.

Pearl of Wisdom: *Theistic evolution is a failed attempt to combine evolutionary theory with creationism.*

Young-Earth Creationism

According to young-earth creationism, the universe was created—mature and fully functioning—during six literal days 10,000 or less years ago.

Young-earth creationism disagrees with evolution and theistic evolution by denying that macroevolution (evolution of one species into another) had anything to do with origins. It disagrees with progressive creationism by affirming that the days of Genesis were literal 24-hour days.

This view posits that when God created the universe, He did so instantaneously. Psalm 33 tells us, "By the word of the LORD the heavens were made...For he spoke, and it came to be; he commanded, and it stood firm" (verses 6,9; see also Genesis 1:3,6,9,14,20,24). Hebrews 11:3 likewise tells us that "the universe was created by the word of God." These verses do not describe a slow process of evolution.

This viewpoint interprets the Genesis account in a plain, straightforward, literal fashion. The text of Genesis gives every indication that it is to be taken as a historical account. No marks of poetry or saga or myth are evident. The text of Scripture must not be mythologized to make it fit with a current scientific theory.

———

Pearl of Wisdom: *If we interpret Genesis as a myth because of perceived scientific problems, what is to prevent us from interpreting other passages the same way, such as the accounts of the incarnation and resurrection?*

Cain's Wife

In Genesis 4:17 we read that "Cain knew his wife, and she conceived and bore Enoch." Many people wonder where Cain found a wife, and this question undermines their faith in the book of Genesis. Actually, though, the question is not difficult to answer.

Adam and Eve had other children after the births of Cain, Abel, and Seth. Genesis 5:4 tells us, "The days of Adam after he fathered Seth were 800 years; and he had other sons and daughters." Eight hundred years is a long time to be fruitful and multiply (Genesis 1:28)!

Adam and Eve were the first man and woman, and God had commanded them and their descendants to be fruitful and multiply, so Cain probably married one of his many sisters. Given the long life spans at that time, he could have married a niece or even a grandniece.

In the early years of the human race, no genetic defects had yet developed as a result of the fall of man. By the time of Abraham, God had not yet declared this kind of marriage to be contrary to His will (see Genesis 20:12). Apparently, incest was not prohibited until the time of Moses (Leviticus 18:7-17; 20:11-12,14,17,20-21).

***

Pearl of Wisdom: *We can trust even the finer details in the book of Genesis.*

The Universal Flood

The flood of Noah's day was universal, covering all the earth. The Bible indicates that "the waters prevailed so mightily on the earth that all the high mountains under the whole heaven were covered" (Genesis 7:19). The waters rose so greatly on the earth that they covered the mountains to a depth of more than 20 feet (verse 20). Moreover, the flood lasted some 377 days (nearly 54 weeks), indicating more than just local flooding.

The Bible also affirms that every living thing that moved on the earth perished: "Everything on the dry land in whose nostrils was the breath of life died. He blotted out every living thing that was on the face of the ground, man and animals and creeping things and birds of the heavens. They were blotted out from the earth. Only Noah was left, and those who were with him in the ark" (verses 22-23). This surely describes a universal flood.

Further, the universal view best explains the worldwide distribution of diluvial deposits. A universal flood would also explain the sudden death of many woolly mammoths frozen in Alaskan and Siberian ice. Investigation shows that these animals died suddenly by choking or drowning and not by freezing.

Finally, more than 270 universal flood legends exist among people of various religions and cultural backgrounds all over the world. These people attribute the descent of all races to Noah.

Pearl of Wisdom: *The evidence for a universal flood in Noah's day is substantial and convincing.*

Jesus Was a Real Person

The biblical accounts are based on eyewitness testimony (Luke 1:1-4). John writes, "That which was from the beginning, which we have heard, which we have seen with our eyes, which we have looked at and our hands have touched—this we proclaim concerning the Word of life" (1 John 1:1 NIV). In 2 Peter 1:16, we read, "We did not follow cleverly devised myths when we made known to you the power and coming of our Lord Jesus Christ, but we were eyewitnesses of his majesty."

Certainly the resurrection of Jesus Christ was attested by multiple eyewitnesses. Jesus' followers claimed, "This Jesus God raised up, and of that we all are witnesses" (Acts 2:32). Speaking to some Jews, Peter claimed, "You killed the Author of life, whom God raised from the dead. To this we are witnesses" (3:15). The Jewish leaders tried to stop the disciples from testifying, but they responded, "Whether it is right in the sight of God to listen to you rather than to God, you must judge, for we cannot but speak of what we have seen and heard" (4:18-20). Peter later said to some Gentiles, "We are witnesses of all that he did both in the country of the Jews and in Jerusalem. They put him to death by hanging him on a tree, but God raised him on the third day and made him to appear" (10:39-40).

Pearl of Wisdom: *The sheer volume of eyewitnesses of Jesus Christ makes it impossible to claim He was a mythical character.*

Jesus Never Married

S ome critics of Christianity, including Dan Brown in *The Da Vinci Code*, claim Jesus was married to Mary Magdalene. They appeal to the Gospel of Philip, which allegedly speaks of Jesus kissing Mary on the mouth.

However, the New Testament never mentions Jesus getting married. Moreover, in 1 Corinthians 9:5, Paul defends his right to get married: "Do we not have the right to take along a believing wife, as do the other apostles and the brothers of the Lord and Cephas?" If Jesus had been married, surely the apostle Paul would have cited Jesus' marriage as the number one precedent.

Scripture reveals that Jesus' marriage is yet future. In fact, He will one day marry the bride of Christ—the church (Revelation 19:7-9).

As for the Gospel of Philip, the document says "Jesus kissed her often on the—" and the manuscript is broken at that point. Brown and others have assumed the missing word must be *mouth*, but it could just as easily be *head*, *cheek*, or even *hand*. Nothing in that context demands that Jesus kissed Mary on the mouth. Besides, this spurious Gospel nowhere states that Jesus was even married. Most important, this document dates to about AD 275, hundreds of years later than the canonical Gospels. It can hardly be considered a reliable source of information about Jesus.

Pearl of Wisdom: *We would be unwise to trust late, forged documents instead of the early, historically verified Gospels—Matthew, Mark, Luke, and John.*

Jesus: A Good Moral Teacher?

S ome people have been fooled by the fashionable claim that Jesus was simply a good moral teacher who came to provide an example of the right way to live. But of course, no mere teacher would claim that the destiny of the world lay in His hands or that people would spend eternity in heaven or hell depending on whether they believed in Him for salvation (John 6:26-40). This would not be an example of morality but of lunacy.

For Jesus to convince people that He was God (John 8:58) and the Savior of the world (Luke 19:10) when He really wasn't would be the ultimate immorality. So to say that Jesus was just a good moral teacher and nothing more makes no sense.

Jesus, the eternal God, was born into the world as a man not primarily to be a moral influence, but rather to die for the sins of humankind. He affirmed that He came into the world for the very purpose of dying (John 12:27), and He perceived His death as a sacrificial offering for the sins of humanity (Matthew 26:26-28). He took His sacrificial mission with utmost seriousness, for He knew that without Him, humanity would certainly perish (Matthew 16:25; John 3:16) and spend eternity apart from God in a place of great suffering (Matthew 10:28; 11:23; 23:33; 25:41; Luke 16:22-28).

Pearl of Wisdom: *Jesus wasn't just a moral teacher. He was the Savior of immoral humanity.*

Jesus and the Messianic Prophecies

From Genesis to Malachi, the Old Testament abounds with anticipations of the coming Messiah. Numerous predictions—fulfilled to the crossing of the *t* and the dotting of the *i* in the New Testament—relate to His birth, life, ministry, death, resurrection, and glory. Jesus Himself often indicated to listeners that He was the specific fulfillment of messianic prophecy.

For example, He affirmed, "All this has taken place that the Scriptures of the prophets might be fulfilled" (Matthew 26:56). On another occasion, when Jesus was with some disciples, we read that "beginning with Moses and all the Prophets, he interpreted to them in all the Scriptures the things concerning himself" (Luke 24:27). He claimed, "Everything written about me in the Law of Moses and the Prophets and the Psalms must be fulfilled" (Luke 24:44). He informed some Jews, "If you believed Moses, you would believe me; for he wrote of me" (John 5:46). On another occasion, He affirmed, "Today this Scripture has been fulfilled in your hearing" (Luke 4:21).

Hundreds of prophecies predicted things like Jesus' virgin birth (Isaiah 7:14), His birthplace of Bethlehem (Micah 5:2), the Holy Spirit's anointing on Him (Isaiah 11:2), His ministry of miracles (Isaiah 35:5-6), His betrayal for 30 shekels (Zechariah 11:12), His piercing for the sins of humanity (Zechariah 12:10), His atonement (Isaiah 53:1-3), His crucifixion (Psalm 22:16; Isaiah 53:12), and His resurrection (Psalm 16:10; 22:22).

Pearl of Wisdom: *The hundreds of messianic prophecies in the Old Testament zero in on one person: the Messiah, Jesus Christ.*

Messianic Prophecies and the Jews

I f you want to show a Jewish person that Jesus is the Messiah, begin with broad messianic prophecies and then narrow the field with increasingly specific prophecies. You might use circles to graphically illustrate your points.

- *Circle 1: the Messiah's humanity.* The Messiah had to become a human being. This is a very large circle (Genesis 3:15).

- *Circle 2: the Messiah's Jewishness.* The Messiah had to be Jewish—a descendant of Abraham, Isaac, and Jacob (Genesis 12:1-3).

- *Circle 3: the Messiah's tribal identity.* The Messiah had to come from the tribe of Judah (Genesis 49:10).

- *Circle 4: the Messiah's family.* The Messiah had to be from David's family (2 Samuel 7:16).

- *Circle 5: the Messiah's birthplace.* The Messiah had to be born in Bethlehem (Micah 5:2).

- *Circle 6: the Messiah's life, rejection, and death.* Isaiah 53 reveals that the Messiah was to be despised and rejected by His fellow Jews, be put to death following a judicial proceeding, and be guiltless.

- *Circle 7: chronology.* Daniel 9:24-26 reveals that Jerusalem and the temple would be rebuilt, the Messiah would come, He would die but not for Himself, and the city and the temple would be destroyed.

Pearl of Wisdom: *Jesus is truly the divine Messiah.*

The Angel of the Lord

Appearances of the angel of the Lord in Old Testament times were actually preincarnate appearances of Jesus Christ. (*Preincarnate* means "before becoming a human being.")

When the word *angel* is used in reference to Christ in the Old Testament, the word indicates not a created being (like other angels), but—true to its Hebrew root—a messenger, or one who is sent. Christ as the angel of the Lord was sent by the Father as a messenger to accomplish specific tasks in Old Testament times.

Three lines of evidence identify Christ as the angel of the Lord:

1. The angel of Yahweh is God. This angel appeared to Moses in a burning bush and claimed, "I am the God of your father, the God of Abraham, the God of Isaac, and the God of Jacob" (Exodus 3:6).

2. The angel of Yahweh is distinct from Yahweh. Zechariah 1:12 portrays the angel of Yahweh interceding to another person called Yahweh on behalf of the people of Jerusalem and Judah, thereby pointing to trinitarian distinctions (see Hebrews 7:25; 1 John 2:1).

3. The angel of Yahweh and Jesus exhibit notable parallels. Both were sent into the world by God (Judges 13:8-9; John 3:16-17). The two had similar ministries, such as delivering those who were enslaved (Exodus 3; Hebrews 2:14-15).

Pearl of Wisdom: *Christ was heavily active among God's people even in Old Testament times.*

Melchizedek

S ome today believe Melchizedek was a preincarnate appearance of Christ. They believe Hebrews 7:3 supports this view: "He is without father or mother or genealogy, having neither beginning of days nor end of life, but resembling the Son of God he continues a priest forever." These interpreters say that this verse seems to describe an eternal person, so Melchizedek must be the preincarnate Christ.

Many scholars rebut this view, however, suggesting that this verse simply means that the Old Testament Scriptures have no record or account of Melchizedek's parents or birth. In this light, the silence of Scripture on these matters is divinely intended in order to render Melchizedek as an ideal *type* of Christ's eternality. (A type is a representation of something yet to come.) These scholars also note that Melchizedek is *like* the Son of God. Hebrews does not say he is the Son of God Himself (Hebrews 7:3).

Melchizedek was probably an actual historical person who served as a type of Christ, foreshadowing certain things about Christ, including His eternality. Melchizedek's name is made up of two words meaning "king" and "righteous." Melchizedek was also a priest. Thus, Melchizedek foreshadows Christ as a righteous king-priest. Melchizedek was also king of Salem, and Salem means "peace."

Pearl of Wisdom: *Melchizedek, as a type of Christ, points forward to Christ as the righteous King-Priest of peace.*

Jesus and the Archangel Michael

Some people confuse the archangel Michael with Jesus. We can easily clear this up.

- Colossians 1:16 says of Christ, "For by him all things were created, in heaven and on earth, visible and invisible, whether thrones or dominions or rulers or authorities—all things were created through him and for him." In ancient rabbinic (Jewish) writings, the terms *thrones, dominions, rulers,* and *authorities* referred to various kinds of angels. So this verse indicates that Christ Himself created all the angels and therefore could not have been the archangel Michael.

- In Daniel 10:13, Michael is called "one of the chief princes." He is one among a group of chief princes and not a unique personality. But Jesus is unique (John 3:16) and is "King of kings and Lord of lords," not a mere chief prince (Revelation 19:16).

- Hebrews 1:5 tells us that no angel can ever be called God's son. Jesus is the Son of God (John 3:16), so He cannot possibly be the archangel Michael.

- Hebrews 2:5 says the world is not (and will not be) in subjection to an angel. Christ is repeatedly called the ruler of God's kingdom (He is the King of kings), so He cannot be the archangel Michael (Matthew 2:1-2; 9:35; Luke 1:32-33; Revelation 19:16).

- Finally, Michael does not have the authority to rebuke Satan (Jude 9), but Jesus does (see Matthew 17:18; Mark 9:25), so Jesus cannot be Michael.

Pearl of Wisdom: *Jesus was not a created angel, but was rather the Creator of the angels.*

Jesus, the Christ

S ome misguided individuals claim that humans can become the Christ just as Jesus was the Christ. Jesus was allegedly the prototype for the rest of us.

This view is as arrogant as it is fallacious. Jesus alone is the Christ. The Old Testament presents hundreds of prophecies regarding the coming of a single Messiah (see Genesis 12:1-3; 2 Samuel 7:12-16; Psalm 16:10; 22:16,22; Isaiah 7:14; 11:2; 35:5-6; 53:3-5; Micah 5:2; Zechariah 12:10). The New Testament counterpart for *Messiah* is *Christ* (John 1:41). Jesus alone fulfilled these hundreds of prophecies, so He alone is the Christ, the divine Messiah.

Peter recognized Jesus as the unique Christ (Matthew 16:16), as did Martha (John 11:25-27). Further, on two occasions, Jesus made His identity as the Christ the primary issue of faith (Matthew 16:13-20; John 11:25-27).

After Jesus was arrested, He stood before Caiaphas the high priest, who demanded, "Tell us if you are the Christ, the Son of God." Jesus answered forthrightly, "Yes, it is as you say" (Matthew 26:63-64). He paid for that answer with His life. But as promised, the divine Messiah rose from the dead (John 2:19-21).

When Jesus was acknowledged as being the Christ in the New Testament, He never said, "You too have the Christ within." Instead He warned that others in the future would come falsely claiming to be the Christ (Matthew 24:5).

Pearl of Wisdom: *Jesus is utterly unique, and He alone is the Christ, our divine Messiah.*

Jesus Is God

The Bible offers many proofs of the deity of Christ. One of my favorites is the correlation of Old Testament references to God and New Testament references to Jesus. For example, in the Old Testament, God Almighty flatly asserts, "I am the LORD, who made all things, who alone stretched out the heavens, who spread out the earth by myself." In the New Testament, we see that Jesus Himself was the agent of creation (see John 1:3; Colossians 1:16).

In Isaiah 43:11, God Almighty asserts, "I, I am the LORD, and besides me there is no savior." In the New Testament, Jesus is referred to as "our great God and Savior" (Titus 2:13).

Isaiah 6:1-5 records a vision of God Almighty that the prophet Isaiah received in the temple: "I saw the LORD sitting upon a throne, high and lifted up; and the train of his robe filled the temple. Above him stood the seraphim. Each had six wings: with two he covered his face, and with two he covered his feet, and with two he flew. And one called to another and said: 'Holy, holy, holy is the LORD of hosts; the whole earth is full of his glory!'" Yet John 12:41 tells us that Isaiah actually beheld the glory of Jesus. No wonder Jesus was often worshipped as God, just as the Father was (Matthew 2:11; 8:2; 9:18; 15:25; 28:9; John 9:38; Hebrews 1:6)!

Pearl of Wisdom: *Never doubt it for a minute: Jesus is God!*

Jesus and the Names and titles of God

Divine names and titles are often ascribed to Jesus in Scripture. For example, in the New Testament, Thomas saw the wounds of the resurrected Jesus and cried out, "My Lord and my God!" (John 20:28). Paul later made reference to "Christ, who is God over all" (Romans 9:5) and who existed "in the form of God" (Philippians 2:5-8). Jesus is the one in whom "the whole fullness of deity dwells bodily" (Colossians 2:9). In Titus, Paul recognizes Jesus as "our great God and Savior" (2:13). Hebrews 1:8 records the Father's words to the Son: "Your throne, O God, is forever and ever."

Names of deity are also used of Jesus Christ in the Old Testament. For example, Isaiah 9:6 refers to Him as "Wonderful Counselor, Mighty God, Everlasting Father, Prince of Peace." The phrase *Mighty God* is literally *Elohim*.

In Isaiah 40:3 we read, "A voice cries: 'In the wilderness prepare the way of the LORD; make straight in the desert a highway for our God.'" This verse was fulfilled when John the Baptist prepared the way for the coming of Jesus Christ (see Matthew 3:3; Mark 1:3; Luke 3:4; John 1:23). The significant thing is that *LORD* and *God* in this verse are literally *Yahweh* and *Elohim*. Jesus is *Yahweh* and *Elohim*!

Pearl of Wisdom: *Scripture uses the same divine names and titles for the Father and for Jesus Christ.*

Jesus Is Equal to God

Jesus claimed to be equal to God in a number of ways. One was by claiming for Himself the prerogatives of God. He said to a paralytic, "My son, your sins are forgiven" (Mark 2:5). The scribes responded, "Who can forgive sins but God alone?" (see also Isaiah 43:25). To prove that His claim was not an empty boast, He healed the man.

Another prerogative Jesus claimed was the power to raise and judge the dead, affirming that "the dead will hear the voice of the Son of God, and those who hear will live...and come out, those who have done good to the resurrection of life, and those who have done evil to the resurrection of judgment" (John 5:25,29). He asserted that "as the Father raises the dead and gives them life, so also the Son gives life to whom he will" (John 5:21). But the Old Testament says God alone is the giver of life (Deuteronomy 32:39) and the only Judge (Deuteronomy 32:35).

Jesus also claimed He should be honored as God. He asserted that all people should "honor the Son, just as they honor the Father. Whoever does not honor the Son does not honor the Father who sent him" (John 5:23).

Further, Jesus instructed the disciples, "Believe in God; believe also in me" (John 14:1). If Jesus were not equal to the Father, placing Himself on an equal par with Him as an object of men's faith would have been blasphemy.

Pearl of Wisdom: *When Jesus lived on the earth, He obviously knew He was God in the same sense the Father is.*

Jesus and God's Authority

J esus believed His words were as authoritative as God's. He often repeated the phrase, "You have heard that it was said to those of old...But I say to you" (Matthew 5:21-22). Moreover, Jesus never said "Thus saith the Lord," as did the prophets. Rather, He always said, "Truly, I say to you." He affirmed, "All authority in heaven and on earth has been given to me" (Matthew 28:18-19).

God had given the Ten Commandments to Moses, but Jesus said, "A new commandment I give to you, that you love one another" (John 13:34). Jesus said, "Until heaven and earth pass away, not an iota, not a dot, will pass from the Law until all is accomplished" (Matthew 5:18), but He later said of His own words, "Heaven and earth will pass away, but my words will not pass away" (Matthew 24:35). Clearly, Jesus considered His words to have equal authority with God's declarations in the Old Testament. Jesus never retracted anything He said, never guessed or spoke with uncertainty, never made revisions, never contradicted Himself, and never apologized for what He said.

Jesus' teachings had a profound effect on people. His listeners always seemed to surmise that these were not the words of an ordinary man. When Jesus taught in Capernaum, for example, the people "were astonished at his teaching, for his word possessed authority" (Luke 4:32).

Pearl of Wisdom: *The Gospels clearly show that Jesus regarded Himself and His message as inseparable. Jesus' teachings had ultimate authority because He was (and is) God.*

Jesus, the Son of God

Scripture indicates that Christ is eternally the Son of God. Though *son of* can mean "offspring of," it can also mean "of the order of." The phrase is often used this way in the Old Testament. For example, "sons of the prophets" meant "of the order of prophets" (1 Kings 20:35). "Sons of the singers" meant "of the order of singers" (Nehemiah 12:28). Likewise, the phrase "Son of God" means "of the order of God" and represents a claim to undiminished deity.

Ancient Semitics and Orientals used the phrase *son of* to indicate likeness, sameness of nature, and equality of being. So when Jesus claimed to be the Son of God, His Jewish contemporaries fully understood that He was making a claim to be God in an unqualified sense. Indeed, the Jews insisted, "We have a law, and according to that law he ought to die because he has made himself the Son of God" (John 19:7). Recognizing that Jesus was identifying Himself as God, the Jews wanted to kill Him for committing blasphemy.

Hebrews 1:2 says God created the universe through His Son, implying that Christ was the Son of God prior to the creation. Moreover, Christ as the Son existed before all things (Colossians 1:17,13-14). The Scriptural teaching that the Son of God was sent into the world implies He was the Son before He was sent (see John 3:16-17).

Pearl of Wisdom: *Jesus, as the Son of God, is absolute deity.*

Jesus, the Son of Man

If Jesus is the Son of God, why is He also called the Son of Man? This may appear to be a contradiction at first glance, but it isn't. Even if the phrase Son of Man were solely a reference to Jesus' humanity, it would not constitute a denial of His deity. When Jesus became a human being, He didn't cease to be God. His incarnation was not a subtraction of deity, but an addition of humanity. Jesus clearly asserted His deity on many occasions (Matthew 16:16-17; John 8:58; 10:30). But in addition to being divine, He was also human in the incarnation (Philippians 2:6-8). He had two natures—divine and human—conjoined in one person.

Furthermore, Scripture indicates that Jesus was not denying He was God when He referred to Himself as the Son of Man. Indeed, the term *Son of Man* is used of Christ in contexts where His deity is overtly evident. For example, the Bible indicates that only God has the prerogative of forgiving sins (Isaiah 43:25; Mark 2:7). But Jesus as the Son of Man exercised this prerogative (Mark 2:10). Likewise, at the second coming, Christ will return to earth as the Son of Man in clouds of glory to reign on earth (Matthew 26:63-64). Christ, as the Son of Man, is the divine Messiah (see Daniel 7:13)!

Pearl of Wisdom: *Jesus is both the Son of God and the Son of Man, and we learn much about our glorious divine Messiah from both terms.*

Christ's Humanity

Christ's humanity, like His deity, is an essential Christian doctrine. As the perfect mediator between God and man, Christ in the incarnation was both fully divine and fully human. To deny either constitutes a heresy (see 1 John 4:3; 2 John 7).

Christ's development as a human was normal in every respect, with two major exceptions: Christ always did the will of God, and He never sinned. As Hebrews 4:15 tells us, in Christ "we do not have a high priest who is unable to sympathize with our weaknesses, but one who in every respect has been tempted as we are, yet without sin." Indeed, Christ is "holy, innocent, unstained" (Hebrews 7:26). We see Christ's humanity in these scriptural facts:

Jesus had human parents (Matthew 1:18-19) and relatives (Mark 6:3; John 7:5), and He experienced a human birth (Matthew 1:23; Luke 1:24,26,31; 2:6,7,22-23; Galatians 4:4;) and normal human growth (Matthew 2:11; Luke 2:16; 2:40; 2:42-50; 2:52). He had human ethnicity, for He was Jewish (Genesis 49:10; John 4:9; Galatians 4:4; Hebrews 7:14). He experienced normal human emotions (John 11:35; Hebrews 5:7), hunger and thirst (Luke 4:2; John 4:1-7; 19:28), fatigue (Mark 6:31; John 4:6), pain (Matthew 26:46; Mark 15:25-34; John 19:28), and death (Luke 24:40; John 20:27; Acts 2:24).

Pearl of Wisdom: *When Jesus became a man, He revealed God to us, became Mediator between us and God, became our faithful High Priest, and—most important—died on the cross for our sins. Praise Him!*

The Virgin Birth

Christ was miraculously conceived in Mary's womb when the Holy Spirit overshadowed her (Matthew 1:18,20-25; Luke 1:26-38). The eternal Son of God's divine nature was joined, within Mary's womb, with a human nature by a direct supernatural act of God.

In reality, of course, the *conception* of Christ in Mary's womb was supernatural. Christ's actual birth was quite normal, aside from the protecting and sanctifying ministry of the Holy Spirit. The virgin birth was necessary for four primary reasons.

1. The virgin birth prevented Jesus from receiving a sin nature from Joseph (see 2 Corinthians 5:21; 1 Peter 2:22-24; Hebrews 4:15; 7:26).

2. The Old Testament referred to the Messiah as God and as man (see Isaiah 7:14; 9:6).

3. Jesus is our Kinsman-Redeemer. In Old Testament times the next of kin always functioned as the kinsman-redeemer of a family member who needed redemption from jail. Jesus became related to us by blood so He could function as our Kinsman-Redeemer and rescue us from sin. This necessitated the virgin birth.

4. Finally, the virgin birth was necessary to fulfill the prediction in Genesis 3:15 that our Deliverer would come from the seed of the woman.

Pearl of Wisdom: *The incarnation is a wonderfully profound mystery. It is worthy of deep contemplation and should inspire us to praise!*

Jesus' Two Natures

Before the incarnation, Jesus was one person with one nature (a divine nature). After the incarnation, Jesus was still one person, but now He had two natures—a divine nature and a human nature (Philippians 2:5-11).

The word *nature*, when used of Christ's divinity, refers to all that belongs to deity, including all the attributes of deity. When used of Christ's humanity, *nature* refers to all that belongs to humanity, including all the attributes of humanity. Christ in the incarnation was fully God and fully man.

One person. Though Jesus in the incarnation had both a human and a divine nature, He was only one person. He referred to Himself with singular pronouns (*I, me,* and *mine*).

Two natures. The relationship of Christ's two natures is complex. The attributes of one nature are never attributed to the other, but the attributes of both natures are properly attributed to His one person. Thus Christ at the same moment in time had what seem to be contradictory qualities. He was finite and yet infinite, weak and yet omnipotent, increasing in knowledge and yet omniscient.

Forever human and divine. When Christ became a man in the incarnation, He did not enter into a temporary union of the human and divine natures in one person that ended at His death and resurrection. Rather, the Scriptures make clear that Christ's human nature continues forever (Acts 1:11; Matthew 26:64).

Pearl of Wisdom: *Christ in the incarnation was 100 percent God and 100 percent man.*

Christ Emptied Himself in the Incarnation

Some wrongly assume that when Philippians 2:6-9 indicates that Jesus "made himself nothing" in the incarnation, He gave up His divine attributes. This is a complete misunderstanding of the passage. Christ's self-emptying amounts to three primary things: He veiled His preincarnate glory, He voluntarily didn't use some of His divine attributes on some occasions, and He condescended to take on a human nature.

During His time on earth, Christ veiled the glory that was His for all eternity as God. He never surrendered His glory, for He displayed it briefly at the transfiguration (Matthew 17). Had He not veiled it, however, people would not have been able to behold Him (see Isaiah 6:5; Revelation 1:17).

Christ also voluntarily didn't use some of His divine attributes on some occasions so that He could accomplish His objectives. Christ could never have actually surrendered any of His attributes, for then He would have ceased to be God. But He could (and did) voluntarily choose not to use some of them on some occasions during His time on earth in order to live among us and our limitations (Matthew 24:36).

Finally, Christ condescended to take on the likeness (literally, the form or appearance) of a man and the form (the very nature) of a bondservant. Christ was thus truly human. This humanity was subject to temptation, distress, weakness, pain, sorrow, and limitation.

Pearl of Wisdom: *The incarnation is best appreciated by considering the dazzling heights from which Christ came.*

The Incarnation Lasts Forever

When Christ became a man in the incarnation, He did not enter into a temporary union of the human and divine natures that ended at His death. Rather, Christ's human nature continues forever. The miracle of the incarnation lasts forever.

Scripture tells us that Christ was raised immortal in the very same human body in which He died (Acts 2:31; 1 John 4:2). The risen Christ even instructed His frightened disciples, "See my hands and my feet, that it is I myself. Touch me, and see. For a spirit does not have flesh and bones as you see that I have" (Luke 24:39). Christ rose from the dead with a physical human body.

Later, Christ ascended into heaven in the very same physically resurrected human body as several of His disciples watched. Some angels then said to the watching disciples, "This Jesus, who was taken up from you into heaven, will come in the same way as you saw him go into heaven" (Acts 1:11). In the future, Christ will gloriously return as the "Son of Man"—a messianic title that points to His humanity (Matthew 26:64).

At the same time, we must recognize that even though Jesus has fully retained His humanity and will one day return as the glorified God-man, the glory that He now has in heaven is no less than the resplendent glory that has been His as God for all eternity past (see John 17:5; see also Isaiah 6:1-5; John 12:41).

Pearl of Wisdom: *Even today, Jesus is the glorified God-man (see Revelation 1:13-16).*

Jesus' Temptation

The fact that Jesus was tempted (Matthew 4) is not a proof against His full deity, as some cultists allege. In the incarnation, Jesus took on an additional nature—a human nature. It was in His humanity that He was subject to temptation. However, He was also fully God, so the temptation stood no chance of success because of these attributes of His divine nature:

- He is immutable (Hebrews 13:8) and does not change.

- He is omniscient (John 6:30), knowing all the consequences of sin.

- He is omnipotent (for example, Colossians 1:16) and is therefore able to resist sin.

- He was tempted and yet was without sin (Hebrews 4:15).

- He had no sin nature and was perfectly holy from birth (Luke 1:35).

- There is an analogy between the written Word of God (the Bible) and the living Word of God (Christ). Just as the authorship of the Bible involved humans (Matthew, Mark, Luke, and John, for example) and God (the Holy Spirit) and is completely without error, so Christ is fully divine and fully human and is completely without (and unable to) sin.

This, of course, does not mean Christ's temptations were unreal. Christ was genuinely tempted, but the temptations stood no chance of luring Him to sin. Picture it like this: A canoe can genuinely attack a U.S. battleship, but it stands no chance of success.

Pearl of Wisdom: *Because Christ was tempted, He understands our temptations.*

Jesus' Three Primary Offices

Jesus, the divine Messiah, fulfilled the three offices of Prophet, Priest, and King. As a Prophet, Jesus gave major discourses such as the Upper Room Discourse (John 14–16), the Olivet Discourse (Matthew 24–25), and the Sermon on the Mount (Matthew 5–7). He also spoke as a prophet on many occasions on the subject of the kingdom of God.

As our divine High Priest, Jesus represents God the Father to us and represents us to God the Father. As the ultimate High Priest, Jesus performed the ultimate sacrifice—He shed His own blood on our behalf (Hebrews 7:27). Jesus also prays on our behalf (Hebrews 7:25), just as Old Testament high priests prayed for the people.

Scripture addresses Jesus' kingship from Genesis to Revelation. Genesis 49:10 prophesied that the Messiah would reign as a King, something also promised in the Davidic covenant (2 Samuel 7:16; see also Psalm 2:6; 110). Daniel 7:13-14 tells us the Messiah-King will have an everlasting dominion. These and many other Old Testament passages point to Christ's role as sovereign King.

In New Testament times, but before Jesus was even born, an angel appeared to Mary and informed her that her son would "reign over the house of Jacob forever; his kingdom will never end" (Luke 1:32-33 NIV; see also Matthew 2:1-2). Christ will one day come as King of kings and Lord of lords (Revelation 19:16).

Pearl of Wisdom: *As Prophet, Jesus revealed what we need to know. As Priest, He made our salvation possible. As King, He reigns over us. Jesus is awesome!*

Jesus, Our Savior

The Old Testament indicates that only God is Savior (Isaiah 43:11). So when the New Testament refers to Jesus as the Savior (Luke 2:11; John 4:42), it makes a strong statement about His divine nature.

In Titus 2:13, Paul encourages Titus to await the blessed hope, the "glorious appearing of our great God and Savior, Jesus Christ." The careful reader will notice that Titus 2:10-13; 3:4,6 uses the phrases *God our Savior* and *Jesus our Savior* interchangeably four times.

Jesus claimed to be equal with the Father as the proper object of men's trust. Jesus told the disciples, "Let not your hearts be troubled. Believe in God; believe also in me" (John 14:1). Had Jesus not been God, this would have been blasphemy.

Jesus, as Savior, affirmed that He came into the world (John 12:27) for the very purpose of dying. He perceived His death as a sacrificial offering for the sins of humanity (Matthew 26:26-28.) Jesus took His sacrificial mission with utmost seriousness, for He knew that without Him, humanity would certainly perish (Matthew 16:25) and spend eternity apart from God in a place of great suffering (Luke 16:22-28).

Jesus therefore described His mission this way: "The Son of Man did not come to be served, but to serve, and to give his life a ransom for many" (Matthew 20:28 NIV). "The Son of Man came to seek and to save what was lost" (Luke 19:10 NIV).

Pearl of Wisdom: *Jesus is our God and Savior.*

Jesus, the Divine Word

In John 1:1, Jesus is called "the Word." The Greek noun for *Word* in this verse is *Logos*. Christ, the *Logos*, is portrayed as a preexistent, eternal Being.

In John's Gospel, the Word is portrayed as a divine person (Jesus) who came into the world to reveal another person (the Father) to the world (John 1:18). This Word was the source of all life (John 1:3) and nothing less than God Himself (John 1:1). This is an amazing assertion, given John's staunch monotheism—the belief in only one God.

John begins his Gospel, "In the beginning was the Word" (John 1:1). The verb *was* in this verse is an imperfect tense in the Greek, indicating continued existence. When the time-space universe came into being, Christ, the divine Word, was already existing in a loving, intimate relationship with the Father and the Holy Spirit. When everything else came into being, Christ, the divine Logos, already existed.

Later in John 1, we are told that "the Word became flesh and dwelt among us" (John 1:14). This verse uses a Greek word that literally means "to pitch one's tent"—probably a subtle reference to the Old Testament tabernacle. The glory of God dwelt within the tabernacle in Old Testament times (Exodus 40:34-38), and in New Testament times the glory of God dwelt within the tabernacle of "the Word made flesh" (John 1:14).

Pearl of Wisdom: *The word* Logos *has rich and awe-inspiring connotations regarding the deity of Christ.*

Christ, Our Divine Advocate

Scripture teaches that Jesus is our Advocate. In 1 John 2:1-2 we read, "My little children, I am writing these things to you so that you may not sin. But if anyone does sin, we have an advocate with the Father, Jesus Christ the righteous. He is the propitiation for our sins, and not for ours only but also for the sins of the whole world" (1 John 2:1-2). The word *advocate* here carries the idea of a defense attorney. Jesus Himself is our defense attorney (see also Romans 8:34; 1 Timothy 2:5; Hebrews 7:25). A defense attorney becomes necessary when someone has been charged with a crime or a wrongdoing.

Who is our accuser? Revelation 12:10 refers to Satan as "the accuser of our brothers" (see Job 1:9; 2:5; Zechariah 3:1). This is illustrated in the book of Job. Satan went before God's throne and brought accusations against Job (Job 1–3). Satan does the same thing with you and me. I can picture it this way:

Satan walks up to God's throne (the Judge) and says, "God, how can you call Ron Rhodes a Christian? Did you see what he just did? He sinned! He's as fallen as they come!"

At that moment, Jesus Christ—my defense attorney—steps up to the throne and says, "Father, Ron Rhodes trusted me for salvation in 1971."

The Father immediately renders His verdict and says, "Case dismissed!"

Pearl of Wisdom: *Jesus is your defense attorney. Rejoice in this fact. Never forget it. Jesus is on your side, and He will defend you.*

Jesus and the Indian Gurus

Contrary to the claims of some today, Jesus did not go to India to learn from Indian gurus. Scripture reveals that Jesus was raised in Nazareth (Luke 4:16). During these childhood years, He studied the Old Testament, as did other Jewish boys His age (see Luke 2:52).

Upon reaching adulthood, Jesus was well-known in His community as a long-standing carpenter (Mark 6:3) and as a carpenter's son (Matthew 13:55). This would not have been the case had Jesus just returned from India. The local community's obvious familiarity with Jesus is more than evident in Luke 4:22.

Others were offended that Jesus was attracting so much attention. These seemed to be treating Him with a contempt born of familiarity (Matthew 13:54-57). These people seemed to be thinking, *We've known Jesus since He was a child, and now, He's standing before us claiming to be the Messiah. What nerve and audacity He has!* They would not have responded this way if they hadn't had regular contact with Him for a prolonged time.

Among those who became angriest at Jesus were the Jewish leaders. They accused Him of many offenses, but they never accused Him of teaching or practicing anything He would have learned in the East. Had Jesus actually gone to India to study under gurus, His opponents could have used this to discredit His claim to be the promised Jewish Messiah. If the Jewish leaders could have accused Jesus of this, they certainly would have.

Pearl of Wisdom: *Jesus was a Jew who grew up among Jews and was trained as a Jew in Nazareth.*

Jesus' Parables

The word *parable* literally means "a placing alongside of" for the purpose of comparison. A parable is a teaching tool. Jesus often told a story from real life—about a woman who lost a coin, a shepherd watching over sheep, or a worker in a vineyard—and used that story to illustrate a spiritual truth.

When Jesus places such a story alongside a spiritual truth, the comparison helps us to understand His teaching more clearly. Jesus' story of the good shepherd (John 10:11,14), for example, helps us understand that Jesus watches over us and guides us, just as a shepherd watches over and guides sheep.

The New Testament contains several kinds of parables:

A simile involves a likeness that employs the words *like* or *as*. It uses something we already know in the natural world as a word picture to illustrate a spiritual truth. In Matthew 10:16, Jesus said, "I am sending you out like sheep among wolves."

A metaphor implies a likeness. In John 10:7 (NIV), Jesus said, "I am the gate for the sheep." This metaphor teaches that Jesus is the way of salvation.

Jesus also told stories to illustrate spiritual truth. For example, in Luke 15:11-32, Jesus told the story of the prodigal son to show that God accepts repentant sinners and that we should too.

Pearl of Wisdom: *Jesus, the Master Teacher, often told stories and parables to help us understand profound spiritual truths.*

Jesus' Deity and the Bible

Cultists often cite a barrage of biblical verses as they try to prove that Jesus is lesser than the Father, but in each case they misinterpret the passage in question.

- Isaiah 9:6 refers to Jesus as "Mighty God." This does not mean He is a lesser God than God Almighty, for Yahweh Himself is also called "Mighty God" in Isaiah 10:21.

- In John 14:28, Jesus says the Father is greater than Him. But He was speaking positionally (the Father was in heaven; Jesus was on earth, about to be crucified).

- Colossians 1:15 calls Jesus "the Firstborn." This phrase throughout the Bible indicates preeminence. Jesus is preeminent over creation because He created it.

- When Jesus said in Mark 13:32 that He does not know the hour of His return, He was speaking only from His human nature. Christ in His divine nature is omniscient (see Matthew 11:27; John 7:29; 8:58; 16:30; 17:25). To fulfill His messianic mission on earth, Jesus voluntarily chose not to use some of His divine attributes on some occasions.

- Revelation 3:14 indicates Jesus was the "beginning of God's creation." The word *beginning* teaches that Jesus created God's creation (see John 1:3).

Pearl of Wisdom: *Jesus, our Savior, is absolute deity.*

Jesus Did What His Father Did

In John 5:19, Jesus said, "Truly, truly, I say to you, the Son can do nothing of his own accord, but only what he sees the Father doing. For whatever the Father does, that the Son does likewise." Jesus may seem to be implying that He is not fully divine. However, the biblical teaching on the Trinity clears things up.

Jesus is fully equal to the Father in His divine nature, but a functional hierarchy nevertheless exists between the persons of the Trinity, with the Father in authority over the Son. To illustrate, my son David has my identical nature (human), but I am in authority over him. Similarly, Jesus has the same nature as the Father (a divine nature), but the Father is in authority over Him.

The first-century Jewish setting is significant. Jewish boys understood that they were to imitate their fathers. Of course, Jewish sons shared their fathers' nature (both were human). Similarly, John 5:19 portrays Jesus as imitating the Father, but He nevertheless has the same nature as the Father (a divine nature).

This verse actually includes a veiled claim to deity, for it plainly tells us that "whatever the Father does, that the Son does likewise." The Father is God, and who besides God can do what God does? Jesus does what only God can do, so Jesus Himself is quite obviously God!

Pearl of Wisdom: *Jesus, as God, does what the Father does!*

Jesus Said What His Father Said

I n John 8:28, Jesus said, "When you have lifted up the Son of Man, then you will know that I am he, and that I do nothing on my own authority, but speak just as the Father taught me." To understand this verse, we must consider verses that indicate that Jesus as God is all-knowing (Matthew 9:4; 11:27; John 1:48; 2:24-25; 4:16-19; 6:64; 7:29; 8:55). John 8:28 cannot be taken to mean that Jesus is devoid of this divine attribute.

At the very beginning of John's Gospel, we learn that Jesus became a human being to reveal who God is: "No one has ever seen God [the Father]; the only God [Jesus Christ], who is at the Father's side, he has made him known" (John 1:18). The perfect revelation of God the Father came in the person of God the Son. As the divine Revealer, what Jesus did and what He said were rooted in His relationship to the Father (John 8:28).

Pearl of Wisdom: *Jesus never did or said anything alone—nothing in opposition or contradiction to the Father—but rather did all things in conjunction with the Father. The Father and the Son share the same divine power, the same divine will, and the same divine nature. They are fully equal to each other.*

Jesus and the Time of His Return

In Mark 13:32, Jesus said of the second coming, "Concerning that day or that hour, no one knows, not even the angels in heaven, nor the Son, but only the Father." Does this verse prove Jesus is not omniscient?

No. Many other verses prove Jesus is omniscient (for example, Matthew 11:27; 17:27; John 2:25; 7:29; 8:55). One must keep in mind, however, that in the incarnation, Jesus had two natures—a divine nature and a human nature. When Jesus became a man in order to fulfill His messianic mission among us, He voluntarily chose not to use some of His divine attributes on some occasions (see Philippians 2:5-11). Mark 13:32 is apparently one of those occasions.

More broadly, the Gospels clearly show that Christ operated at different times under the major influence of one or the other of His two natures. Indeed, Christ operated in the human sphere to the extent that it was necessary for Him to accomplish His earthly purpose as determined in the eternal plan of salvation. At the same time, He operated in the divine sphere on numerous occasions in openly demonstrating that He was (is) the divine Messiah. In Mark 13:32, Jesus was apparently speaking strictly from the vantage point of His humanity. If Jesus had been speaking from the perspective of His divinity, He would not have said the same thing.

Pearl of Wisdom: *In His messianic mission, Christ chose not to use some of His divine attributes on some occasions.*

The Kingdom of God
and the Kingdom of Heaven

The terms *kingdom of God* and *kingdom of heaven* are essentially interchangeable. The Gospels of Mark, Luke, and John use *kingdom of God* (for example, Mark 1:15; Luke 9:2). Matthew, however, uses *kingdom of heaven* 34 times but *kingdom of God* only four times. Why so? The apparent reason is that Matthew was a Jew writing to Jews, and he was showing sensitivity to the Jewish preference of avoiding using God's name when possible to make sure to not use this name in vain (Exodus 20:7). The other Gospel writers were not writing to a Jewish audience, so they used the term *kingdom of God*.

Scripture uses *kingdom of God* and *kingdom of heaven* in two primary senses: a present sense and a future sense. In the present sense, God spiritually rules over His people, who have been delivered from the kingdom of darkness and transferred to the kingdom of Jesus Christ (Colossians 1:13). The kingdom exists wherever Christians are submitting to the kingship and rule of God (1 Corinthians 4:20).

The future aspect of the kingdom relates to the future millennial reign of Jesus Christ on earth. Following the second coming, Christ will institute a kingdom of perfect peace and righteousness on earth that will last for a thousand years. After this reign of true peace, the eternal state begins (see Revelation 21–22).

Pearl of Wisdom: *God reigns both now and in the future.*

The Resurrection: The Heart of Biblical Christianity

The apostle Paul wrote to the Corinthians, "If Christ has not been raised, then our preaching is in vain and your faith is in vain" (1 Corinthians 15:14). The Greek word for *vain* refers to something that is useless or empty. Our faith means nothing if Christ is not risen from the dead.

Paul also wrote, "If Christ has not been raised, your faith is futile and you are still in your sins" (verse 17). The Greek word for *futile* indicates something that is without results. Our faith is meaningless if Christ is not risen.

It all boils down to this: If the resurrection of Christ did not occur, the apostles were false witnesses; our faith is vain, useless, empty, and futile; and we are all still lost in our sins. Moreover, the dead in Christ have truly perished forever, and you and I are the most pitiful people on the face of the earth—to say nothing of the fact that we have no hope beyond the grave.

The good news is that Christ is indeed risen, as we will see later in this book. For now, we simply note that Christ "presented himself alive to them after his suffering by many proofs, appearing to them during forty days and speaking about the kingdom of God" (Acts 1:3).

Pearl of Wisdom: *Christ is risen indeed. Your faith rests on a solid foundation.*

Evidence of the Resurrection

The evidence for the resurrection of Jesus Christ is substantial.

- The circumstances at the tomb reveal a missing body. And the Roman guards had fled their guard duty—an act punishable by the death penalty.

- Jesus appeared first to a woman, Mary Magdalene (John 20:1). In ancient Jewish culture, no one would make up a resurrection account in this way, for a woman's testimony was considered weightless.

- After the crucifixion, the disciples were full of doubt and fear. Suddenly they became willing to die for their claims. Only the resurrection explains the change.

- Only the resurrection explains the conversion of hardcore skeptics, such as the apostle Paul, James, and doubting Thomas.

- Only the resurrection explains the growth and survival of the Christian church amid Roman oppression.

- Too many appearances occurred over too many days to too many people for the resurrection to be easily dismissed (Acts 1:3).

- Jesus appeared to 500 people at one time, many of whom were still living and could have disputed Paul's resurrection claims (1 Corinthians 15:6). They did not do this, however, because the appearance of Christ was well attested.

Pearl of Wisdom: *Fear not, for Christ is risen. You and I will be too!*

Jesus Rose Physically

Scripture is clear that Jesus' resurrection from the dead was physical. The resurrected Christ said to His fearful disciples, "See my hands and my feet, that it is I myself. Touch me, and see. For a spirit does not have flesh and bones as you see that I have" (Luke 24:39). Notice three things here: (1) The resurrected Christ indicates that He is not a spirit, (2) He indicates that His resurrection body is made of flesh and bones, and (3) His physical hands and feet represent physical proof of His material resurrection from the dead.

Jesus had told the Jews, "Destroy this temple, and in three days I will raise it up." The temple He was speaking about was His own body (John 2:19-21). Moreover, the resurrected Christ ate food on four different occasions to prove He had a physical body (Luke 24:30,42-43; John 21:12-13; Acts 1:4).

The resurrected Christ was touched and handled by different people (Matthew 28:9; Luke 24:39; John 20:17). Paul affirmed that the body that dies is the very same body that is raised in life (1 Corinthians 15:35-44). In the New Testament, the Greek word for *body* (*soma*), when used of a person, always means a physical body. There are no exceptions to this. So all references to Jesus' resurrection body (*soma*) in the New Testament must be taken to mean a resurrected physical body.

Pearl of Wisdom: *Because Christ rose physically, you and I will be resurrected physically as well.*

The Resurrection—a Conspiracy?

Some have claimed that Jesus conspired with Joseph of Arimathea, Lazarus, and an anonymous man to convince His disciples that He was the Messiah. He allegedly manipulated events to make them appear as if He fulfilled numerous prophecies. Regarding the resurrection, Jesus allegedly took some drugs and feigned death but was revived later. Unfortunately, the crucifixion wounds ultimately proved fatal. The plotters then disposed of Jesus' body. The appearances of Christ were simply a case of mistaken identity.

This theory is full of holes. First, Christ's life and teaching were of the highest moral character. To say Jesus was deceitful and fooled people into believing He was the Messiah breaches all credulity. Moreover, He couldn't have conspired to fulfill many prophecies—such as His birth in Bethlehem (Micah 5:2), His virgin birth (Isaiah 7:14), and the identity of His forerunner, John the Baptist (Malachi 3:1).

Plotters could hardly have stolen Jesus' dead body to dispose of it. The tomb had a massive stone blocking it, it had a seal of the Roman government, and it was guarded by trained Roman guards.

The idea that appearances of Christ were a case of mistaken identity is ridiculous. Jesus appeared to too many people (including 500 at a single time—1 Corinthians 15:6) on too many occasions (dozens) over too long a time (40 days) for this to be the case.

Pearl of Wisdom: *Conspiracy theories often lack one thing: evidence.*

The Wrong Tomb?

Even today, some people try to explain away Christ's resurrection by saying that the women and the disciples went to the wrong tomb—and when they didn't see His dead body, they merely assumed He rose from the dead.

To believe in this theory, we'd have to conclude that the women went to the wrong tomb, that Peter and John ran to the wrong tomb, that the Jews then went to the wrong tomb, followed by the Jewish Sanhedrin and the Romans who went to the wrong tomb and then guarded the wrong tomb. We'd also have to say that Joseph of Arimathea, the owner of the tomb, also went to the wrong tomb. As well, the angel from heaven appeared at the wrong tomb (see Matthew 27:60; 28:1-2).

To believe in this theory we would have to dismiss virtually all of Christ's postresurrection appearances over a 40-day period (Acts 1:3)—including the appearance to more than 500 people at a single time, many who were still alive when Paul wrote his account (1 Corinthians 15:6). We would also be left wondering why Christ's followers were willing to undergo great persecution and even death to defend the truth of Christianity and Christ's resurrection from the dead. People who accept this theory are grasping at straws in their attempt to deny the resurrection.

Pearl of Wisdom: *The preposterous suggestion that all these first-century people (and an angel) went to the wrong tomb shows the hardness of some people's hearts today as they reject the truth of the resurrection.*

Did Jesus Swoon on the Cross?

S ome people have speculated that Jesus did not really die on the cross. He was nailed to the cross, suffered from loss of blood, and went into shock. But He didn't die. He merely fainted (or swooned) from exhaustion. The disciples mistook Him for dead and buried Him alive in a tomb. Suddenly, the cold tomb woke Jesus from His state of shock. When Jesus emerged from the tomb and met the disciples, they reasoned He must have been raised from the dead.

This theory is highly imaginative. Consider the claims: Jesus went through six trials and was beaten beyond description. He was so weak that He couldn't even carry the wooden crossbar. Huge spikes were driven through His wrists and feet, causing a substantial loss of blood. A Roman soldier thrust a spear into His side so that blood and water came out. And then four experienced Roman executioners goofed and mistakenly pronounced Jesus dead.

More than a hundred pounds of gummy spices were applied to Jesus' body, and during this process, no one saw Jesus breathing. A large stone weighing several tons was rolled against the tomb, Roman guards took their post there, and a seal was wrapped across the entrance. Jesus awoke in the cool tomb, split off the garments, pushed the several-ton stone away, fought off the Roman guards, and appeared to the disciples. (I don't think so.)

Pearl of Wisdom: *Some people are so hardened against Christianity that they are willing to accept any rationalization against the clear evidence.*

Jesus' Body Was Not Stolen

Some people have suggested that the dead body of Jesus was stolen, and the disciples simply assumed He had risen from the dead. Such a scenario lacks credibility. The tomb was secured with a stone that weighed several tons, sealed by the Roman government, and guarded by Roman guards.

Here's the bottom line: Raiding the tomb would not have been an easy task. Besides, the biblical text indicates the disciples were scared, discouraged, and disheartened (Mark 16:10). They were in no frame of mind to attack the Roman guards and steal the body.

Certainly neither the Romans nor the Jews would have stolen the body. When Christians began claiming Christ had risen from the dead, they would have loved to be able to produce Jesus' dead body, but they were unable to do so because they did not have it.

Further, why would Christians steal the body and then, instead of recanting their resurrection story in order to save their lives, suffer imprisonment, torture, and death to defend their plot? Why engage in such a mad, self-defeating, futile endeavor?

Also, consider the noble character of these men. Christ's disciples had been raised from early childhood to obey the Ten Commandments, including the commandment against bearing false witness (Exodus 20:16).

***

Pearl of Wisdom: *Some critics claim the New Testament contains fairy tales, but these same critics make up their own fairy tales to explain away the evidence.*

The Disciple's Memories and Jesus' Resurrection

Some people claim that Jesus' resurrection can be explained in terms of distorted memories among His followers. They were, after all, subject to tremendous social pressures, their emotions were undeniably tense, and they were gullible. Perhaps all this led to their distorted memories.

But this view is not supported by a shred of evidence. One could easily make this same kind of argument against any event of ancient history. If we used this methodology of skepticism consistently, we could know very little if anything about ancient history.

Further, were people in biblical times actually gullible? As C.S. Lewis noted, Joseph knew enough about biology to know that women don't just become pregnant by themselves. Likewise, the disciples in the boat became afraid because they understood enough of the laws of nature to know that people don't just walk on water! They knew enough to be aware that nothing can be viewed as abnormal until one has first grasped the norm. People in biblical times knew enough of the norm not to be gullible.

Still further, would critics have us believe that multitudes of Jews left Judaism, joined the cause of Christ, and ended up being tortured and even brutally killed for their faith in Christ, all because of distorted memories? Are we to believe that the 500 who saw the resurrected Jesus at the same time (1 Corinthians 15:6) were all suffering from memory problems? Such a view is beyond credulity.

Pearl of Wisdom: *The distorted memory interpretation of the resurrection is itself brimming with distortion.*

Mass Hallucinations?

Some people claim Jesus' followers were hallucinating when they saw Jesus after the resurrection. However, hallucinations are by nature individual experiences. They generally happen to individuals. First Corinthians 15:6, by contrast, indicates that the resurrected Jesus appeared to 500 people at the same time. All 500 people could not possibly have seen the same hallucination at the same time.

Moreover, Jesus appeared to too many people (many different kinds of people) on too many occasions (literally dozens) over too long a time (40 days) for this view to be feasible. Also, the resurrected Jesus was seen doing a number of different things—walking with people, eating with people, speaking with people, and being touched by people. The hallucination theory cannot explain this wide diversity of personal interactions.

If Jesus' resurrection involved hallucinations, the Roman and Jewish authorities could have easily put an end to it all by producing Jesus' dead body. However, this was not a viable option because the body was missing from the tomb.

Finally, these Jewish people believed there would be only a single resurrection at the end of time—a general resurrection. A resurrection of a single individual prior to this general resurrection was completely foreign to their theology. For countless Jews to experience the same hallucination of a single individual being resurrected, when as Jews, they believed in a general resurrection at the end of time, stretches all credulity.

Pearl of Wisdom: *The hallucination theory of the resurrection seems itself like a hallucination.*

The Resurrection of Our Bodies

I am sometimes asked about the bodies of people who have been cremated, blown up in a war, eaten by wild animals, or attacked by sharks. Can God physically resurrect such people from the dead?

Absolutely. Second Corinthians 5:1 promises, "For we know that if the tent that is our earthly home is destroyed, we have a building from God, a house not made with hands, eternal in the heavens." The way in which our "earthly tent" (body) is destroyed is not important; all that matters is that God, with His matchless power, will raise it from the dead. Keep in mind that even those who are buried eventually dissolve into dust and bones. So regardless of whether we are buried or cremated (or our bodies are somehow destroyed), we can all look forward to a permanent resurrection body that will never be subject to death and decay.

Our God has all the elements of the earth at His disposal, so nothing can prevent Him from commanding the earth, fire, and water to give up what they seem to have destroyed. God, the Creator of the entire universe (Genesis 1; John 1:3; Colossians 1:16), will experience no difficulty in resurrecting our bodies from the dead (see John 6:39-40,44,54; 1 Corinthians 6:14; 1 Thessalonians 4:13-17; Revelation 20:4-6).

Pearl of Wisdom: *Regardless of what happens to your body in death, you will be resurrected!*

The Tents We Live In

Paul compares our present earthly bodies to tents and our permanent resurrection bodies to buildings (2 Corinthians 5:1-4). He was speaking in terms that his listeners would have readily understood. After all, the temporary tabernacle of Israel's wilderness wanderings—essentially, a giant tent—was eventually replaced with a permanent building (a temple) when Israel entered the promised land. In like manner, believers' temporary "tents" (their bodies) will be replaced one day with an eternal, immortal, imperishable body (see 1 Corinthians 15:42,53-54).

Paul's statement in 2 Corinthians 5:4 is particularly relevant: "While we are still in this tent [of our present mortal body], we groan, being burdened—not that we would be unclothed [without a body], but that we would be further clothed [with a resurrection body], so that what is mortal [our earthly body] may be swallowed up by life [resurrection]." Being "unclothed"—being without a physical body as a result of death—is a state of incompletion, and for Paul, it carries a sense of nakedness. Even though departing to be with Christ in a disembodied state is far better than life on earth (Philippians 1:21), Paul's true yearning was to be clothed with a physically resurrected body (see 2 Corinthians 5:6-8).

Meanwhile, as Paul said, we groan (2 Corinthians 5:4). Why so? Because our bodies are burdened by sin, sickness, sorrow, and death. We yearn for a permanent remedy—the resurrection body.

Pearl of Wisdom: *Don't fret over your tent; just rejoice in your future building!*

In Jesus' Name

In John 16:24 Jesus said, "Until now you have asked nothing in my name. Ask, and you will receive, that your joy may be full." Some have taken these words to mean that by prayer we can unconditionally receive anything we want from Jesus.

These words, however, should not be taken in isolation from what Jesus and the apostles taught elsewhere about prayer. In John 15:7, for example, Jesus said, "If you abide in me, and my words abide in you, ask whatever you wish, and it will be done for you." We are also told that "whatever we ask we receive from him, because we keep his commandments and do what pleases him" (1 John 3:22). Moreover, we are told, "This is the confidence that we have toward him, that if we ask anything according to his will he hears us. And if we know that he hears us in whatever we ask, we know that we have the requests that we have asked of him" (1 John 5:14-15). Finally, we are told that if we ask for something with wrong motives we will not receive what we asked for (James 4:3). These are important qualifications to keep in mind!

———

Pearl of Wisdom: *We will receive what we pray for in Jesus' name if we abide in Christ, obey His commandments, ask with the right motive, and make requests that match God's will for our lives.*

Our Supreme Love

In Luke 14:26, Jesus said, "If anyone comes to me and does not hate his own father and mother and wife and children and brothers and sisters, yes, and even his own life, he cannot be my disciple." Jesus may initially appear to be saying that we should have the emotion of hate for our families for His sake. But I do not think that is what He was intending.

Jesus' ethic leaves no room for hating anyone. We are to love even our enemies (Luke 6:27). As well, the fifth commandment instructs us, "Honor your father and your mother" (Exodus 20:12), and the New Testament repeats the commandment (Ephesians 6:1-3; Colossians 3:20).

Jesus in Luke 14:26 is apparently using a vivid hyperbole (an exaggeration or extravagant statement used as a figure of speech). In understanding Jesus' point, one must keep in mind that in the Hebrew mind-set, to hate means to love less (see Genesis 29:31-33; Deuteronomy 21:15). Jesus is apparently communicating that our supreme love must be for Him alone. Everything else—and everyone else—must take second place.

This is in keeping with what Jesus said in Matthew 10:37 (NIV): "Anyone who loves his father or mother more than me is not worthy of me; anyone who loves his son or daughter more than me is not worthy of me." Measuring our supreme love for Christ against other lesser loves may make these lesser loves seem like hate by comparison.

Pearl of Wisdom: *Our supreme love must be for Christ alone.*

Of Pearls and Pigs

I n Matthew 7:6 Jesus said, "Do not give dogs what is holy, and do not throw your pearls before pigs, lest they trample them underfoot and turn to attack you." The words *dogs* and *pigs* portray that which is vicious and unclean. The terms seem appropriate ways to describe the enemies of the gospel.

Jesus here instructs His followers that in their relationships with enemies of the gospel, they were to be cautious, recognizing that these enemies may turn on them and even kill them. The spiritual information we give to others should always be in accordance with their capacity to receive it. Perhaps one reason Jesus exhorted the disciples to purchase a sword to take with them was that they could be attacked by enemies of the gospel (Luke 22:36).

The bottom line, then, is this: We must be cautious in what we say and not throw our pearls of wisdom before those who have little or no spiritual capacity to receive them. We must be cautious not to treat the sacred as if it were profane. We should be careful not to pass on holy revelation to unholy people who will have nothing but disdain for the things of Christ (compare with Luke 10:10-11).

Even Jesus put this maxim into practice. He gave no answer to Herod Antipas when Herod "questioned him at some length" (Luke 23:9).

Pearl of Wisdom: *Be cautious about passing on the sacred to profane people.*

Lead Us Not into Temptation

Jesus taught His followers to pray, "Lead us not into temptation, but deliver us from evil" (Matthew 6:13). Some may think Jesus is implying that God could lead us into temptation. But I do not think that is His intent.

James 1:13 instructs, "Let no one say when he is tempted, 'I am being tempted by God,' for God cannot be tempted with evil, and he himself tempts no one." Clearly, God is not the source of our temptations. In the next verse, James says we are tempted when we are lured and enticed by our own sinful desires.

Scholars suggest two possible explanations of Jesus' words in the Lord's Prayer. Some believe that all Jesus was saying is that we should ask God to order our lives and guide our steps so we are not brought into situations in which we will find ourselves tempted to do evil. We should ask God to keep our spiritual radar active so we can steer ourselves away from tempting circumstances.

Others believe Jesus may be instructing us to pray, *Let us not succumb to temptation.* This would be right in line with 1 Corinthians 10:13: "No temptation has overtaken you that is not common to man. God is faithful, and he will not let you be tempted beyond your ability, but with the temptation he will also provide the way of escape, that you may be able to endure it."

Pearl of Wisdom: *We ought to pray that God will keep us from tempting circumstances, and pray for divine assistance whenever we encounter temptations.*

Learn from the Fig Tree

J esus was hungry and saw a fig tree by the side of the road. As He came close to it, He saw that it had no figs, so He cursed it, and it withered (Matthew 21:19). Jesus may appear to be responding in anger to the tree. But He often used parables and word pictures to teach. With the fig tree, He was apparently performing a living parable—an acted-out parable—to teach His disciples an important truth. His cursing of the fig tree was a dramatic visual aid.

The fig tree had leaves on it (Matthew 21:19), so from a distance, it gave the appearance of being fruitful. Closer examination revealed that it had no fruit at all. Jesus cursed the fig tree to teach the disciples that God will judge those who give an outer appearance of fruitfulness but in fact are not fruitful at all (like the Pharisees).

Another interpretation is possible. The account of Jesus' cleansing of the temple in Mark's Gospel (Mark 11:15-19) is sandwiched between the two sections of Scripture dealing with the fig tree (verses 12-14 and 20-25). Jesus may have been teaching that from a distance, the temple appeared fruitful in the work of God. Closer inspection revealed mere religion without substance, full of hypocrisy, bearing no spiritual fruit, ripe for judgment.

———

Pearl of Wisdom: *Our commitment to Jesus Christ ought to show itself in the way we live!*

Two Senses of Forgiveness

In Matthew 6:14-15, Jesus said, "If you forgive others their trespasses, your heavenly Father will also forgive you, but if you do not forgive others their trespasses, neither will your Father forgive your trespasses." This passage seems to indicate that our salvation is in jeopardy if we fail to forgive others. This points to the need to understand the two senses of forgiveness in the New Testament.

First, those who have trusted in Christ are forgiven once and for all. Their eternal salvation is secure. God affirms in Hebrews 10:17, "I will remember their sins and their lawless deeds no more." Psalm 103:11-12 also tells us that "as high as the heavens are above the earth, so great is his steadfast love toward those who fear him; as far as the east is from the west, so far does he remove our transgressions from us." In other words, God is putting an immeasurable distance between Himself and our sins!

Another sense of forgiveness relates specifically to our daily fellowship with God. Bible expositors believe this is what we see in Matthew 6:14-15. The idea is this: If we do not forgive others, our fellowship with God is broken because our fellowship with Him hinges on our forgiveness of others. Our daily fellowship with God remains broken until the time we extend forgiveness to others.

Pearl of Wisdom: *Do you need to forgive someone? Why not take care of it right now so that your daily fellowship with God will be unhindered?*

God the Holy Spirit

Some people seem to think the Holy Spirit is in some sense divine but not necessarily God. One doctrine that comes through loud and clear in the New Testament is that the Holy Spirit is indeed God.

In Acts 5 we find an account of Ananias and his wife, Sapphira, selling some land, pretending to bring all of the profits to the apostles, but secretly retaining some of the proceeds for themselves. So Peter said to Ananias, "Why has Satan filled your heart to lie to the Holy Spirit and to keep back for yourself part of the proceeds of the land?" Peter then affirmed, "You have not lied to men but to God." Lying to the Holy Spirit is equivalent to lying to God.

Many other evidences for the Holy Spirit's deity are sprinkled throughout Scripture. For example, in 2 Corinthians 3:17-18 the Holy Spirit is called "Lord." The Holy Spirit is often identified with Yahweh (Acts 7:51; 1 Corinthians 2:12; Hebrews 3:7-9) and is spoken of as divine (Matthew 12:32; 1 Corinthians 3:16; Ephesians 2:22). As well, the Holy Spirit is often referred to as the "Spirit of God," thus indicating His full deity (Genesis 1:2; Exodus 31:3; Romans 8:9; 1 Corinthians 2:11,14). Further, the Holy Spirit has all the attributes of deity—such as omnipresence (Psalm 139:7), omniscience (1 Corinthians 2:10), omnipotence (Romans 15:19), holiness (John 16:7-14), and eternalness (Hebrews 9:14).

Pearl of Wisdom: *It will be in the best interest of your spiritual life to learn as much as you can about the Holy Spirit!*

The Holy Spirit Is a Person

I sometimes encounter people who consider the Holy Spirit to be a force or an energy, but not a divine person. However, substantive evidence indicates that the Holy Spirit is indeed a person.

For example, the three attributes of personality are mind, emotions, and will—and the Holy Spirit has each of these attributes. Romans 8:27 tells us that God the Father knows what the mind of the Spirit is. We know the Holy Spirit has emotions too, for we are exhorted not to grieve the Holy Spirit by sin (Ephesians 4:30). And we know that the Holy Spirit has a will, for spiritual gifts are distributed among Christians by His will (1 Corinthians 12:11).

The Holy Spirit also does many things in Scripture that only a person can do. For example, He teaches believers (John 14:26), testifies (John 15:26), guides (Romans 8:14), commissions people to service (Acts 13:4), issues commands (Acts 8:29), restrains sin (Genesis 6:3), intercedes (prays) for believers (Romans 8:26), and speaks to people (John 15:26). A mere force or energy could not engage in such acts.

Still further, the Holy Spirit is treated as a person throughout Scripture. For example, the Holy Spirit can be lied to (Acts 5:3) or obeyed (Acts 13:2), and He is sent by the Father (John 14:26). Such things can be said only of a person and not a force.

Pearl of Wisdom: *As Jesus promised, the Holy Spirit is personally with you as your Comforter and Advocate (John 14:16,26).*

Sealed by the Holy Spirit

Paul informs us that we are "sealed for the day of redemption" (Ephesians 4:30). Indeed, we are "sealed with the promised Holy Spirit" at the moment we believe in Jesus (1:13).

In ancient Rome, scrolls or documents sent from one location to another were sealed with wax that was imprinted with a Roman stamp. The authority of the Roman government protected that document against unauthorized opening. The seal could not be broken until the document reached its final destination.

In the same way, God Himself seals believers with the Holy Spirit for the day of redemption. This seal guarantees that you and I will be "delivered" into eternal life—on the day of redemption. The Holy Spirit, as our seal, represents complete security.

In Ephesians 1:13, the Greek words carry the idea that we have been stamped or marked with the seal of the long-promised Holy Spirit. This stamp, or mark, stays with us—guaranteeing that we will enter heaven.

I live in Texas. Each spring the cattle ranchers round up all their one-year-old calves for branding. The brand is placed directly on the calf's flank. This is the rancher's mark of ownership. Once the brand is applied, no one can dispute that the calf belongs to that rancher.

In the same way, God has placed His mark of ownership on us—the Holy Spirit. No one can remove us from His ownership anytime before the day of redemption.

Pearl of Wisdom: *You are sealed by the Holy Spirit, and that guarantees your entrance into heaven.*

The Holy Spirit: A Deposit of What Is to Come

Paul referred to our earthly bodies as tents and our future resurrection bodies as buildings (2 Corinthians 5:1-3). While still in our mortal bodies, however, we groan, for these bodies are wearing down (verse 4). Moreover, we ideally prefer to immediately receive resurrection bodies instead of temporarily becoming disembodied spirits. This is so, despite the fact that being a disembodied spirit with Christ in heaven is "better by far" than our present lives on earth (Philippians 1:23).

In this context, Paul said God has given us the Holy Spirit as a deposit of what is to come (2 Corinthians 5:5 NIV). The Greek word translated *deposit* refers to a pledge that guaranteed final possession of an item. It was sometimes used of an engagement ring, which acted as a guarantee that the marriage would take place. The Holy Spirit is a deposit in the sense that His presence in our lives guarantees our eventual total transformation and glorification into the likeness of Christ's glorified resurrection body (Philippians 3:21). The Holy Spirit in us is a guarantee of what is to come.

This helps us to maintain an eternal perspective. Our present bodies are wearing down. One day, they will simply fall down like a flimsy tent. By contrast, our resurrection bodies in heaven will never again wear down. The Holy Spirit in our lives is a guarantee that this reality will one day be ours.

Pearl of Wisdom: *Rejoice, Christian, for the best is yet to come!*

Be filled with the Holy Spirit

I n Ephesians 5:18 the apostle Paul instructs us, "Be filled with the Spirit." Notice two things here. First, this is a command and not a mere option. Second, it is in the present tense, which communicates continuing action. Day by day, moment by moment, you and I are to be filled with the Spirit. But what does this mean?

The context provides us with the answer. The verse says, "Do not get drunk with wine, for that is debauchery, but be filled with the Spirit" (Ephesians 5:18). Both drunk and spiritual persons are controlled persons—that is, they're under the influence of either liquor or the Spirit, and as a result they do things that are unnatural to them. In both cases they abandon themselves to an influence and act accordingly.

To be filled with the Holy Spirit means that we will no longer be controlled or governed by self but by the Holy Spirit. It is not a matter of an individual acquiring more of the Holy Spirit, but rather of the Holy Spirit acquiring all of the individual.

Believers become filled with the Holy Spirit when they are fully yielded to the indwelling Holy Spirit. As a result the Holy Spirit controls and empowers them moment by moment.

Pearl of Wisdom: *People who are full of the Holy Spirit behave accordingly. That is, they act in ways that please God.*

Walk in the Holy Spirit

From the time of Adam and Eve's fall into sin (Genesis 3), all people have been born into the world with a sin nature. This sin nature becomes manifest through numerous kinds of sin. In our own strength, we do not have the power to resist the evil inclinations of our sin nature. But we can have victory over the sin nature by depending on the Holy Spirit. Galatians 5:16 tells us, "Walk by the Spirit, and you will not gratify the desires of the flesh."

In that verse, the word *walk* (which means *live*) is a present-tense verb, indicating continuing action. We are to persistently and continually walk in dependence on the Holy Spirit. As we do this, we will live in a way that is pleasing to God.

As we depend on the Holy Spirit, we not only enjoy victory over sin but also find the fruit of the Spirit cropping up in our lives. Galatians 5:22-23 tells us that "the fruit of the Spirit is love, joy, peace, patience, kindness, goodness, faithfulness, gentleness, [and] self-control."

Many theologians have noted that the qualities listed in Galatians 5:22-23 provide an accurate profile of Jesus Christ Himself. The character of our Lord is reproduced in our lives as we depend on the Holy Spirit. In this way, we progressively take on the family likeness (as members of God's forever family).

Pearl of Wisdom: *As we depend on the Holy Spirit, we progressively become more and more like Jesus Christ.*

Spiritual Gifts and Natural Talents

Spiritual gifts are special abilities that the Holy Spirit sovereignly gives to individual believers for the purpose of edifying the body of Christ (1 Corinthians 12:11). Some gifts empower people to teach, pastor, or evangelize. Other gifts bring supernatural wisdom, knowledge, or faith. Gifts may bring individual instances of healing or miraculous power. Through gifts of the Spirit, people may prophesy, distinguish between spirits, speak in different tongues, or interpret those tongues (Romans 12:3-8; 1 Corinthians 12:8-10; Ephesians 4:7-13).

Spiritual gifts are different from natural talents. Natural talents are from God but are transmitted through parents; spiritual gifts come directly from God the Holy Spirit (Romans 12:3,6; 1 Corinthians 12:4). People possess natural talents from the moment of birth, but they receive spiritual gifts when they become Christians. Natural talents generally benefit people on the natural level; spiritual gifts bring spiritual blessing to people and edify believers (Ephesians 4:11-13).

But gifts and talents share similarities as well. Both must be developed and exercised. Otherwise one will not become proficient in their use. As well, both natural talents and spiritual gifts can be used for God's glory. For example, a Christian might have the spiritual gift of teaching. He might also have the natural talent of playing the guitar. This person could exercise his spiritual gift of teaching and his natural talent by writing and performing songs that teach about God.

Pearl of Wisdom: *God has given you a specific spiritual gift for blessing the body of Christ! Are you using it?*

The Spiritual Gifts Today

Most Christians generally hold to one of two views as to whether all the spiritual gifts are for today:

Many Christians, particularly charismatics and Pentecostals, believe all the spiritual gifts listed in the New Testament exist today (including speaking in tongues). They affirm that Jesus is the same yesterday, today, and forever (Hebrews 13:8), so the gifts haven't changed either. They assert that no New Testament verse proves the spiritual gifts have passed away. And they acknowledge that the New Testament was written for believers of all ages, so they conclude that spiritual gifts are for Christians of all ages.

Other Christians, known as cessationists, believe that some gifts (like speaking in tongues) passed away in the first century. They teach that 1 Corinthians 13:8 indicates that tongues would, at some point, cease. They suggest that the discussion of speaking in tongues in the New Testament may be descriptive and not prescriptive—that is, it may describe what took place in the first century but not prescribe what will take place in every century. Tongues were a sign-gift of the apostles, and since the apostles passed away (Acts 1:22), the sign-gift of tongues passed away too. The sign-gifts confirmed the apostles' message (Acts 2:22; 3:3-11), and once their message was delivered, confirmation was no longer needed (Hebrews 2:3-4).

Pearl of Wisdom: *Despite different opinions, the important thing is that all Christians use their spiritual gifts to bless the body of Christ.*

Slain in the Spirit

Sometimes we witness a televangelist touching someone on the forehead, and the person is knocked out cold, allegedly by the power of the Holy Spirit. Such people are said to be slain in the Spirit.

However, not only is the phrase *slain in the Spirit* not found in the Bible, the experience is not in the Bible either. Scripture does record instances of people falling to their knees as they witness God's glory (Isaiah 6:1-5). But the idea of being touched by another person who is so "anointed" by the Spirit that a mere touch of his hand knocks someone out cold is not biblical.

How do we explain such an experience? It may be psychological or emotional. People may so strongly expect to be knocked out by the Spirit through the ministry of an anointed preacher that when the preacher touches them, down they go.

The powers of darkness may also be involved in this experience (2 Thessalonians 2:9). Some people affiliated with Eastern religions claim to be able to make people unconscious merely by touching them.

Many who believe in this phenomenon like to cite certain passages in its support, such as Genesis 15:12-21, Numbers 24:4, 1 Samuel 19:20, and Matthew 17:6. But in every case they are reading their own meaning into the text.

Pearl of Wisdom: *We ought to test all claims regarding experiences against the Scriptures (Acts 17:11).*

Holy Laughter

In some churches, you might walk into a service and find that everyone is laughing hilariously—with some even rolling on the floor in uncontrollable, hysterical laughter. This is claimed to be a mighty manifestation of the Holy Spirit. Examining the phenomenon in the light of Scripture, however, leads me to reject it for several reasons.

- The Bible admonishes us to test all things against Scripture (1 Thessalonians 5:21; Acts 17:11). No verse in the Bible says that when the Holy Spirit comes upon a person, he breaks out into uncontrollable laughter.

- One fruit of the Holy Spirit is self-control (Galatians 5:23). In the holy laughter phenomenon, people laugh uncontrollably, even when there is nothing funny to laugh about.

- A leader in the holy laughter movement said people were laughing at his meeting even when he was preaching on hell. But Scripture tells us that God takes no joy at the perishing of the wicked (Ezekiel 18:23,32).

- In 1 Corinthians 14:33, the apostle Paul speaks of the need for order in the church: "Everything should be done in a fitting and orderly way" (1 Corinthians 14:40 NIV).

- During the ministry of our Lord Jesus (who had the Holy Spirit without measure), people never broke out into uncontrolled laughter. Neither did Peter's or Paul's ministry result in laughter.

Pearl of Wisdom: *Scripture alone is our barometer of truth!*

We Are Social Beings

When God created Adam, He said Adam's loneliness was "not good" (Genesis 2:18). God made man as a social being. People are created to enter into and enjoy relationships with others.

The most important relationship man was created to enter into is with God Himself. The human heart has a hunger that none but God can satisfy, a vacuum that only God can fill. We were created with a need for fellowship with God. We are restless and insecure until this becomes our living experience.

Why is this? The answer is that God created man in His image (Genesis 1:26). Many have debated down through the centuries what this means, but one thing is certain: Man is a personal, social, and relational being. We were specifically engineered with a capacity to interact with the Creator on a personal level (see Genesis 3:8; 5:24; 6:9).

As God has a social nature, so He has endowed man with a social nature. And because man has been endowed with a social nature, man in his deepest heart seeks companionship with his Creator. He yearns for this relationship so the void in his heart can be filled.

Certainly many have tried (and will continue to try) to fill that void with earthly things—human relationships, power, prestige, and the like. But until man comes into the relationship with God that he was created for, the void will remain ever present.

Pearl of Wisdom: *God desires to fellowship daily with you and me.*

Adam as the Head

The creation account illustrates Adam's headship. For example, as soon as the woman was created, Adam named the woman: "She shall be called Woman, because she was taken out of Man" (Genesis 2:23). This is significant, because to name someone in ancient times implied having authority over the one named (for example, see Genesis 17:5; 2 Kings 23:34; Daniel 1:7).

When God gave instructions about moral responsibility, He gave these instructions to Adam alone (Genesis 2:16-17). And after Adam and Eve fell, God first summoned Adam, not Eve, even though she had initially led him into sin. "Adam, where are you?" God said immediately following the fall (Genesis 3:9). In Romans 5:12, we learn that Adam was held solely responsible for the fall even though Eve played a significant role. This implies Adam's headship.

Certainly one of Adam's failures in the fall was his abdication of responsibility for leadership. Instead of obeying God and leading his wife, he disobeyed God and followed his wife's lead (by eating the fruit). For this reason, God begins His sentence against Adam, "Because you have listened to the voice of your wife…" (Genesis 3:17). In the fall, therefore, God's intended order of authority was reversed.

Pearl of Wisdom: *Our God is a God of order, and He has set up authority structures in society (with the government), in the church (with elders), and in the family unit (with the man or husband acting as servant-leader of the household).*

The Races of Humanity

God created all races of humanity. All human beings are completely equal because of their common creation (Genesis 1:28), their common sin problem (Romans 3:23), God's love for everyone (John 3:16-17), and God's provision of salvation for all (Matthew 28:19). Paul affirmed that God "made from one man every nation of mankind to live on all the face of the earth, having determined allotted periods and the boundaries of their dwelling place" (Acts 17:26). Malachi 2:10 affirms, "Have we not all one Father? Has not one God created us?" Moreover, Revelation 5:9 tells us that God's redeemed will be from "every tribe and language and people and nation." This means racial discrimination has no place, for all people are equal in God's sight.

Related to this, Genesis 3:20 tells us that Adam "called his wife's name Eve, because she was the mother of all living." In the original Hebrew of this verse, Eve sounds like the word for *life-giver* and resembles the word for *living*. So we find a play on words. The main idea, though, is that regardless of the color of our skin, Eve is our common mother, just as Adam is our common father.

As for differences in skin color, scientists tell us they are related to genetics as the human races grew from generation to generation. The Bible nowhere says that dark skin is a sign or indicator of inferiority. Contrary to this, the Shulammite woman is called "dark" and "lovely" (Song of Solomon 1:5).

Pearl of Wisdom: *God created and loves all races of humankind.*

What Is the Soul?

The word *soul* is used in several ways in Scripture. For example, the Hebrew word for the soul (*nephesh*) can refer to a living being. Genesis 2:7 explains that when God created man, he "became a living soul" (Genesis 2:7 KJV).

The Old Testament also uses *nephesh* to refer to the seat of the emotions and experiences. Man's *nephesh* can be sad (Deuteronomy 28:65), grieved (Job 30:25), distressed (Genesis 42:21), troubled (Psalm 6:3), and cheered (Psalm 86:4). Clearly, man's soul can experience a wide range of emotional ups and downs. In this sense, the word *soul* seems to refer to at least part of a person's personality.

The word *soul* can also refer to man's immaterial nature. Genesis 35:18 is an example: "As her soul was departing (for she was dying), she called his name Ben-oni; but his father called him Benjamin." This seems to be equivalent to the Greek word for *soul* in the New Testament, *psuche*. In fact, *psuche* is often used to translate the Hebrew term *nephesh* into Greek. In Revelation 6:9-10, the souls of dead martyrs are conscious in the presence of God. In this sense, the word *soul* (*psuche*) is interchangeable with the word *spirit* (see Luke 23:46; Acts 7:59).

———

Pearl of Wisdom: *The moment you and I die, our spirit-soul departs the body and goes directly to heaven in the presence of Jesus (Philippians 1:21-23; 2 Corinthians 5:6-8).*

We Are Not Divine

Many today—especially cultists—claim that humans are divine. From a scriptural perspective, nothing could be further from the truth.

One must ask, if the essence of human beings is God, and if God is an infinite, changeless being, then how is it possible for people (if they are a manifestation of divinity) to go through a changing process of enlightenment by which they discover their divinity? The fact that people come to realize they are God proves they are not God. For if they were God, they would never have passed from a state of ignorance of their divinity to a state of awareness of it.

Further, if people were divine, we would expect them to display the same qualities God does. However, when we compare the attributes of humankind with those of God, we find more than ample testimony for the truth of Paul's statement in Romans 3:23 that human beings "fall short of the glory of God." For example, God is all-knowing (Matthew 11:21), but man is limited in knowledge (Job 38:4); God is all-powerful (Revelation 19:6), but man is weak (Hebrews 4:15); God is everywhere-present (Psalm 139:7-12), but man is confined to a single space at a time (John 1:50); God is holy (1 John 1:5), but even man's "righteous" deeds are as filthy garments before God (Isaiah 64:6); God is eternal (Psalm 90:2), but man was created at a point in time (Genesis 1:1,21,27).

———

Pearl of Wisdom: *If man is a god, one could never tell it by his attributes!*

Christianity and a Woman's Value

The ancient Jews believed women were inferior to men in all things. Jesus, however, elevated women in a patriarchal society. In a Jewish culture where women were discouraged from studying the law, Jesus taught women right alongside men as equals (Matthew 14:21; 15:38). When He taught, He often used women's activities to illustrate the character of the kingdom of God, such as baking bread (Luke 13:20-21) and grinding corn (Luke 17:35). Some Jewish rabbis taught that a man should not speak to a woman in a public place, but Jesus not only spoke to a woman—who, incidentally, was a Samaritan—but also drank from her cup in a public place (John 4:1-30). The first person He appeared to after being resurrected from the dead was Mary and not one of the male disciples (Luke 24).

Moreover, Galatians 3:28 tells us that there is neither male nor female in Jesus Christ. First Peter 3:7 says men and women are fellow heirs of grace. Ephesians 5:21 speaks of mutual submission between husband and wife. In John 7:53–8:11, Jesus wouldn't permit the double standard of punishing the woman caught in adultery and letting the man go free. In Luke 10:38, Jesus let a woman sit at His feet, which was a place reserved for the male disciples. Verses such as these show that in God's eyes, men and women are spiritually equal.

However, God has established male leadership in the family and in the church (Ephesians 5:22; 1 Corinthians 11:3; 14:34; 1 Timothy 2:11).

Pearl of Wisdom: *Jesus was the great equalizer among men and women.*

The Saddest Event in Scripture

The *fall* is a theological term that refers to the sin of the first man and woman, Adam and Eve, and the subsequent plunging of the human race into a state of sin and corruption. The effects of Adam and Eve's sin were not isolated to them. Their actions affected the entire human race. As a result of their decision to disobey God's command, every human being is born into the world in a state of sin (Psalm 51:5; Romans 5:12).

In fact, because of Adam and Eve's sin, everyone is born totally depraved. This does not mean all people are as bad as they can be, or that they commit all the sins that are possible, or that they are incapable of doing kind things to others. Rather, it means that all people are contaminated in every part of their being by sin, and no one can earn merit before a just and holy God (see Galatians 2:16). People are too entrenched in sin to be able to impress God by what they consider to be good works.

Before the fall, only four levels of authority existed: God, man, woman, and animals. In the fall, this is inverted into precisely the opposite: animal (serpent), woman, man, God. Eve listened to the serpent instead of Adam, and Adam listened to Eve instead of God.

Pearl of Wisdom: *You and I are fallen—but we're also redeemed! We may be horrible sinners, but we have a great Savior!*

Missing the Target

A key meaning of *sin* in the Bible is "to miss the target." The target is God's law. Sin is failure to live up to God's infinite standards. No one is capable of fulfilling all of God's laws at all times (Romans 3:23).

I've often illustrated this truth with a story about a contest to see who can throw a rock to the moon. I'm sure that a Major League Baseball player would be able to throw the rock much farther than I could—but not even the MVP is capable of throwing a rock all the way to the moon. All of us fall short.

In the same way, some people may be more righteous than others. But all of us fall short of God's infinitely high and perfect standards. None of us can measure up to His infinite holiness (Isaiah 53:6). It is simply impossible.

When we measure ourselves against other people, we might not appear evil. However, human sin shows up most clearly when measured against God's infinite holiness. Consider the prophet Isaiah—a relatively righteous man. When he beheld God in His infinite holiness, his own personal sin came into clear focus, and he could only say, "Woe is me! For I am lost; for I am a man of unclean lips" (Isaiah 6:5).

Pearl of Wisdom: *All of us woefully miss the target of God's infinite standards, so let's rejoice in the fact that our Savior, Jesus Christ, has redeemed us!*

Fallen in Sin

Some people believe they're not sinners. When I talk to such people, I ask them if they respect Jesus' teachings. They almost always say yes, so I show them what Jesus had to say on the subject.

I explain that Jesus taught that human beings have a grave sin problem that is altogether beyond their means to solve. He taught that people are by nature evil (Matthew 12:34; Luke 11:13) and that they are capable of great wickedness (Mark 7:20-23; Luke 11:42-52). He said all people are utterly lost (Luke 19:10), are sinners (Luke 15:10), and are in need of repentance before a holy God (Mark 1:15; Luke 15:10).

Then I mention that Jesus often described human sin with metaphors that illustrate the havoc that it can cause in one's life. He described human sin as blindness (Matthew 15:14; 23:16-26), sickness (Matthew 9:12), slavery (John 8:34), and living in darkness (John 3:19-21; 8:12; 12:35-46). He also taught that this is a universal condition and that all people are guilty before God (see Luke 7:37-48). Moreover, He taught that not only external acts but also inner thoughts render a person guilty of sin (Matthew 5:28).

I remind them that by human standards, they might come out looking pretty good. But all of us, when measured against Jesus' infinitely high standards, fall short, and our need of a Savior is acute.

Pearl of Wisdom: *Praise the Savior! He took what was ours (sin) and gave us what was His (eternal life).*

Bad News, Good News

In our day, talking about sin is not politically correct. Many seeker-sensitive churches rarely even mention the word. Sin is an outdated and offensive concept. People might not come to church if they are offended.

The truth is, such a viewpoint is absurd. Suppose a medical doctor were to say to you that disease is a totally outdated concept. Though you see widespread evidence for disease—with people suffering all kinds of deadly illnesses—the doctor assures you that disease does not exist. Such a doctor would do you very little good. If you were sick, he wouldn't be able to help you because he wouldn't accurately diagnose your problem.

In the same way, some people today avoid talking about sin even though the evidence for sin among human beings is everywhere around us. Watch the evening news tonight. You'll find overwhelming empirical evidence to confirm that people have made a mess of this world as a result of sin.

More importantly, if people do not recognize a sin problem, they will never go to the cure of man's spiritual ills—Jesus Christ, the Savior. A weak view of sin always produces a weak view of salvation. A weak view of sin blinds people to the need for a Savior.

Pearl of Wisdom: *A weak view of sin always produces a weak view of salvation.*

Mortal and Venial Sins

Some people distinguish between mortal sins (deadly sins) and venial sins (lesser sins). The problem with such a view is that if we think that most of our sins are venial sins, we may view ourselves as essentially good people. We may not see our dire need of a Savior.

The Bible makes no such distinction between mortal sins and venial sins. Some sins are indeed worse than others (Proverbs 6:16-19), but Scripture never says that only certain kinds of sin lead to spiritual death. All sin leads to spiritual death, not just one category of sins (Romans 3:23).

The truth is that every single sin a person commits is a mortal sin in the sense that it brings about spiritual death and separates us from God. Scripture reveals that even the smallest sin makes us legally guilty before God and warrants the death penalty (Romans 6:23).

Besides, Scripture is quite clear that every one of us is unrighteous before God. Romans 3:10-12 tells us, "None is righteous, no, not one...no one seeks for God. All have turned aside...no one does good, not even one." If words mean anything, we're all in dire trouble and need a Savior!

Pearl of Wisdom: *Though sin has alienated the human race from God, Jesus—by His work on the cross—has ended that alienation and brought us near to God: "Now in Christ Jesus you who once were far off have been brought near by the blood of Christ" (Ephesians 2:13).*

When Christians Sin

When we Christians sin, the Holy Spirit convicts us, and we experience a genuine sense of conviction, which Scripture calls a godly sorrow (2 Corinthians 7:8-11). If we fail to properly relate this sorrow to the forgiveness we have in Christ, we feel guilty and estranged from God. So what do we do when the Holy Spirit convicts us of sin?

Scripture encourages us to confess that sin to God (1 John 1:9). The Greek word for *confess* literally means "to say the same thing." So when we confess our sin to God, we're saying the same thing about our sin that God says about it. We're agreeing with God that what we did was wrong. No excuses! And following our confession, we can thank God that our sin is already forgiven because Jesus paid for it on the cross. Instantly our fellowship with the Father is restored. Our goal from that point forward is to walk in the power of the Holy Spirit so we'll have the power to resist such sins in the future (Galatians 5:16).

If Christians refuse to respond to the Holy Spirit's conviction and choose to continue sinning, God—with a motive of love—brings discipline into their lives to bring them to a point of confession (Hebrews 12:4-11). God's desire is that fellowship be restored.

Pearl of Wisdom: *The Christian will either respond to God's light or to His heat.*

The Temptations of This World

A temptation is an enticement to sin and disobey God. Scripture warns that we are to beware of the reality of temptations (Galatians 6:1) and make every effort not to let evil get the best of us (Romans 12:21). We are not to let sin control us (Romans 6:12) and must be cautious not to lose our secure footing (2 Peter 3:17). If we get too close to the fire, metaphorically speaking, we may get burned (Proverbs 6:27-28).

Scripture exhorts us to keep alert and pray (Matthew 26:41). Indeed, we are to pray daily that we not succumb to temptation (Matthew 6:9-13) and are not overcome (Luke 22:40). Such temptations emerge from our sinful nature (James 1:13-15).

The temptation to desire wealth has ensnared many (1 Timothy 6:9-10). So has an inappropriate desire for sex (1 Corinthians 7:5). We must not let Satan outsmart us (2 Corinthians 2:11), for he is a master tempter (Matthew 4:3; 1 Thessalonians 3:5).

Thankfully, God can prevent us from falling (Jude 24). Scripture reveals that when we are tempted, God will make a way of escape for us (1 Corinthians 10:13). Dependence on God's Spirit is essential (Galatians 5:16). Scripture also indicates that Jesus, our faithful High Priest, helps us in the midst of our temptations (Hebrews 2:14,18).

Pearl of Wisdom: *Though temptations assault us daily, God gives us the strategies and strength to overcome them.*

The Unforgivable Sin

S ome Christians fear that they have committed the unforgivable sin. This sin is clearly described for us in Matthew 12:32, and modern Christians are not likely to have committed it. The verse reads, "Whoever speaks a word against the Son of Man will be forgiven, but whoever speaks against the Holy Spirit will not be forgiven, either in this age or in the age to come."

The Old Testament prophesied that when the Messiah came, He would perform specific miracles in the power of the Holy Spirit, such as giving sight to the blind and opening deaf ears (Isaiah 35:5-6). But the Jewish leaders claimed Christ did such miracles in the power of the devil, the unholy spirit (Matthew 12:24). This was the sin against the Holy Spirit.

Matthew 12 thus describes a unique situation among the Jewish leaders. The actual committing of this sin requires the presence of the Messiah on earth doing His messianic miracles. The circumstances of Matthew 12 cannot be reduplicated exactly today, so the unforgivable sin probably cannot either.

The people who blasphemed the Spirit opposed Jesus' messiahship so vehemently that they accused him of sorcery instead of believing the Holy Spirit's miraculous signs, which confirmed that Jesus is the Messiah. This is truly a damning sin, for no other provision for man's sin can replace the work of the Messiah as attested by the Spirit.

Pearl of Wisdom: *Don't let the devil torture you with thoughts of being unforgiven by God!*

The Eternal Plan of Salvation

God is all-knowing—He knows all things, both actual and possible (Matthew 11:21-23), past (Isaiah 41:22), present (Hebrews 4:13), and future (Isaiah 46:10). This means that before humanity was even created, God already knew that Adam and Eve would fall into sin. God was omnisciently aware of this, so He devised the plan of salvation before He even created humankind.

Before the world began—indeed, in eternity past—God determined how He would bring about salvation for human beings. The plan would be based upon Jesus, the Lamb of God, who would die on the cross for human sin. Revelation 13:8 (NIV) thus refers to Him as "the Lamb that was slain from the creation of the world" (see also 17:8; 1 Peter 1:20). Ephesians 1:4 (NIV) assures us that God "chose us in him before the creation of the world to be holy and blameless in his sight."

Because the plan of salvation was formulated in eternity past and is worked out in human history, we must view human history from the standpoint of eternity. We must recognize a uniform plan, guided by God, which in the course of human history has been unfolding and will one day find its culmination when Christ comes again (Revelation 19).

Pearl of Wisdom: *What has happened in the past, what is happening now, and what will happen in the future is all evidence of the unfolding of the purposeful redemptive plan devised by the personal God of the Bible.*

The Trinity, and Our Salvation

Each of the three persons in the Trinity were involved in our salvation. The Father devised the plan (Ephesians 1:4). He sovereignly decreed it in eternity past (Romans 8:29-30) but carried it out in time. That which was eternally determined before the ages, happened in the ages. The plan includes the means of salvation (Jesus' death on the cross), the objective (the forgiveness of sins), and the persons to benefit (believers). Jesus referred to this plan when speaking to Nicodemus: "God did not send his Son into the world to condemn the world, but in order that the world might be saved through him" (John 3:17).

Jesus' task in the eternal plan included coming to earth as God's ultimate revelation (Hebrews 1:1-2), dying on the cross as a sacrifice for the sins of humankind (John 3:16), rising from the dead (1 Peter 3:21), and being the Mediator (or go-between) between the Father and humankind (1 Timothy 2:5). We were purchased with the precious blood of Christ, a Lamb without blemish or defect (Revelation 5:9).

The Holy Spirit's role was to inspire Scripture (2 Peter 1:21), regenerate believers (give them new life—spiritual life) (Titus 3:5), seal believers for the day of redemption (Ephesians 4:30), empower believers to overcome sin and live righteously (Galatians 5:22-23), and give them spiritual gifts (1 Corinthians 12:11).

Pearl of Wisdom: *Our God is an awesome God, and He has provided an awesome salvation.*

Divine Election and God's Foreknowledge

lection is the sovereign act of God of choosing certain individuals to salvation before the foundation of the world. Christians hold two different views on this issue. The first is that God's election is based on His foreknowledge of who would respond favorably to His gospel message. Several arguments are offered in favor of this view:

- God's salvation has appeared to all people, not merely the elect (Titus 2:11).

- Christ died for all (1 Timothy 4:10; 2 Peter 2:1; 1 John 2:2).

- People are free to turn to God (Isaiah 31:6; Acts 3:19), repent (Matthew 3:2; Luke 13:3,5), and believe (John 6:29; Acts 16:31).

- Election rests on God's foreknowledge of our response (Romans 8:28-30).

The second view is that God sovereignly elected without the use of foreknowledge:

- The Father gave certain ones to Christ (John 6:37; 17:2,6,9).

- No one comes to Christ unless the Father draws him (John 6:44).

- God chose Jacob rather than Esau before they were born (Romans 9:10-16).

- Salvation originated with God's choice (Ephesians 1:5-8; 2:8-10).

Pearl of Wisdom: *Regardless of whether this view is correct, we can all rejoice that Christians have been elected—personally chosen—by God.*

Divine Election and God's Sovereignty

A second view of divine election is based on God's sovereign choice with no consideration of human freewill decisions. Here are some arguments in favor of this view:

- Election is by God's choice (Acts 13:48).

- People are given to Christ (John 6:37; 17:2) as the Father draws them (John 6:44).

- God called some people before they were born (Jeremiah 1:5; Galatians 1:15).

- Election is necessary in light of man's depravity (Jeremiah 13:11; Romans 3:10-20).

Two primary arguments have been suggested against this view:

- A limited election implies a limited atonement as well. However, this conclusion seems to be refuted (John 1:29; 3:16; Hebrews 2:9; 1 John 2:2).

- Sovereign election makes God responsible for "reprobation" (the unsaved being "elected" to hell). However, those not included in election suffer only their due reward. God does not elect a person to hell.

Pearl of Wisdom: *A moderating view is that there is no chronological or logical priority of election and foreknowledge. Both foreknowledge and predetermination are simultaneous, eternal, and coordinate acts of God. Whatever He knows, He determines. Whatever He determines, He knows.*

Limited Atonement

L imited atonement is the view that Christ's atoning death was only for the elect and not for all people. Here are some of the verses that are used to support this viewpoint: Matthew 1:21 states that "he will save his people from their sins." Matthew 20:28 says Christ came "to give his life as a ransom for many." Jesus said, "I lay down my life for the sheep" (John 10:15). He purchased the church with His blood (Acts 20:28). He was sacrificed "to bear the sins of many" (Hebrews 9:28). Proponents of limited atonement offer a number of arguments:

- Scripture often limits those for whom Christ laid down His life.

- The elect were chosen before the foundation of the world (Ephesians 1:4), so how could Christ have died for all human beings?

- Christ is defeated if He died for all men and all men are not saved.

- If Christ died for all people, God could not fairly send people to hell for their sins.

- When terms such as *all, world,* and *whosoever* are used in Scripture in reference to those for whom Christ died (for example, John 3:16), they refer to the elect.

Pearl of Wisdom: *Regardless of whether Christians agree with this doctrine, they can certainly rejoice that Christ died for them!*

Unlimited Atonement

Unlimited atonement is the doctrine that Christ's redemptive death was for all persons—both the elect and the unelect. A number of verses are cited in support of this viewpoint. For example, 1 Timothy 2:4-6 affirms that God "desires all people to be saved." First Timothy 4:10 refers to Christ as "the Savior of all people, especially of those who believe." First John 2:2 affirms of Christ, "He is the propitiation for our sins, and not for ours only but also for the sins of the whole world." Isaiah 53:6 tells us that "All we like sheep have gone astray; we have turned every one to his own way; and the Lord has laid on him the iniquity of us all." (Notice that the same *all* who went astray are the *all* for whom the Lord died.) In 2 Peter 2:1 we read that Christ died even for false teachers.

My personal belief is that seemingly restrictive references can be logically fit into an unlimited scenario much more easily than universal references can be made to fit into a limited atonement scenario. No one denies that Christ died for God's sheep and His people. The question is, did He die exclusively for them? Certainly if Christ died for the whole of humanity, there is no logical problem in saying that He died for a specific part of the whole (see Galatians 2:20).

Pearl of Wisdom: *Let's each rejoice that Christ died for us!*

Scripture and the Gospel

The gospel is the good news of salvation in Jesus. The single best definition of the gospel is found in 1 Corinthians 15:3-4: "For I delivered to you as of first importance what I also received: that Christ died for our sins in accordance with the Scriptures, that he was buried, that he was raised on the third day in accordance with the Scriptures." The gospel thus has four primary components: Man is a sinner, Christ is the Savior, Christ died as man's substitute, and Christ rose from the dead. This is the gospel Paul and the other apostles preached.

People have had several misconceptions about the gospel:

- Some have taught that people must plead for mercy to be saved. However, this idea is never found in Scripture. Salvation comes by faith in Christ (John 3:16; Acts 16:31).

- Some have taught that we must follow Christ's example and live as He lived in order to be saved. However, we simply do not have it in us to live as Christ lived. Only the Holy Spirit working in us can imitate Christ in our lives (Galatians 5:16-23).

- Some have communicated that prayer is necessary to be saved (the "prayer of repentance"). Prayer may be a vehicle for the expression of one's faith, but faith brings about salvation (Acts 16:31).

Pearl of Wisdom: *Let's remember that salvation is a free gift that we receive by faith in Christ (Ephesians 2:8-9). This truly is good news!*

Jesus Is the Only Way

Many people today—even some Christians—claim that Jesus is one of many ways to salvation. This line of thinking embraces the idea that all the world religions teach the same basic truths.

Some years ago, I heard Christian philosopher Ravi Zacharias say that many people believe the various religions are essentially the same and only superficially different. The truth is, he said, that the various religions are essentially different and are only superficially the same. I think he is right.

One cannot read the Bible for long without seeing that Jesus did not just claim to have a way to God. Rather, He claimed to *be* God (John 8:58; 10:30). Moreover, Jesus and His message were inseparable. Jesus' teachings had absolute authority because He was and is God. This is not the case with the leaders of the other world religions.

Jesus claimed that what He said took precedence over all others: "I am the way, and the truth, and the life. No one comes to the Father except through me" (John 14:6). A bold Peter likewise asserted in Acts 4:12, "Salvation is found in no one else, for there is no other name under heaven given to men by which we must be saved" (see also 1 Timothy 2:5). Moreover, Jesus sternly warned His followers against following a different "Christ" (Matthew 24:4-5). Jesus proved the veracity of all He said by rising from the dead (Acts 17:31), something that no other religious leader did.

Pearl of Wisdom: *Salvation is found only in the person of Jesus Christ.*

Are Christians Narrow-Minded?

Some people assert that Christians are being narrow-minded in claiming Jesus is the only way. We can respond to this assertion in several ways. But I always like to ask, is being narrow always bad?

Many things in life are narrow that are not bad. For example, when I fly to Los Angeles, I want the pilot not only to land in Los Angeles but on the right runway. I want my wife, Kerri, to remain faithful to her one and only husband (me) her entire life. Sometimes only one road leads out of the forest, only one operation can save your life, or only one antidote works against a poison. These things are all narrow, but they are good!

God's way of salvation is narrow (by faith in Christ alone), but God's heart is infinitely wide. That is, God is full of love for all people—men and women, rich and poor, fat and thin, kings and peasants, the social elite and social outcasts (see Ezekiel 18:23; Isaiah 45:22; 1 Timothy 2:3-4). He offers the same gift to everyone—a singular gift of salvation in Jesus Christ. Jesus Himself wants all people to receive this wonderful gift (see Matthew 28:19; John 3:17), as did the apostles (Acts 26:28-29; Romans 1:16).

Pearl of Wisdom: *Never shy away from sharing this narrow gift with the people you meet!*

Are Christians Arrogant?

Sometimes unbelievers claim that Christians are being arrogant when they claim that Jesus is God's exclusive way of salvation. However, we should remember that when Christians make this claim, they are not suggesting that they think they are better than anyone else. They are putting themselves in the same camp as the rest of humanity in affirming that all people—Christians included—need the true Savior. Accepting and proclaiming God's one way of salvation is therefore not arrogance; it is genuine humility—like one beggar showing another beggar where to find bread. All of us are lost; all of us need the one true Savior, Jesus Christ.

Christians have nothing in themselves that saves or makes them special. Christians readily admit that the way of Jesus saves, not their way. Christians merely repeat Jesus' own claim: "I am the way, and the truth, and the life. No one comes to the Father except through me" (John 14:6; see also Acts 4:12; 1 Timothy 2:5).

Christians are therefore not the authors of Jesus' words or even the editors. They are only the mail carriers. Merely delivering the mail is not being arrogant. Rather, mocking and speaking against God's holy revelation of salvation in Jesus Christ—that's arrogant.

Pearl of Wisdom: *Regardless of what false accusations may come from unbelievers, let's continue to humbly share the good news with others.*

Lost People and the Gospel

S ome have suggested that perhaps people who don't know God are not lost. However, if they are not lost, Christ's postresurrection commands to His disciples are a mockery. In Luke 24:47, for example, Christ commanded "repentance and forgiveness of sins should be proclaimed in his name to all nations" (see also Matthew 28:19). These verses might well be stricken from the Scriptures if human beings without Christ are not lost.

If those without Christ do not need Him and His salvation, neither do we. Conversely, if we need Him, so do they. Scripture makes it very plain: "There is salvation in no one else, for there is no other name under heaven given among men by which we must be saved" (Acts 4:12; 1 Timothy 2:5).

Of course, God has given a certain amount of revelation to every single person in the world. God has written His moral law on every human heart so it perceives the difference between right and wrong (Romans 2:15). God has also given witness of Himself in the stellar universe above (Romans 1:20). This general revelation makes all people accountable (see Psalm 19:1-6; Romans 1:20). Those who respond positively to this general revelation receive more specific revelation from God (such as a visit from a missionary) (see Acts 10). Many such missionaries report conversions.

Pearl of Wisdom: *God desires all to be saved (1 Timothy 2:4) and does not want anyone to perish (2 Peter 3:9). He surely takes no pleasure in the death of the unsaved (Ezekiel 18:23).*

Christ's Substitutionary Atonement

G od did not arbitrarily decide to overlook human sin or wink at unrighteousness (Romans 3:23; 5:18; 6:23). Christ atoned for our sin by becoming our substitute—He died in our place. A number of biblical factors establish this truth.

- God's justice requires a perfect sacrifice. He cannot overlook sin (Habakkuk 1:13).

- Our depravity requires a perfect substitute, for we fall short of God's perfect standard.

- The Old Testament sacrifices implied a substitutionary atonement (Leviticus 1:3-4).

- Christ was wounded for our transgressions and crushed for our iniquities (Isaiah 53:5).

- Jesus became our ransom. He delivered us, paying compensation by becoming our substitute.

- Christ's death was for us, which implies substitution (see John 10:15; Romans 12:17).

- *Propitiation,* or "atoning sacrifice," when used of Christ's death, implies a substitution (1 John 2:2).

- The appeasing of God's wrath by Christ's death implies a substitutionary death (Romans 3:25).

Pearl of Wisdom: *Jesus took the rap for us. What an awesome Savior!*

Did Jesus Become Sin for Us?

In 2 Corinthians 5:21 we read, "For our sake he made him to be sin who knew no sin, so that in him we might become the righteousness of God." Some Christians have concluded that Jesus actually became sin—or became sinful—on our behalf. However, the apostle Paul's intended meaning is that Jesus was always without sin actually, but at the cross He was made to be sin for us judicially. Jesus never committed a sin personally, but He was made to be sin for us substitutionally.

Just as the righteousness that is imputed to Christians in justification is extrinsic to them, so the sin that was imputed to Christ on the cross was extrinsic to Him. In no sense did it contaminate His essential nature. The innocent one (Jesus) was punished voluntarily as if He were guilty. As a result, the guilty ones (you and me) are gratuitously rewarded as if we were innocent. That's a great exchange!

In a nutshell, then, the whole redemptive plan entails substitution; salvation cannot happen without it. By His utterly selfless sacrificial death on the cross, our sinless Savior—the unblemished Lamb of God—paid the penalty for our sins and thereby canceled the debt of sin against us, thus wondrously making possible our reconciliation with God.

———

Pearl of Wisdom: *Exultation and praise are appropriate responses of the redeemed. "To Him who loves us and released us from our sins by His blood...to Him be the glory and the dominion forever and ever" (Revelation 1:5-6 NASB).*

Born Again, Justified, Reconciled, Forgiven, and Adopted

Scripture uses various salvation words to describe the wonder and all-encompassing nature of our salvation.

Born again. This Bible phrase can also be translated *born from above.* It refers to the act of God by which He gives eternal life to the one who believes in Christ (Titus 3:5; John 3:1-5; 1 Peter 1:23).

Justified. God declares righteous all those who believe in Jesus. Because of Christ's work on the cross—taking our place and bearing our sins—God acquits believers and pronounces a verdict of not guilty.

Reconciled. By believing in Jesus, who paid for our sins at the cross, we are reconciled to God. The alienation and estrangement that formerly existed is gone (2 Corinthians 5:19).

Forgiven. God promised, "I will remember their sins and their lawless deeds no more" (Hebrews 10:17). We are told, "For as high as the heavens are above the earth, so great is his steadfast love toward those who fear him; as far as the east is from the west, so far does he remove our transgressions from us" (Psalm 103:11-12). That means God puts infinity between Himself and our sins!

Adopted. Believers are adopted into God's forever family. We become sons of God (Romans 8:14). God adopts into His family any who believe in His Son, Jesus. Because of this new relationship with God, believers are called "heirs of God" and "coheirs with Christ" (Romans 8:17).

———

Pearl of Wisdom: *The breadth and depth of our salvation are wondrous indeed.*

Only by God's Grace

The word *grace* literally means "unmerited favor." *Unmerited* means this favor cannot be earned. Grace, theologically speaking, refers to the undeserved, unearned favor of God. Romans 5:1-11 tells us that God gives His incredible grace to those who actually deserve the opposite—that is, condemnation.

Eternal life cannot be earned. It is a free gift of grace that comes from believing in Jesus Christ. Jesus said, "Truly, truly, I say to you, whoever believes has eternal life" (John 6:47). "The free gift of God is eternal life in Christ Jesus our Lord" (Romans 6:23).

True grace is sometimes hard for people to grasp. After all, our society is performance oriented. Good grades depend on how well we perform in school. Climbing up the corporate ladder depends on how well we perform at work. Nothing of any real worth is free in our society. But God's gift of salvation is a grace-gift. It is free! Ephesians 2:8-9 affirms, "For by grace you have been saved through faith. And this is not your own doing; it is the gift of God, not a result of works, so that no one may boast."

This does not mean that this free gift was free for God. The price God paid to provide our salvation was the very death of His Son (2 Corinthians 5:21). Such is the wonder of God's grace.

Pearl of Wisdom: *As surely as human effort fails, God's grace prevails!*

Trust in Christ and Be Born Again

We have seen that being born again literally means to be born from above. It refers to God giving eternal life to the one who believes in Christ (Titus 3:5). The new birth places one into God's eternal family (1 Peter 1:23).

In John 3, Jesus talks with Nicodemus about the need to be born again. Here we find a Pharisee—a Jewish leader—who was probably trusting in his physical descent from Abraham for entrance into the Messiah's kingdom.

Jesus denied such a possibility. Parents can transmit to their children only the nature they themselves possess. All human parents have a sin nature, so all parents transmit this same nature to their children. All people are born in sin. And what is sinful cannot enter the kingdom of God (John 3:5). The only way people can enter God's forever family is by experiencing a spiritual rebirth, and this is precisely what Jesus emphasized to Nicodemus.

The moment we place our trust in Jesus, the Holy Spirit infuses our dead human spirits with the eternal life of God, and we are reborn spiritually. One moment we are spiritually dead; the next moment we are spiritually alive. At the moment of the new birth, the believer receives a new spiritual nature or capacity that expresses itself in spiritual concerns and interests. What a great blessing!

Pearl of Wisdom: *Better not to have been born than not to be born twice!*

Change Your Mind About Jesus

The Greek word for repentance, *metanoe*, means "to change one's mind." The context in the Bible always indicates what one must change the mind about.

Repentance as it relates to Jesus Christ, for example, means to change our mind about Him—who He is (God in human flesh) and what He's done (died on the cross for our sins). Repentance in this sense refers to changing our mind about the particular sin of rejecting Christ.

As the book of Acts opens, the Jews have rejected Jesus as being the divine Messiah. So when Peter admonished them to repent and believe in Jesus (Acts 2:38; 3:19), he was actually encouraging them to change their minds about Jesus and believe in Him as the Messiah-Savior so their sins could be forgiven.

Saul, in the New Testament, is another good example. Saul—a vitriolic anti-Christian—is first introduced in Acts 7:58, where he approved of Stephen's stoning. Saul was also responsible for many Christians being thrown in jail (26:10). While en route to Damascus to persecute more Christians (9:2), he saw a light from heaven, and he found himself in a conversation with the resurrected Jesus (9:4,27; 22:14-15). He not only repented of his view of Jesus but also became the greatest witness of Christ ever (as the apostle Paul).

People everywhere are called to change their minds about Jesus. Salvation is found in Him alone.

Pearl of Wisdom: *One of our goals as witnesses for Christ should be to help people change their minds about who Jesus is and what He's done for us at the cross.*

A Clean Slate

Humankind's dilemma of falling short of God pointed to the need for a solution—and that solution is found in justification (Romans 3:24). The word *justified* is a legal term and refers to the process of being declared righteous or acquitted. Negatively, the word means that one is once and for all pronounced not guilty before God. Positively, the word means that one is once and for all pronounced righteous. When people trust in Christ for salvation, they are pronounced not guilty and forever righteous (Romans 3:25,28,30). This is a singular and instantaneous judicial act of God (Romans 3:25,28,30; 8:33-34).

This legal declaration is external to us. It does not hinge on our personal level of righteousness. It does not hinge on anything we do. It hinges solely on God's declaration. It is a once and for all judicial pronouncement that takes place the moment we place our faith in Christ. Even while we are yet sinners and are experientially not righteous, we are nevertheless righteous in God's sight because of forensic justification (Romans 3:25,28,30).

The Jews previously tried to earn right standing with God by works, but Paul indicated that God's acquittal and declaration of righteousness (justification) is given "by his grace as a gift" (Romans 3:24). The word *grace* means "unmerited favor." Because of God's unmerited favor, human beings can freely be declared righteous before God.

Pearl of Wisdom: *You and I are sinners who have forever been acquitted and declared righteous. Rejoice!*

Instant Forgiveness

Because of the salvation Christ accomplished at the cross, those who place their faith in Him are completely forgiven of all their sins (Acts 16:31). And I mean *all*.

Psalm 103:11-12 tells us, "For as high as the heavens are above the earth, so great is his steadfast love toward those who fear him; as far as the east is from the west, so far does he remove our transgressions from us." There is a definite point that is north and another that is south—the North and South Poles. But there are no such points for east and west. Regardless of how far we go to the east; we will never arrive where east begins because by definition east is the opposite of west. The two never meet. They never will meet and never could meet because they are defined as opposites. To remove sins "as far as the east is from the west" is to put them where no one can ever find them. That is the forgiveness God grants believers.

Scripture says that Christ took the certificate of debt of each of our lives and nailed it to the cross (Colossians 2:14). In ancient days, whenever someone was found guilty of a crime, the offender was put in jail and a certificate of debt—listing his sins—was posted on the jail door. Upon release, the offender's certificate was stamped "Paid in Full." Jesus' sacrifice paid in full the price for our sins.

Pearl of Wisdom: *God has forgiven us, so we should also forgive others (Matthew 18:22,35; Luke 17:4).*

Christians Are "in Christ"

Scripture graphically demonstrates that our salvation does not depend on our good works by proclaiming that believers are "in Christ" (Ephesians 2:7). The moment you trust in Christ, a wonderful thing happens. You are identified with Christ. You are joined in spiritual union to Him. The Father accepts Christ perfectly, so He also accepts you perfectly because you are in Christ.

As we might expect, Satan tries to blind our minds to this glorious and liberating truth. His goal is to keep us from focusing on our standing "in Christ" and focus instead on the need to perpetually do good works in order to earn favor with God. When we fail to live up to the standards of God's law in the Bible, Satan shifts his attention to accusing our consciences and making us feel like worms before God (Revelation 12:10). He wants us to feel guilt and despondency over our consistent failure to meet God's demands.

This in turn leads to a sense of alienation from God. If we think that God has something against us because of some sin we've committed, we naturally back off and alienate ourselves from Him (Genesis 3:8).

The fact is, though, that Christians who give in to this line of thinking have forgotten that they are in Christ and that the Father sees believers as being in Him. So never, ever forget this pivotal spiritual truth!

———

Pearl of Wisdom: *Do not allow yourself to be blinded by Satan's lies regarding your status of being in Christ.*

Secure Salvation

When people trust in Christ and become part of God's forever family, they are saved forever (Romans 8:28-30). Regardless of what children of God do from then on, they are saved.

That does not mean Christians can get away with anything. If children of God sin and refuse to repent, God brings discipline—sometimes very severe discipline—into their lives to bring them to repentance (Hebrews 12:4-11). Christians will either respond to God's light or to His heat.

Ephesians 4:30 says we are sealed for the day of redemption by the Holy Spirit. This seal—which indicates ownership, authority, and security—cannot be broken. The seal guarantees our entry into heaven.

Further, the Father keeps us in His sovereign hands, and no one can take us out of His hands (John 10:28-30; 13:1). God has us in His firm grip, and God's plans cannot be thwarted (Isaiah 14:24).

Still further, the Lord Jesus Himself regularly intercedes and prays for us (Hebrews 7:25). His work of intercession, as our divine High Priest, is necessary because of our weaknesses, our helplessness, and our immaturity as children of God. He knows our limitations. He is therefore faithful to make intercession for us (see Luke 22:31-32).

Additionally, Romans 8:29-39 portrays an unbroken chain that spans from the predestination of believers to their future glorification in heaven. This indicates the certainty of all believers reaching heaven.

———

Pearl of Wisdom: *You and I can rest secure in our salvation!*

The Book of Life

In Revelation 3:5, Jesus said, "The one who conquers will be clothed thus in white garments, and I will never blot his name out of the book of life." One might surmise that Jesus is here implying that Christians' names could potentially be blotted out of the book of life. But I do not think this is the intent of His words.

Many clear passages of Scripture point to the security of believers' salvation. The same John who wrote the book of Revelation wrote elsewhere about the security of salvation of each individual believer (see John 5:24; 6:35-37,39; 10:28-29). So however Revelation 3:5 is interpreted, I do not think it should be taken to mean that believers can lose their salvation.

This passage may seem to imply that believers' names could be erased from the book of life, but it actually only gives a positive affirmation that their names will not be erased. Jesus' statement may thus be considered not a threat but indeed an assurance that saved people's names will always be in the book of life.

This seems consistent with what other verses communicate about the book of life. For example, in Luke 10:20 Jesus said to the disciples, "Do not rejoice in this, that the spirits are subject to you, but rejoice that your names are written in heaven." In Hebrews 12:23 (NIV) we read of "the church of the firstborn, whose names are written in heaven."

Pearl of Wisdom: *You and I are secure in our salvation.*

Will Everyone Be Saved?

Universalism, the idea that all people will be saved in the end, is a false doctrine. Certain passages—John 12:32; Philippians 2:11; and 1 Timothy 2:4—are typically twisted out of context in support of this viewpoint. Such passages, interpreted properly, do not support universalism.

John 12:32 says that Christ's work on the cross makes possible the salvation of both Jews and Gentiles. Notice, however, that the Lord in the same passage warned of judgment of those who reject Christ (verse 48).

Philippians 2:10-11 assures us that someday all people will acknowledge that Jesus is Lord, but not necessarily that He is Savior. (Even those in hell will have to acknowledge Christ's lordship.)

First Timothy 2:4 expresses God's desire that all be saved but does not promise that all will be. This divine desire is realized only in those who exercise faith in Christ (Acts 16:31).

In Matthew 13:49, Jesus said that at the close of the age, "the angels will come out and separate the evil from the righteous." Notice that two classes are mentioned—unbelievers and believers (the evil and the righteous). Matthew 25:32 then tells us that following the second coming, the nations will be gathered before Jesus, "and he will separate people one from another as a shepherd separates the sheep from the goats." Believers and unbelievers are called sheep and goats. The sheep will enter into God's kingdom (verse 34), but the goats will go into eternal punishment (verse 46).

Pearl of Wisdom: *In the end, there are two classes of people (the saved and the unsaved) who experience two different destinies (heaven or hell).*

The Law Cannot Save

If salvation is a free gift we receive by faith in Christ, why did God give us the law (including the Ten Commandments)? That's an important question.

God did not give us the law as a means of attaining salvation. Romans 3:20 emphasizes that "by works of the Law no human being will be justified in his sight." So why did God give us the law?

- God gave us the law to show us what sin is. The law shows us God's holy standards and the consequences of not measuring up to them.

- The law provokes sin all the more in us. It was given "to increase the trespass" (Romans 5:20). God wants us to become so overwhelmed with the sin problem that we cannot deny its reality and our need for a Savior.

- Most important, the law is like a tutor that leads us to Christ (Galatians 3:24-25). The law does this by showing us our sin and then pointing to the marvelous grace of Christ.

- Once we have come to Christ—trusting in Him as our Savior— the law has done its job, and it no longer holds sway over us. For believers, "Christ is the end of the law so that there may be righteousness for everyone who believes" (Romans 10:4 NIV).

Pearl of Wisdom: *The law has an important role in bringing us to Christ. Now that it has done so, we keep our eyes upon Jesus.*

Sinless Perfection

In Matthew 5:48 we read, "You therefore must be perfect, as your heavenly Father is perfect." Surely this verse does not mean we can actually attain sinless perfection in this life. Such an idea is foreign not only to Matthew's Gospel but to all of Scripture. First John 1:8 asserts, "If we say we have no sin, we deceive ourselves, and the truth is not in us." This epistle was written to Christians (1 John 2:12-14,19), so it seems obvious that Christians should never claim moral perfection.

The great saints of the Bible seemed to all recognize their own intrinsic sinfulness (see Isaiah 6:5; Daniel 9:4-19; Ephesians 3:8). If anyone could have attained perfection, certainly Isaiah, Daniel, and Paul would have been contenders. But none of them succeeded, for each still had a sin nature (Romans 7:13-20).

So how can we make sense of Matthew 5:48? The context of this verse deals with the law of love. The Jewish leaders of Jesus' day said we should love those near and dear to us (Leviticus 19:18) but hate our enemies. Jesus refutes this idea, instructing us to love even our enemies. After all, Jesus said, God's love extends to all people (Matthew 5:45). God is our righteous standard, so we should seek to be as He is. We are to be perfect (or complete) in loving, just as He is perfect.

Pearl of Wisdom: *As we depend on the Holy Spirit, God's kind of love is progressively reproduced in our lives (see Galatians 5:22-23).*

Speaking in Tongues

S ome today claim that speaking in tongues is a prerequisite for salvation. They allege that speaking in tongues is the definitive evidence of the baptism of the Holy Spirit, and this baptism is necessary for salvation.

Such a view is imbalanced. Scripture reveals that the Holy Spirit bestows spiritual gifts on believers (1 Corinthians 12:11), but He does not give every Christian the same gift. Here's what we learn about speaking in tongues from Scripture.

Contrary to what is sometimes claimed, speaking in tongues is not an evidence of the baptism of the Holy Spirit. After all, not all the Corinthians spoke in tongues (1 Corinthians 14:5), but all of them had been baptized (12:13).

The fruit of the Holy Spirit (Galatians 5:22-23) does not include speaking in tongues. Therefore, Christlikeness does not require speaking in tongues.

Most of the New Testament writers are silent on speaking in tongues. Only three books—Acts, 1 Corinthians, and Mark—mention the phenomenon. (And the reference in Mark 16:17 is not in the two best Greek manuscripts.) Significantly, many of the other New Testament books speak a great deal about the Holy Spirit but fail to even mention speaking in tongues. To say, then, that speaking in tongues is necessary for salvation is to force something into Scripture that simply is not there!

Other gifts are more important than speaking in tongues, and Scripture encourages us to seek those (1 Corinthians 12:28,31).

———

Pearl of Wisdom: *Some people make way too big a deal over speaking in tongues. Don't buy into the hype!*

Baptism and Salvation

I do not believe baptism is necessary for salvation. Baptism is important, and it should be among the first acts of obedience to God following our conversion. But our faith in Christ is what saves us (Acts 16:31; John 3:16), not baptism.

Recall that when Jesus was crucified, two thieves were crucified with Him. One of them placed his faith in Christ while he was hanging on his cross. Jesus said to him, "Truly, I say to you, today you will be with me in Paradise" (Luke 23:43). The thief had no opportunity to jump down from the cross and get baptized, but he was still saved.

In Acts 10 we find Cornelius—a devout Gentile—placing faith in Christ and becoming saved. Yet the account in Acts 10 makes it clear that Cornelius was saved prior to being baptized in water. After all, at the moment Cornelius believed in Christ, the gift of the Holy Spirit was poured out on him (Acts 10:45), thereby indicating salvation.

Finally, in 1 Corinthians 1:17 the apostle Paul said, "Christ did not send me to baptize but to preach the gospel." Here a distinction is made between the gospel and being baptized. We are told elsewhere that it is the gospel that brings salvation (1 Corinthians 15:2). Because baptism is not a part of that gospel, it is not necessary for salvation.

Pearl of Wisdom: *Let's not forget the purpose of baptism. Baptism is essentially a public profession of faith. It says to the whole world, "I am a believer in Christ and have identified my life with Him."*

Is Healing Guaranteed in the Atonement?

Some people believe Isaiah 53:4-5 teaches that healing is guaranteed in the atonement. One must keep in mind, however, that the Hebrew word for healing (*napha*) can refer not only to physical healing but also to spiritual healing. The context of Isaiah 53:4-5 indicates that spiritual healing is in view in this passage. Verse 5 states, "He was wounded for our transgressions; he was crushed for our iniquities...With his stripes we are healed." *Transgressions* and *iniquities* indicate that spiritual healing from the misery of sin is in view.

God doesn't always physically heal people. Paul couldn't heal Timothy's stomach problem (1 Timothy 5:23), nor could he heal Trophimus (2 Timothy 4:20) or Epaphroditus (Philippians 2:25-27). Paul spoke of his own bodily illness (Galatians 4:13-15) and a "thorn in the flesh" that God allowed him to retain (2 Corinthians 12:7-9). In none of these cases did anyone act as if healing were guaranteed in the atonement.

Finally, Scripture reveals that our present bodies are perishable and weak (1 Corinthians 15:42-44), and "our outer self is wasting away" (2 Corinthians 4:16). Death and disease will be a part of the human condition until we receive resurrection bodies that are immune to such frailties (1 Corinthians 15:51-55).

Pearl of Wisdom: *When we get sick, we should pray for healing (James 5:15) but not hesitate to visit the doctor (Matthew 9:12). All the while, trust in God (2 Corinthians 12:9).*

Spreading the Good News of Jesus Christ

The word *evangelism* comes from the Greek verb *evangelizomai*, which means, "proclaim the good news." So evangelism involves proclaiming to other people the gospel (or good news) of salvation in Jesus Christ (Luke 15; John 3:16; Romans 5:8). Evangelism is not a task for professionals only (pastors and ministers). Rather, all Christians are called to be ambassadors for Christ (2 Corinthians 5:17-21).

As for the content of the gospel message, the apostle Paul described it in 1 Corinthians 15:3-4: "For I delivered to you as of first importance what I also received: that Christ died for our sins in accordance with the Scriptures, that he was buried, that he was raised on the third day in accordance with the Scriptures." The gospel, according to this passage, has four primary components: human beings are sinners, Christ is the Savior, Christ died as man's substitute, and Christ rose from the dead.

Let's remember that the Lord does not want anyone to perish (2 Peter 3:9). We are to be Christ's witnesses in the world (Luke 24:45-49; Acts 1:8), ever remembering that a single lost sheep is worthy of finding (Matthew 18:12-14). One plants and another waters (1 Corinthians 3:6-9), but we all ought to keep in mind Paul's words to young Timothy to "do the work of an evangelist" (2 Timothy 4:5).

Pearl of Wisdom: *We should all perpetually be about the business of helping people enter the kingdom (Luke 5:10).*

The Church—Universal and Local

The universal church is the ever-enlarging fellowship of born-again believers who comprise the universal body of Christ over whom He reigns as Lord (1 Corinthians 12:13). The members of the church vary in age, sex, race, wealth, social status, and ability, but they are all joined together as one people (Galatians 3:28). This body is comprised only of believers in Christ. People become members of this universal body simply by believing in Christ.

The word *church* is translated from the Greek word *ekklesia*. This Greek word comes from two smaller words: *ek* (out from among) and *klesia* (to call). Combining the two words, *ekklesia* means "to call out from among." The church represents those whom God has called out from among the world. And those God has called come from all walks of life. All are welcome in Christ's church.

Though there is one universal church, there are many local churches scattered all over the world (see, for example, 1 Corinthians 1:2; 1 Thessalonians 1:1). Most people who attend local churches are believers, but some unbelievers are inevitably present. Attending local churches is strongly urged in the New Testament. Hebrews 10:25 specifically warns us about neglecting to meet together.

Pearl of Wisdom: *We are to live the Christian life within the context of the family of God and not in isolation (Ephesians 3:14-15; Acts 2). The Bible knows nothing of "lone ranger Christians."*

Israel and the Church

Israel and the church share some similarities: Both are part of the people of God, both are part of God's spiritual kingdom, and both participate in the spiritual blessings of the Abrahamic covenant and the new covenant (Genesis 12:1-3; Jeremiah 31:31-37). However, notable distinctions also exist:

- Israel predates Moses; the church began on Pentecost (Acts 1:5; 1 Corinthians 12:13).

- Israel is earthly and political (Exodus 19:5-6); the universal church is the invisible, spiritual body of Christ (Ephesians 1:3).

- Israel is composed of Jews; the church is composed of both Jews and Gentiles.

- People can be born Jewish; people enter the church only through rebirth (John 3:3-5).

Some Christians today believe the New Testament church is spiritual Israel—a continuation of Old Testament ethnic Israel. But this view has problems: (1) A consistent historical-grammatical hermeneutic demands that the unconditional land and throne promises be literally fulfilled in Israel (Genesis 13:1-7). (2) John the Baptist offered a literal kingdom to national Israel (Matthew 3:2), as did Jesus (Matthew 19:28) and Peter (Acts 3:19-21). (3) The apostle Paul was clear that national Israel will be restored before Christ returns (Romans 11:1-2,29). Such events are never said to be fulfilled in (or pertain to) the church.

Pearl of Wisdom: *Confusing the church with Israel can lead to a variety of interpretive errors.*

The Sabbath and the Lord's Day

The Hebrew word for *Sabbath* means "cessation." The Sabbath was a holy day and a day of rest for both man and animals (Exodus 20:8-11). This day was to commemorate God's rest after His work of creation (Genesis 2:2). God set the pattern for living—working six days and resting on the seventh. Keeping the Sabbath was a sign that showed submission to God, and honoring it brought great blessing (Isaiah 58:13). Some Christians today believe Sabbath observance (on Saturday) is still mandatory.

Other Christians believe worship should be on the Lord's Day (Sunday). They offer a number of reasons: (1) Keeping the Sabbath is the only one of the Ten Commandments not repeated after the day of Pentecost (Acts 2). (2) New Testament believers are not under the Old Testament law (Romans 6:14; Galatians 3:24-25). (3) Jesus rose from the grave and appeared to some of His followers on a Sunday (Matthew 28:1). (4) Jesus continued His appearances on succeeding Sundays (John 20:26). (5) The descent of the Holy Spirit took place on a Sunday (Acts 2:1). (6) The early church was thus given the pattern of Sunday worship, and this they continued to follow regularly (Acts 20:7; 1 Corinthians 16:2). (7) Jesus appeared to John on "the Lord's day" (Revelation 1:10). (7) Colossians 2:16 instructs us not to let anyone pass judgment on us regarding Sabbath days.

Pearl of Wisdom: *I opt for Sunday worship. However, this is a matter over which Christians can agree to disagree in an agreeable way.*

Musical Instruments in Church

Some churches—such as some branches of the Church of Christ, old-order Amish, and some Mennonites—do not use musical instruments in church services. The New Testament does not refer to musical instruments in worship, so they believe worship should be noninstrumental.

Other churches disagree. They believe that to prohibit musical instruments simply because they are not mentioned in New Testament church services is an argument from silence—which is not a valid argument. Omission does not mean exclusion.

In the Old Testament, a wide variety of musical instruments were used in temple worship (1 Chronicles 25). Indeed, many of the Psalms were originally designed for musical accompaniment. Psalm 4, for example, was to be accompanied "with stringed instruments." Scripture tells us that "David and all the house of Israel played music before the LORD on all kinds of instruments" (2 Samuel 6:5 NKJV).

Many today believe that since musical instruments were used predominantly in Old Testament worship, including in temple worship, then certainly God's people in New Testament times—many of them Jewish converts to Christianity—can follow this same pattern. No verse in the New Testament prevents it. Besides, Revelation 5:8 indicates that harps will be used in heaven in worship of God.

Pearl of Wisdom: *If musical instruments were used in worship in the past and will be used in worship in the future, we are probably free to worship God with instruments in the present.*

Traditional and Contemporary Music in Worship

These are some of the advantages of traditional hymns over contemporary songs:

- The lyrics are typically more rich, poetic, and doctrinal.

- Many were written by spiritual giants, like Martin Luther and Charles Wesley, and new generations should be introduced to this rich heritage.

- Contemporary music might be problematic for longtime churchgoers.

- Contemporary music is often loud and could detract from worship.

- Contemporary music can become showy and detract from worship.

On the other hand...

- Unchurched people can relate to contemporary music.

- Martin Luther used the contemporary music of his day.

- Some contemporary hymns share the strengths of older hymns.

- Many believers enjoy contemporary songs on recordings and radio.

- Some contemporary songs are effective in worship services.

Pearl of Wisdom: *Perhaps worship services can make room for both traditional music and contemporary music.*

Grace-Giving, and Tithing

The Hebrew word translated *tithe* literally means "a tenth." In Old Testament times, tithing was commanded by God on the basis that "the earth is the Lord's and the fullness thereof, the world and those who dwell therein" (Psalm 24:1). Through the tithe, the people of God acknowledged that God owned all things and was sovereign over them. Withholding tithes and offerings from God was tantamount to robbing God (Malachi 3:8-10).

No verse in the New Testament specifies that believers should give 10 percent of their income to the church. Yet this should not be taken to mean that church members should not support the church financially. The New Testament emphasis seems to be on what might be called *grace-giving*. We are to freely give as we have freely received. And we are to give as we are able (2 Corinthians 8:12). For some, this will mean less than 10 percent. But for others whom God has materially blessed, this will mean much more than 10 percent.

To develop a right attitude about giving to the church, we must first give ourselves to the Lord. The early church is our example: "They gave themselves first to the Lord and then by the will of God to us" (2 Corinthians 8:5). Only when we have given ourselves to the Lord will we have a proper perspective on money.

Pearl of Wisdom: *God is not interested in our money until He first has our hearts.*

Women in Ministry

These are some reasons people encourage the ordination of women:

- Women could be ordained and remain under the authority of a male senior pastor.

- Miriam the prophetess helped Moses shepherd Israel (Exodus 15).

- Other female prophetesses are mentioned in Scripture (Acts 21:9).

- Many gifted women ministered with Jesus and the apostles (Mark 15:41; Acts 18:18,26).

- Priscilla (wife of Aquila) helped train Apollos (Acts 18).

- Women can receive the spiritual gift of teaching (1 Corinthians 12:28-29).

- Women can be "fellow workers" in ministry (Romans 16:3).

On the other hand...

- The disciples and apostles established a pattern of male leadership.

- Genesis to Revelation demonstrates a pattern of male leadership.

- Elders were required to be the husband of one wife (Titus 1:6).

- Paul said women should not teach or have authority over men (1 Timothy 2:11-14).

- Paul said women are to keep silent in church (1 Corinthians 14:33-36).

Pearl of Wisdom: *Christians on both sides of the debate ought to show charity in their attitudes toward one another.*

The Significance of Baptism

B aptism was not a new concept in the first century. Whenever people converted to Judaism in biblical times, they were immersed in water as a sign of their ritual cleansing. Christianity gave baptism an even deeper significance.

Christians hold three views regarding the significance of baptism. The first is the sacramental view espoused by Roman Catholics and Lutherans. In this view, God conveys grace to believers through the sacrament. Believers' sins are remitted, and they receive a new nature.

The covenantal view explains that New Testament baptism is a counterpart to Old Testament circumcision. This view does not see baptism as a means of salvation. Rather, baptism is a sign of God's covenant to save humankind, and it is a means of entering into that covenant and enjoying its benefits.

A third view (my view) is the symbolic view. This view says that baptism neither produces salvation nor conveys grace. Rather, it is a symbol that points to the believer's identification with Jesus. It is a public testimony that shouts to the world that a change in status has occurred in the person's life. Formerly, the person was identified with the world and was lost, but now the person is identified with Jesus. Immersion into the water and rising out of it symbolizes death to the old life and resurrection to the new life in Christ (Romans 6:1-4).

Pearl of Wisdom: *Let's take advantage of every opportunity to demonstrate our identification with Jesus Christ.*

The Proper Mode of Baptism

Christians disagree about the proper mode of baptism. Those who argue for sprinkling say that a secondary meaning of the Greek word *baptizo* is "to bring under the influence of." This fits sprinkling better than immersion. Moreover, baptism by sprinkling better pictures the coming of the Holy Spirit upon a person. Further, immersion would have been impossible in some of the baptisms portrayed in Scripture. In Acts 2:41, for example, immersing all 3000 people who were baptized would have been difficult (Acts 8:38; 10:47; 6:33).

Those who hold to the immersion view (like I do) respond by pointing out that the primary meaning of the Greek word *baptizo* is "to immerse." Moreover, the prepositions normally used in conjunction with *baptizo* (such as *into* and *out of* the water) clearly picture immersion and not sprinkling. The Greek language has perfectly acceptable words for *sprinkling* and *pouring*, but these words are never used in the context of baptism in the New Testament.

The ancient Jews practiced baptism by immersion. The Jewish converts to Christianity—including the disciples, who came out of Judaism—would have been likely to follow this precedent. Arguments that there was not enough water to accomplish immersion are weak and unconvincing; archaeologists have uncovered ancient pools all over Jerusalem.

———

Pearl of Wisdom: *Ultimately, God accepts the believers on the basis of their faith in Christ and their desire to obey Him, not on the basis of how much water covers the body at the moment of baptism.*

Infant Baptism

Some Christians say infant baptism is analogous to Old Testament circumcision (see Genesis 17:12; Colossians 2:11-12). They reason that if young boys were circumcised (the sign of the old covenant), then children should be baptized as well (the sign of the new covenant). Moreover, household baptisms in the New Testament must have included infants (see Acts 16:33). Jesus Himself blessed the children (Mark 10:13-16) and said that to such belong the kingdom.

Other Christians (myself included) disagree with this view. In the biblical pattern, a person gets baptized following conversion (see Acts 2:37-41; 8:12; 10:47; 16:29-34; 18:8; 19:4-5). Moreover, no household baptism specifies the presence of infants. Some verses indicate the entire household was composed of believers (Acts 18:8). Every baptism we witness in the New Testament involved an adult. We never witness Jesus or a disciple baptizing an infant. Moreover, baptism is presented in the New Testament as an outward symbol of an inward reality (Romans 6:3-6), but how can one outwardly symbolize what one has not inwardly experienced? Further, circumcision is a false analogy to baptism, for circumcision was only for young boys, whereas baptism is for boys and girls. And circumcision was a sign of the old covenant, but baptism is not a sign of the new covenant—the Lord's Supper is (1 Corinthians 11:25).

Pearl of Wisdom: *Any child who has actually trusted in Christ is a candidate for baptism.*

The Significance of the Lord's Supper

The Roman Catholic view is known as transubstantiation. This view says the elements actually change into the body and blood of Jesus at the prayer of consecration of the priest. It is said to impart grace to the recipient. A problem with this view is that Jesus was present with the disciples when He said the bread and wine were His body and blood (Luke 22:17-19), thereby indicating His language was figurative. Moreover, drinking blood is forbidden in Scripture (Leviticus 3:17). Further, Jesus' human body cannot be omnipresent (in Catholic churches around the world).

The Lutheran view is known as consubstantiation. This view says that Christ is present in, with, and under the bread and wine. There is a real presence of Christ but no change in the elements.

The Reformed view is that Christ is spiritually present at the Lord's Supper, and it is a means of grace. A dynamic presence of Jesus in the elements is made effective in believers as they partake.

The memorial view (my view) is that the elements do not change and that the ordinance does not communicate grace. The bread and wine are symbols and reminders of Jesus in His death and resurrection (1 Corinthians 11:24-25). It also reminds us of the gospel (11:26), the second coming (11:26), and our oneness as the body of Christ (10:17).

Pearl of Wisdom: *Every time we celebrate the Lord's Supper, we ought to deeply meditate about Jesus' death and resurrection.*

The Vast Spiritual World

The writer of Hebrews defines faith as "the assurance of things hoped for, the conviction of things not seen" (Hebrews 11:1). But most of us tend to believe only what our five senses tell us. The spiritual world is not subject to any of these, so we often act as if it does not exist.

The eyes of faith can perceive this unseen reality. The spiritual world lies all about us, enclosing us, embracing us, altogether within our reach. This spiritual world will come alive to us the moment we begin to reckon on its reality.

In 2 Kings 6:8-23, Elisha was completely surrounded by enemy troops, yet he remained calm and relaxed. His servant, however, must have been climbing the walls at the sight of this hostile army with vicious-looking warriors and innumerable chariots on every side.

Undaunted, Elisha said to him, "Do not be afraid, for those who are with us are more than those who are with them" (2 Kings 6:16). Elisha then prayed to God, "'O LORD, please open his eyes that he may see.' So the LORD opened the eyes of the young man, and he saw, and behold, the mountain was full of horses and chariots of fire all around Elisha" (verse 17). God was protecting Elisha and his servant with a whole army of magnificent angelic beings!

Pearl of Wisdom: *The eyes of faith recognize that God acts on our behalf even when our physical eyes see only challenges.*

Angels and Spirits

Polls reveal that some 15 percent of Americans think angels are the spirits of dead people—an idea perpetually popularized in books, television, and movies. The big problem with this view is the scriptural teaching that Christ Himself created all the angels—and He created them as angels (Colossians 1:16; see also John 1:3).

We see the distinction between people and angels reflected in a number of biblical passages. For example, Psalm 8:5 indicates that man was made lower than the angels but shall be made higher in the afterlife (in heaven). In Hebrews 12:22-23, the "innumerable angels" are clearly distinguished from the "spirits of the righteous made perfect." First Corinthians 6:3 tells us that a time is coming when believers (in the afterlife) will actually judge angels. As well, 1 Corinthians 13:1 draws a distinction between the tongues (or languages) of human beings and those of angels. Clearly, human beings and angels are portrayed as different classes of beings in the Bible.

Of course, angels and people have some similarities. For example, angels and humans are created beings, both are finite and limited, both depend on God for their continued existence and well-being, and both are responsible and accountable to God for their actions (see John 16:11; 1 Corinthians 6:3; Hebrews 9:27). So yes, angels and humans are similar in some ways, but they are different classes of beings altogether.

Pearl of Wisdom: *Be careful not to derive your theology from Hollywood.*

Angels and the Sons of God

The Bible sometimes calls angels "sons of God" (Job 1:6; 2:1; 38:7). This title simply means that they were created directly by the hand of God. Angels do not give birth to baby angels (Matthew 22:30), and we never read of "sons of angels."

If the phrase *sons of God* in Genesis 6:2-4 is a reference to fallen angels, as many Bible expositors believe, then even fallen angels are called *sons of God* in the sense that He created them. Of course, they were not originally created as fallen angels. These particular angels rebelled against God sometime after their creation and became fallen (see Isaiah 14; Ezekiel 28).

All of this is completely unlike the meaning of *Son of God* in reference to Christ. When used of Christ, the term refers to likeness or sameness of nature. Christ, the Son of God, is in fact God. This is why, when Jesus claimed to be the Son of God, the Jews tried to kill Him for committing blasphemy (John 5:18; 19:7).

Pearl of Wisdom: *We will go far astray unless we distinguish between Jesus as the Son of God and created angels, who are called sons of God.*

Angels—God's Invisible Servants

These are some of the characteristics of angels that we find in the Bible:

- *Incorporeal.* Angels do not have physical bodies, so they are invisible (Hebrews 1:14).

- *Localized.* They have to move from one place to another (Daniel 9:21-23).

- *With or without wings.* Some Bible verses describe angels as having wings (Isaiah 6:1-5; Ezekiel 1:6; Revelation 4:8), whereas others do not (Hebrews 13:2).

- *Can appear as human beings.* (Genesis 18; Hebrews 13:2)

- *Powerful.* Scripture uses the word *mighty* (Psalm 103:20; 2 Thessalonians 1:7).

- *Holy* (Job 5:1; 15:15; Psalm 89:7).

- *Obedient.* They always do only God's bidding (Psalm 103:20).

- *Knowledgeable.* They are a higher order of creatures than humans are (see Psalm 8:5) and have greater knowledge. Their knowledge increases as they watch human activities.

- *Immortal.* They do not die (Luke 20:36) or propagate (Matthew 22:30), so their number remains constant.

Pearl of Wisdom: *Angels are awesome creatures, but we must keep our eyes focused only on Jesus, the Ruler of angels.*

Angels Are Personal Beings

Angels are persons—*spirit* persons (Hebrews 1:14)—with all the attributes of personality: mind, emotions, and will. We know angels have minds because they have great wisdom (2 Samuel 14:20), exercise great discernment (2 Samuel 14:17), and use their minds to look into matters (1 Peter 1:12).

We know the angels have emotions because they gather in "joyful assembly" in the presence of God in heaven (Hebrews 12:22 NIV), "shouted for joy" at the creation (Job 38:7), and rejoice in heaven whenever a sinner repents (Luke 15:7).

Angels certainly give evidence of having a moral will in the many moral decisions they make. For example, an angel exercised his moral will in forbidding John to worship him, acknowledging that worship belongs only to God (Revelation 22:8-9).

In addition to having the basic attributes of personality, angels also engage in personal actions. For example, angels love and rejoice (Luke 15:10), they express desire (1 Peter 1:12), they contend (Jude 9; Revelation 12:7), they engage in worship (Hebrews 1:6), they talk (Luke 1:13), and they come and go (Luke 9:26). Angels also have personal names, such as Michael and Gabriel. Clearly, angels are every bit as much persons as human beings are.

Pearl of Wisdom: *Once you and I are in heaven, we will no doubt engage in ongoing personal relations with the angels and with redeemed people of all ages.*

Angels Are Ministering Spirits

Some people in recent days have tried to argue that people can accomplish certain things by invoking and even manipulating angels. Such a belief system panders to human selfishness and pride.

We get to the heart of the true identity of angels in Hebrews 1:14, where we read, "Are they not all ministering spirits sent out to serve for the sake of those who are to inherit salvation?" This brief statement is packed with meaning. The word *ministering* comes from a Greek word meaning "serve." Angels are spirit-servants who render aid to the heirs of salvation according to God's purposes on earth.

What form does this service take? Such ministry can involve protection (Psalm 91:11), guidance (Genesis 19:17), encouragement (Judges 6:12), deliverance (Acts 12:7), supply (Psalm 105:40), and empowerment (Luke 22:43). It also includes occasional rebuke (Numbers 22:32) and judgment (Acts 12:23). Angelic service is usually unseen and unrecognized (2 Kings 6:17; Hebrews 13:2).

Notice that according to Hebrews 1:14, angels are sent to render service to the heirs of salvation. God has specifically sent and appointed angels to carry out tasks on behalf of believers; humans do not invoke or manipulate them. We must never forget that angels assist us because that is what God has ordained. The sent one is never more significant than (and never takes the place of) the divine Sender.

Pearl of Wisdom: *Angels typically work behind the scenes as God's spirit-servants.*

Angels' Various Roles

Scripture makes reference to a "multitude of the heavenly host" (Luke 2:13). Their number is elsewhere described as "myriads of myriads" (Revelation 5:11). (The word *myriad* means "vast number," "innumerable.") Daniel 7:10, speaking of God, says that "ten thousand times ten thousand stood before him." The number "ten thousand times ten thousand" is 100,000,000. This is a number almost too vast to fathom. Job 25:3 (NIV) understandably asks, "Can his forces be numbered?" These many angels are engaged in fulfilling various roles:

- *Messengers.* The word *angel* literally means "messenger." Angels bring revelation, announcements, warnings, and other information to the people of God (see, for example, Daniel 9; Matthew 1).

- *Guardians.* Angels watch over believers. Psalm 91:9-11 affirms that the angels guard believers in all their ways (see also 2 Kings 6:17).

- *Ministers at death.* At the moment of death, when the soul separates from the body, angels escort believers' souls to their eternal inheritance (Luke 16:22).

- *Restrainers of evil.* For example, in Genesis we read about angels that struck some wicked men with blindness so they could not carry out their evil intentions when they came to Lot's house (Genesis 18:22; 19:1,10-11).

- *Executioners of God's judgments.* In Acts 12, an angel executed Herod in judgment (Acts 12:22-23).

Pearl of Wisdom: *We can thank God for the various ministries of angels.*

Elect Angels and Evil Angels

All the angels were originally created good and holy (Jude 6; Genesis 1:31; 2:3). The holy God could not create anything wicked, such as evil angels. All the angels, however, were subjected to a period of probation. Some retained their holiness and did not sin, while others—following Lucifer's lead—rebelled against God and fell into great sin (Revelation 12:4; Ezekiel 28:12-16; Isaiah 14:12-17).

Once the angels were put to the test, their decision seems to have been made permanent. Those who passed the probationary test are permanently confirmed in that original holy state. Those who failed are now permanently confirmed in their evil, rebellious state.

The good angels are called "elect" angels in 1 Timothy 5:21, but not because they sinned and then were elected to be redeemed (remember, these angels never sinned during the probationary period). Rather, they are called "elect" because God intervened to permanently confirm (or "elect") them in their holiness so they could not possibly sin in the future. Good angels are therefore now incapable of sinning. The lines have been drawn, and they are now absolute.

The evil angels who rebelled against God are nonredeemable. Those who followed Satan's rebellion fell decisively and are permanently locked in their evil state without the possibility of redemption. They are destined for eternal suffering (Matthew 25:41).

Pearl of Wisdom: *God's holy angels outnumber the fallen angels by a ratio of two to one (Revelation 12:4). Good odds!*

Not all that Glitters Is Heavenly Gold

Many angel enthusiasts today assume that all angels are good. However, as we saw yesterday, not every angel is a good angel.

In 2 Corinthians 11:14, the apostle Paul explicitly warned that "Satan disguises himself as an angel of light." Satan and demons mimic God's holy angels, and they do so for a malevolent, sinister purpose—to lead people away from the true Christ and God of the Bible (see verse 3). In the process of doing this, they propagate doctrines of demons (1 Timothy 4:1-3).

Paul explicitly warned against accepting any gospel from an angel that goes against the inspired Word of God (Galatians 1:6-8). One would do well to remember that Joseph Smith, the founder of Mormonism, said an angel named Moroni led him to the golden plates containing the Book of Mormon. As well, Muhammad claimed he received the revelations contained in the Koran directly from the angel Gabriel (a demonic impostor). Other religions claiming angelic messengers include the Church of the New Jerusalem, founded by Emmanuel Swedenborg; the Self-Realization Fellowship, founded by Paramahansa Yogananda; and the Unity School of Christianity, founded by Charles and Myrtle Fillmore. We must not forget that true holy angels of God do not promote new religions or give us revelations that contradict God's Word (see Psalm 103:20; Revelation 22:9). The biblical pattern is that God's holy angels always point away from themselves and to the one true God.

Pearl of Wisdom: *We must always beware of Satan's counterfeits!*

Does God Need Angels?

God does not need angels! I don't mean to minimize the importance of what the Bible teaches about angels. My point is simply that God could accomplish His ends without their assistance.

Though God does not need angels, He nevertheless created them—for His own pleasure and glory—to carry out various functions in His universe and before His throne. Among other things, Scripture indicates that God created angels to minister to believers and show His special concern for us (Hebrews 1:14). His use of angels does not detract from His personal love and concern for us; rather, it's an illustration and expression of it.

In the angel craze of the 1980s and '90s, many people acted as if angels exist but a personal God doesn't. Or if they acknowledged God's existence, they pushed Him off of center stage and relegated Him to a place of irrelevance. They failed to realize that the holy angels themselves insist on human beings recognizing that God alone is to remain on center stage. For example, when John beheld a glorious angel and bowed in an act of worship, the angel responded, "You must not do that! I am a fellow servant with you and your brothers the prophets, and with those who keep the words of this book. Worship God!" (Revelation 22:8-9).

Pearl of Wisdom: *The existence of angels is just one more evidence that our God is an awesome God!*

God's Obedient Angels

God's holy angels carry out only His commands. The Bible never portrays an elect, holy angel of God acting independently from God. Scripture most often describes angels as His angels (for example, Psalm 104:4).

The two angelic names mentioned in the Bible—*Michael* and *Gabriel*—end with *el* (God), and this emphasizes the angels' relationship with God. *Michael* means "Who is like God?" This name humbly points to the incomparability of God. It speaks of Michael's complete and unwavering devotion to God and is in stark contrast with Satan, who in his pride declared, "I will make myself like the most High" (Isaiah 14:14).

Gabriel means "Mighty one of God." The name speaks of Gabriel's incredible power as endowed by God. Out of all the angels in the universe, God entrusted to Gabriel alone the greatest messages that ever left the courts of heaven to be delivered to human beings—such as the message of Christ's approaching birth (Luke 1:19-20).

So angels are God's angels, and they exist to carry out His purposes. Psalm 103:20 refers to God's angels as "mighty ones who do his word, obeying the voice of his word." Because the angels are always sent by God on our behalf, our gratitude must be to the God who sent them.

Pearl of Wisdom: *Angels are awesome helpers only because our awesome God has made them so!*

Guardian Angels

Two verses in the New Testament refer to guardian angels. Matthew 18:10 says, "See that you do not despise one of these little ones [children]. For I tell you that in heaven their angels always see the face of my Father who is in heaven." And in Acts 12:15, a woman named Rhoda recognizes Peter's voice outside the door of the house, and the others inside—thinking Peter was still in jail—didn't believe her: "'You are out of your mind.' But she kept insisting that it was so, and they kept saying, 'It is his angel.'"

Some conclude from these two verses that every believer has his or her own guardian angel. Others, however, argue that this is flimsy support for such an idea. For example, the angels of the little ones in Matthew 18:10 are said to be in heaven, not specifically with the little ones. These argue that Scripture seems to indicate that many multitudes of angels are always ready and willing to render help and protection to each individual Christian whenever a need arises.

For example, in 2 Kings 6:17, Elisha and his servant were surrounded by many glorious angels. Luke 16:22 indicates that several angels carried Lazarus's soul to Abraham's bosom. Jesus could have called on 12 legions of angels to rescue Him if He had wanted (Matthew 26:53). Psalm 91:11 says that God "will command his angels concerning you to guard you in all your ways."

Pearl of Wisdom: *God's angels are constantly watching over you.*

Angels in Disguise

T hough angels are by nature incorporeal and invisible, they can never-theless appear as men. In fact, their resemblance to men can be so real-istic that they are mistaken for human beings. Hebrews 13:2 instructs us, "Do not neglect to show hospitality to strangers, for thereby some have entertained angels unawares." In the account of Jesus' ascension into heaven, Acts 1:10-11 says, "While they were gazing into heaven as he went, behold, two men stood by them in white robes, and said, 'Men of Galilee, why do you stand looking into heaven? This Jesus, who was taken up from you into heaven, will come in the same way as you saw him go into heaven.'" These two men were angels.

Abraham once welcomed three men in the plains of Mamre (Genesis 18:1-8). These men walked, talked, sat down, and ate—just like normal men—but they were not men; they were angels (see Genesis 18:22; 19:1). We have no scriptural evidence that angels need food for sustenance. However, based on this passage of Scripture, they can apparently appear as men and eat like men while fulfilling their assigned tasks.

Pearl of Wisdom: *A person who helped you during a time of need may actu-ally have been an angel that appeared as a human. Such appearances evidently can occur today just as they did in biblical times.*

Ezekiel Saw the…UFO?

Ezekiel 1:4-5 reads, "As I looked, behold, a stormy wind came out of the north, and a great cloud, with brightness around it, and fire flashing forth continually, and in the midst of the fire, as it were gleaming metal. And from the midst of it came the likeness of four living creatures."

This chapter is not a reference to a UFO, as is sometimes claimed, but rather a vision of the glory of God. In verse 1, Ezekiel tells us that "the heavens were opened, and I saw visions *of God*" (Ezekiel 1:1). Hebrews 1:1 tells us that "long ago, at many times and in many ways, God spoke to our fathers by the prophets." One of the many ways God communicated to prophets was by visions. And as we learn elsewhere in Scripture, visions are quite often couched in highly symbolic form (see Revelation 1:9-20). Consequently, we often read of strange creatures and their surroundings in such visions.

We know that the living creatures of Ezekiel 1 are angels because they have wings and because they resemble angels found elsewhere in Scripture, such as in Revelation 4:6. Ezekiel closes the chapter by informing us, "Such was the appearance of the likeness of the glory of the LORD. And when I saw it, I fell on my face" (Ezekiel 1:28).

Pearl of Wisdom: *An important interpretive principle is context, context, context!*

Lucifer's Fall

Ezekiel 28 and Isaiah 14 reveal that the angel Lucifer fell from heaven and became Satan. Ezekiel 28:12-16 describes a sinless cherub on the Holy Mount of God that was cast out of the mountain of God and thrown to the earth. This being was full of wisdom, perfect in beauty, and had the seal of perfection. These things cannot be said of a mere human, so many interpreters believe this is a reference to Lucifer.

Lucifer was created in a state of perfection and remained perfect until iniquity was found in him. Verse 17 says, "Your heart was proud because of your beauty; you corrupted your wisdom for the sake of your splendor." Lucifer apparently became so impressed with his own beauty, intelligence, power, and position that he desired for himself the honor and glory that belonged to God alone. The sin that corrupted Lucifer was self-generated pride (see Isaiah 14:12-17).

God judged this mighty angelic being: "I cast you to the ground" (Ezekiel 28:17). As a result of his heinous sin, Lucifer was banished from living in heaven (Isaiah 14:12). He became corrupt, and his name changed from Lucifer (morning star) to Satan (adversary). His power became completely perverted (14:12,16-17). His destiny is the lake of fire (Matthew 25:41).

Pearl of Wisdom: *Pride has led to the downfall of many!*

Satan's Titles

Satan, formerly known as Lucifer, is a fallen angel who is aligned against God and His purposes, and he heads up a vast company of fallen angels, called demons, who are also aligned against God and His purposes. We learn a great deal about Satan, his goals, and activities by his various names and titles in Scripture.

Satan is our *adversary* (1 Peter 5:8) and opposes us in every way he can. He is *Beelzebub* (Matthew 12:24), "lord of the flies," corrupting everything he touches. He is the *devil* (Matthew 4:1), meaning he is our adversary and slanderer. He truly is the *evil one* (1 John 5:19), opposing all that is good.

Satan is the father of lies (John 8:44). He is a murderer (John 8:44) or man killer (see 1 John 3:12,15). He is a roaring lion (1 Peter 5:8-9), strong and destructive, seeking to devour Christians. Toward this end, he is the tempter (Matthew 4:3), inciting Christians to sin. He truly is our enemy (Matthew 13:39), full of hate for God and His children. He is a serpent (Genesis 3:1; Revelation 12:9) who is characterized by treachery, deceitfulness, venom, and murder. He is the accuser of the brethren (Revelation 12:10), accusing them before God (see Zechariah 3:1; Romans 8:33).

Satan is the god (or head) of this evil age (2 Corinthians 4:4). He is the prince of this world (John 12:31; 14:30; 16:11), promoting an anti-God system that conforms to his ideals, aims, and methods.

Pearl of Wisdom: *Satan is an exceedingly dangerous foe.*

Satan's Power

The Bible sometimes uses the same words—*signs* and *wonders*—to describe the power of the devil and the miracles of God (2 Thessalonians 2:9; Revelation 16:14). But can the devil perform miracles like God's?

Although Satan has great powers, his power is nothing like God's power. God is infinite in power, but the devil (like demons) is finite and limited. God can create life (Genesis 1:1,21; Deuteronomy 32:39), but the devil cannot (Exodus 8:19). God can raise the dead (John 10:18; Revelation 1:18), but the devil cannot.

The devil has great power to deceive people (Revelation 12:9), to oppress those who yield to him, and even to possess them (Acts 16:16). He is a master magician and scientist. And with His vast knowledge of God, man, and the universe, he is able to perform false signs (2 Thessalonians 2:9). But only God can perform true miracles.

Only God can control the natural laws He established, though on one occasion he granted Satan the power to bring a whirlwind on Job's family (Job 1:19). Christ has defeated the devil and triumphed over him (Hebrews 2:14-15; Colossians 2:15), thus giving power to His people to be victorious over demonic forces (Ephesians 4:4-11). John thus informed believers, "He who is in you is greater than he who is in the world" (1 John 4:4).

———

Pearl of Wisdom: *The devil can do the supernormal but not the supernatural.*

Bible Warnings About Demons

Scripture reveals that demons are evil and wicked. They are designated "unclean spirits" (Matthew 10:1), "evil spirits" (Luke 7:21), and the "spiritual forces of evil" (Ephesians 6:12). All these terms point to the immoral nature of demons.

Demons, under Satan's lead, disseminate false doctrine (1 Timothy 4:1) and are no doubt behind the kingdom of the cults. As well, they wield influence over false prophets (1 John 4:1-4) and seek to turn men to the worship of idols (see Leviticus 17:7; Deuteronomy 32:17; Psalm 106:36-38). Demons hinder answers to the prayers of believers (Daniel 10:12-20) and instigate jealousy and faction among them (James 3:13-16). Scripture also portrays demons as inflicting physical diseases on people, such as dumbness (Matthew 9:33), blindness (Matthew 12:22), and epilepsy (Matthew 17:15-18). They also afflict people with mental disorders (Mark 5:4-5; 9:22; Luke 8:27-29; 9:37-42). They can cause people to be self-destructive (Mark 5:5; Luke 9:42). They are even responsible for the deaths of some people (Revelation 9:14-19).

God's holy angels are organized according to rank, and fallen angels are too. These ranks include principalities, powers, rulers of the darkness of this world, and spiritual wickedness in high places (see Ephesians 6:12). All fallen angels, regardless of their individual ranks, follow the leadership of their malevolent commander in chief—Satan, the prince of demons.

Pearl of Wisdom: *Demons perpetually seek the downfall of Christians. Christians beware!*

Christians and Demon Possession

D emon possession may be defined as a demon residing within people and exerting direct control and influence over them. This is to be distinguished from mere demonic influence. The work of the demon in the latter case is external; in demon possession, it is from within.

Demon-possessed people may manifest unusual, superhuman strength (Mark 5:2-4). They may act in bizarre ways, such as going nude and living among tombs rather than in a house (Luke 8:27). Possessed people often engage in self-destructive behavior (Matthew 17:15).

According to this definition, Christians cannot be possessed by demons because they are indwelt by the Holy Spirit (1 Corinthians 6:19). I like the way Walter Martin put it. He said that when the devil knocks on the door of the Christian's heart, the Holy Spirit opens it and says, "Get lost!"

Scripture never gives an account of a Christian being demon possessed. We do find examples of Christians being afflicted by the devil, but not possessed by the devil.

Christians have been delivered from Satan's domain. As Colossians 1:13 puts it, God "has delivered us from the domain of darkness and transferred us to the kingdom of his beloved Son." Furthermore, "he who is in you is greater than he who is in the world" (1 John 4:4). This statement would not make much sense if Christians could be possessed by the devil.

Pearl of Wisdom: *Even though a Christian cannot be possessed, he can nevertheless be oppressed or influenced by demonic powers. Be on guard!*

Sickness and Demonic Spirits

I am often asked by Christians if all sicknesses are caused by demonic spirits. I think it is important to take a balanced approach to this issue.

On the one hand, Scripture does portray Satan and demons inflicting physical diseases on people. Such diseases include dumbness (Matthew 9:33), blindness (Matthew 12:22), and epilepsy (Matthew 17:15-18). Demons can also afflict people with mental disorders (Mark 5:4-5; 9:22; Luke 8:27-29; 9:37-42) and can cause people to be self-destructive (Mark 5:5; Luke 9:42).

On the other hand, Scripture also distinguishes between natural illnesses and those caused by demons. For example, we read in Matthew 4:24 that people brought Jesus "all the sick, those afflicted with various diseases and pains, those oppressed by demons, epileptics, and paralytics, and he healed them." This verse seems to distinguish between those who are naturally sick and those who are oppressed by demons (see Luke 7:21; Acts 5:16). Likewise, in Mark 1:32 we read, "That evening at sundown they brought to him all who were sick or oppressed by demons." No mention is made of demon affliction in the cases where Jesus healed the centurion's servant (Matthew 8:5-13), the woman with the hemorrhage of 12 years' duration (9:19-20), the two blind men (9:27-30), the man with the withered hand (12:9-14), and those who touched the fringe of Jesus' garment (14:35-36).

Pearl of Wisdom: *When you get sick, don't presume you are being afflicted by a demon. You may have just caught a bad bug!*

Satan's Counterfeits

Scripture reveals that Satan and his fallen angels seek to thwart the purposes of God and Christ (Revelation 2:10; 1 Peter 5:8; Ephesians 6:11; Matthew 13:39; 1 Timothy 4:1). We also know that they seek to blind the minds of people to spiritual truth (2 Corinthians 4:4; 11:14; 2 Thessalonians 2:9-10).

Some in the church are said to possess the ability to "distinguish between spirits" (1 Corinthians 12:10). The need for this gift reminds us that not all spirits are good. This is why we are called to test everything against Scripture (Acts 17:11; 1 Thessalonians 5:21).

We must never forget that Satan is a masterful counterfeiter. For example, Scripture reveals that Satan has his own church—the "synagogue of Satan" (Revelation 2:9). Satan has his own ministers of darkness that bring false sermons (2 Corinthians 11:4-5). He has formulated his own system of theology—a "doctrines of demons" (1 Timothy 4:1 NASB; Revelation 2:24). His ministers proclaim a counterfeit gospel—"a gospel contrary to the one we preached to you" (Galatians 1:7-8).

Satan has his own throne (Revelation 13:2) and his own worshippers (13:4). He inspires false Christs and self-constituted messiahs (Matthew 24:4-5). He employs false teachers who bring in "destructive heresies" (2 Peter 2:1). He sends out false prophets (Matthew 24:11) and sponsors false apostles who imitate the true (2 Corinthians 11:13).

Pearl of Wisdom: *These are times for great discernment.*

Our Defense Against Satan

We Christians can be thankful that God has made provision for our defense against Satan and his fallen angels. Here are the key components of this defense:

Jesus lives in heaven to make intercession for us (Romans 8:34; Hebrews 7:25), praying for us on a regular basis (John 17:15). God has provided spiritual armor for our defense (Ephesians 6:11-18). Wearing this armor means that our lives will be characterized by such things as righteousness, obedience to the will of God, faith in God, and an effective use of the Word of God.

Scripture instructs us that each believer must be informed and alert to the attacks of Satan (1 Peter 5:8). Paul warns Christians "so that we would not be outwitted by Satan; for we are not ignorant of his designs" (2 Corinthians 2:11). James 4:7 says, "Resist the devil, and he will flee from you." We are to "stand firm" against the devil (Ephesians 6:13-14).

We need to depend on the Holy Spirit, remembering that "he who is in you is greater than he who is in the world" (1 John 4:4). And remember that God has assigned His angels to watch over us (Psalm 91:9-11).

Pearl of Wisdom: *We can successfully defeat the powers of darkness—not in our own strength, but because of what Jesus Christ has already done. We are more than conquerors through Him who loved us (Romans 8:37). Keep your eyes on Jesus!*

The World

The word *world*, when used in Scripture, often refers not to the physical planet (earth), but to an anti-God system headed by Satan. Indeed, 1 John 5:19 tells us that "the whole world lies in the power of the evil one [Satan]."

Before we were Christians, we followed the ways of the world without hesitation (Ephesians 2:2). But when we became Christians, we obtained another master—Jesus Christ—who calls us to be separate from the world (Romans 12:2; 1 Peter 2:11).

The world is portrayed in Scripture as a seducer. It perpetually seeks to attract our attention and devotion away from God. For this reason, the New Testament instructs us not to love the world or anything in the world (1 John 2:15-16).

Numerous things in the world appeal to our sin nature. If we give in to these things—lust for money and material possessions, the quest for fame and power, an appetite for sexual pleasures, and the like—our attention is drawn away from God. These enticements can effectively sidetrack us into the web of worldliness (see 2 Timothy 2:4; James 4:4).

I use the word *web* purposefully. Sometimes I come across a spider web with an insect stuck in its grasp. This enables the spider to move in for the kill. The world system is like a web that seeks to entrap us. This web enables Satan to move in and harm us.

Pearl of Wisdom: *Take measures to avoid being entrapped by the enticements of the world.*

Beware of the Flesh

The term *flesh* describes that force within each of us that is in total rebellion against God. This sin nature was not a part of man when God originally created him. Rather, it entered Adam and Eve the moment they disobeyed God. Since then, all humans have been born into the world with a flesh nature or sin nature that rebels against God (Psalm 51:5).

The flesh in each of us gives rise to things like hatred, discord, jealousy, fits of rage, selfish ambition, dissensions, factions, envy, drunkenness, and the like (Galatians 5:20-21). These kinds of things greatly hinder our relationship with God.

The good news is that the flesh has no right to reign in our lives any longer, and its power is broken when we—by faith—count this as being true (Romans 6:1-14). Moreover, Galatians 5:16 reveals that by continually depending on the Holy Spirit, we will not gratify the desires of the flesh. By contrast, depending on our own resources will only lead to a fall.

True Christians will always desire to be delivered from the sins of the flesh for the sake of their relationship with Christ (see Romans 7:15-20). The Holy Spirit dwells inside of Christians, so they can't be continually happy in sin (2 Corinthians 7:10-11). Sooner or later they will acknowledge their sin and turn back to trusting Christ to deliver them from its power.

Pearl of Wisdom: *Make it your daily goal to walk in the Spirit.*

Christians and the Rapture

The rapture is that glorious event in which the dead in Christ are raised from the dead and living Christians' bodies are instantly renewed—and both groups are caught up to meet Christ in the air (1 Thessalonians 4:13-17). That means that one generation of Christians will never pass through death's door!

Christians differ regarding the timing of the rapture. Pretribulationism says that Christ will rapture the entire church before any part of the tribulation begins. Posttribulationism says that Christ will rapture the church after the tribulation at the second coming of Christ. Midtribulationism says that Christ will rapture the church in the middle of the tribulation period.

Personally, I think the pretrib position is most consistent with the biblical testimony. After all, God has promised to keep the church from the time of testing coming upon the entire earth (Revelation 3:10) and has promised to deliver the church from the wrath to come (1 Thessalonians 5:9).

Of course, this is not an issue worth fighting over. The different views of the rapture may disagree over the timing of end-time events, but they all agree on the big picture: A rapture will occur, and we will live forever with Jesus in heaven. In the long haul—after we've been with Christ for billions of years in heaven—the question of whether the rapture happened before or after the tribulation period will truly seem insignificant.

Pearl of Wisdom: *The rapture could occur during our own generation!*

The Jews and Their Land

When Titus and his Roman warriors overran Jerusalem and its temple in AD 70, the Jews were forced to scatter around the world. Long before, however, God uttered an amazing prophetic promise to the scattered Jews: "I will take you from the nations and gather you from all the countries and bring you into your own land" (Ezekiel 36:24).

In the vision of dry bones recorded in Ezekiel 37, the Lord miraculously brings the bones of the nation back together into a skeleton. The skeleton is wrapped in muscles, tendons, and flesh, and God then breathes life into the body. This is a metaphor of Israel's restoration: "These bones are the whole house of Israel" (verse 11). Herein lies the significance of 1948, the year Israel once again achieved statehood, after a long and worldwide dispersion.

However, in our day Islamists view the very existence of Israel as an aggression. The initial settlement in the land was illegitimate to start with, they say, for the Jews had no right to return to a land under Islamic authority.

Following the Islamic logic of the Fatah and of jihad, any territory that was at some time controlled by a legitimate Islamic authority cannot revert to a non-Islamic authority. This means Israel cannot reemerge on Muslim land. It constitutes a grievous offense to Allah.

Pearl of Wisdom: *At the heart of today's Middle East conflict is the question, to whom does the holy land really belong? Biblically and prophetically, it belongs to the Jews (Genesis 13:14-18).*

Invading Israel

The prophet Ezekiel prophesied that the Jews would be regathered from many nations to the land of Israel in the end times (Ezekiel 36–37). This is why 1948 is so significant. Ezekiel then prophesied that, sometime later, Russia will lead a massive coalition of Muslim nations in an all-out invasion into Israel.

Ezekiel 38:1-6 lists the specific nations in this invading force: Rosh is modern-day Russia; Magog is the geographical area in the southern portion of the former Soviet Union; Meshech and Tubal, as well as Gomer and Beth-togarmah, refer to modern Turkey; Persia is modern Iran; Cush is the Sudan; and Put is modern-day Libya. The primary unifying factor among these nations is that they are all Muslim, with the exception of Russia—which presently has 20 million Muslim citizens.

Ezekiel indicated this invasion would take place "in the latter years" and "in the latter days" (38:8,16). This clearly points to the end times.

God will destroy this invasion force by means of a massive earthquake (Ezekiel 38:19-20), infighting among the invading troops (38:21), a massive outbreak of disease, and torrential rain, hailstones, fire, and burning sulfur (38:22). All this causes one to ponder God's promise in Scripture: "Behold, he who keeps Israel will neither slumber nor sleep" (Psalm 121:4).

Pearl of Wisdom: *This is an exciting time to be alive, as the stage appears to be set for the soon fulfillment of biblical prophecy.*

The Tribulation

Scripture prophetically details what the seven years prior to the second coming of Christ will be like. This is known as the tribulation.

The tribulation will be a definite period of time at the end of the age that will be characterized by great travail (Matthew 24:29-35). It is called "the great tribulation" in Revelation 7:14. It will be of such severity that no period in history—past or future—will equal it (Matthew 24:21). It is called the "time of Jacob's trouble," for it is a judgment on Messiah-rejecting Israel (Jeremiah 30:7 KJV; Daniel 12:1-4). The nations will also be judged for their sin and rejection of Christ (Isaiah 26:21; Revelation 6:15-17). The prophet Daniel is the one who informs us the period will last seven years (Daniel 9:24,27).

Scripture indicates that this horrific time will be characterized by wrath, judgment (Revelation 14:7), indignation (Isaiah 26:20-21), trial (Revelation 3:10), trouble (Jeremiah 30:7), destruction (Joel 1:15), darkness (Amos 5:18), desolation (Daniel 9:27), overturning (Isaiah 24:1-4), and punishment (Isaiah 24:20-21). No passage of Scripture in the Old or New Testaments alleviates the severity of this time that will come on the earth.

Pearl of Wisdom: *Many people (including me) believe that the church will be raptured off the planet prior to the beginning of the tribulation (1 Thessalonians 1:10; 4:13-17; 5:9; Revelation 3:10). Praise the Lord!*

Daniel's "Seventieth Week"

In Daniel 9, God provided a prophetic timetable for Israel. The prophetic clock began ticking when the command went out to restore and rebuild Jerusalem following its destruction by Babylon (Daniel 9:25). According to this verse, Israel's timetable was divided into 70 groups of 7 years, totaling 490 years.

The first 69 groups of 7 years—483 years—counted the years "from the going out of the word to restore and build Jerusalem to the coming of an anointed one, a prince" (Daniel 9:25). The Anointed One is Jesus Christ. *Anointed One* means "Messiah." The day Jesus rode into Jerusalem to proclaim Himself Israel's Messiah was exactly 483 years to the day after the command to restore and rebuild Jerusalem had been given.

At that point God's prophetic clock stopped. Daniel describes a gap between these 483 years and the final 7 years of Israel's prophetic timetable. Several events were to take place during this gap, according to Daniel 9:26: The Messiah will be killed, the city of Jerusalem and its temple would be destroyed (which occurred in AD 70), and the Jews would encounter difficulty and hardship from that time on.

The final "week" of 7 years will begin for Israel when the Antichrist confirms a covenant for seven years (Daniel 9:27). The signing of this peace pact will signal the beginning of the tribulation period. That signature marks the beginning of the seven-year countdown to the second coming of Christ, which follows the tribulation period.

Pearl of Wisdom: *Our awesome God is guiding human history toward its culmination.*

Biblical Prophecy Cleanses the People of God

God did not give us biblical prophecy merely so we would have inside information on what the future holds. Prophecy is to have a cleansing and purifying effect on the people of God.

Many prophecies in the Bible include an exhortation to righteous living. For example, in 1 John 3:2-3 we read, "Beloved, we are God's children now, and what we will be has not yet appeared; but we know that when he appears we shall be like him, because we shall see him as he is. And everyone who thus hopes in him purifies himself as he is pure." Titus 2:12-13 likewise exhorts us to "live self-controlled, upright, and godly lives in the present age, waiting for our blessed hope, the appearing of the glory of our great God and Savior Jesus Christ." In view of the approaching end times, Peter ponders, "What sort of people ought you to be in lives of holiness and godliness, waiting for and hastening the coming of the day of God" (2 Peter 3:11-12).

Such verses reveal a cause-and-effect relationship between believers' anticipation of the second coming and their personal purity. The flip side, of course, is that those who do not have such a prophetic hope may not have as strong a motivation to live in personal purity.

Pearl of Wisdom: *Perpetually focusing your heart and mind on biblical prophecy is a fail-safe formula for maintaining personal purity in life (Romans 13:11-14).*

The Antichrist's Global Domination

The apostle Paul warned of a "man of lawlessness," which is the Antichrist. This individual will perform counterfeit signs and wonders and deceive many during the future tribulation period (2 Thessalonians 2:3,8-10). The apostle John describes him as a beast (Revelation 13:1-10). This description shows his true nature.

This evil individual will rise to prominence during the tribulation period and attempt to dominate the world, destroy the Jews, persecute believers, and set up his own counterfeit kingdom (Revelation 13). He will be a charismatic leader, and many will flock to him as the one who possesses the answers to the world's problems. He will be personally empowered by Satan, the unholy spirit. He will speak arrogant and boastful words that glorify himself, even exalting himself as God (2 Thessalonians 2:4). His assistant, the false prophet, will seek to make the world worship him (Revelation 13:11-12). People around the world will be forced to receive his mark, without which they cannot buy or sell (Revelation 13:16-17). This will be one way the Antichrist will control people. But to receive this mark ensures one of being the recipient of God's wrath.

This beast will be defeated and destroyed by the Lord Jesus at His second coming (Revelation 19:11-16). The destiny of the Antichrist is the lake of fire (Revelation 19:20).

Pearl of Wisdom: *Evil forces are aligned against God, but God will be victorious in the end. One day, all evil—including the Antichrist—will be eternally quarantined, never again able to harass the people of God.*

The Antichrist and Islam

In recent days—and for understandable reasons—many have claimed that the Antichrist who will emerge during the tribulation period will be a Muslim. However, the Bible does not agree.

Daniel 11:36 tells us the Antichrist "shall exalt himself and magnify himself above every god." Second Thessalonians 2:4 likewise affirms that the Antichrist ultimately "opposes and exalts himself against every so-called god or object of worship, so that he takes his seat in the temple of God, proclaiming himself to be God." A Muslim Antichrist claiming to be God would be trashing the Muslim creed, which affirms, "There is one God named Allah, and Muhammad is his prophet." I cannot imagine a true Muslim claiming to be God.

Muslims also teach that "God (Allah) can have no partners." Muslims generally affirm this as a means of arguing against the Trinity. But it is certainly applicable also to human leaders on earth who claim to be God or a partner with Allah.

I also wonder why a Muslim Antichrist would make a covenant with Israel (Daniel 9:24-27) to guarantee its protection. Many prophecy scholars have believed that this covenant is what allows Israel to live in peace and safety so it can rebuild the Jewish temple. I have difficulty believing that a Muslim leader would protect Israel in this regard.

Pearl of Wisdom: *Comparing Scripture with Scripture keeps us on the right track in biblical prophecy.*

The Tribulation and Armageddon

Human suffering will steadily escalate during the tribulation period. First are the seal judgments, involving bloodshed, famine, death, economic upheaval, a great earthquake, and cosmic disturbances (Revelation 6). Then come the trumpet judgments, involving hail and fire mixed with blood, the sea turning to blood, water turning bitter, further cosmic disturbances, affliction by demonic scorpions, and the death of a third of humankind (Revelation 8:6–9:21). Then come the bowl judgments, involving horribly painful sores on human beings, more bodies of water turning to blood, the death of all sea creatures, people being scorched by the sun, total darkness engulfing the land, a devastating earthquake, and much more (Revelation 16). Worse comes to worst, however, when these already traumatized human beings find themselves engaged in a catastrophic series of battles called Armageddon.

The word *Armageddon* literally means "Mount of Megiddo" and refers to a location about 60 miles north of Jerusalem. This is the location of Barak's battle with the Canaanites (Judges 4) and Gideon's battle with the Midianites (Judges 7). This will be the site for the final horrific battles of humankind just prior to the second coming (Revelation 16:16).

Napoleon is reported to have commented that this site is perhaps the greatest battlefield he had ever seen. Of course, the battles Napoleon fought will dim in comparison to Armageddon. Armageddon will be so horrible that no one would survive if Christ didn't intervene (Matthew 24:22).

Pearl of Wisdom: *The human suffering that takes place in the tribulation period represents the cumulative fruit of humankind's rebellion against God.*

The Second Coming of Christ

The second coming will involve a visible, physical, bodily coming of the glorified Jesus. A key Greek word used to describe the second coming in the New Testament is *apokalupsis*. This word means "revelation," "visible disclosure," "unveiling," and "removing the cover" from something that is hidden. The word is used of Christ's second coming in 1 Peter 4:13.

Another Greek word used of Christ's second coming in the New Testament is *epiphaneia* (to appear or to shine forth). In Titus 2:13, Paul speaks of "waiting for our blessed hope, the *appearing* of the glory of our great God and Savior Jesus Christ." In 1 Timothy 6:14, Paul urges Timothy to "keep the commandment unstained and free from reproach until the *appearing* of our Lord Jesus Christ." Significantly, Christ's first coming—which was both bodily and visible ("the Word become flesh")—was called an *epiphaneia* (2 Timothy 1:10). In the same way, Christ's second coming will be both bodily and visible.

The second coming will be a universal experience in the sense that every eye will witness the event. Revelation 1:7 says, "Behold, he is coming with the clouds, and every eye will see him, even those who pierced him, and all tribes of the earth will wail on account of him." Moreover, magnificent signs will appear in the heavens at the second coming (Matthew 24:29-30).

Pearl of Wisdom: *Rejoice, Christian, for the coming of your King draws nigh!*

The Millennium

Most evangelicals hold to one of three theological views regarding the millennial kingdom. According to premillennialism, following the second coming, Christ will institute a literal kingdom of perfect peace and righteousness on earth that will last for a thousand years. Amillennialism, a more spiritualized view, says that when Christ comes, eternity will begin with no prior literal thousand-year reign on earth (Christ reigns spiritually from heaven). The postmillennial view, another spiritualized view, says that through the church's progressive influence over a long time (metaphorically called a thousand years), the world will be "Christianized" before Christ returns.

I believe the premillennial view is the most biblical because it (1) naturally emerges from a literal hermeneutic, (2) best explains the unconditional land promises to Abraham and his descendants, which are yet to be fulfilled (Genesis 13:14-18), (3) makes the best sense of the unconditional Davidic promise regarding the throne (2 Samuel 7:12-17), (4) is most compatible with Old Testament predictions about the coming messianic age, (5) is consistent with the Old Testament concluding in expectation of the messianic kingdom (see Isaiah 9:6; 16:5; Malachi 3:1), (6) best explains the scriptural teaching that Jesus and the apostles would reign on thrones in Jerusalem (Matthew 19:28; 25:31-34; Acts 1:6-7), and (7) is most consistent with the apostle Paul's promise that Israel will one day be restored (Romans 9:3-4; 11:1).

Pearl of Wisdom: *Christ will one day set up a perfect kingdom on earth over which He will rule. It will be glorious!*

Heaven and Earth Will Be Renewed

In the Garden of Eden, where Adam and Eve sinned against God, God cursed the earth (Genesis 3:17-18). So before the eternal state can begin, God must deal with this cursed earth (Revelation 8:13).

The Scriptures often say the old heaven and earth will pass away. "Then I saw a new heaven and a new earth, for the first heaven and the first earth had passed away, and the sea was no more...And he who was seated on the throne said, 'Behold, I am making all things new'" (Revelation 21:1-5).

The Greek word used to designate the newness of the cosmos is *kainos*. This word means "new in nature" or "new in quality." So the phrase "a new heaven and a new earth" refers not to a cosmos that is totally other than the present cosmos. Rather, the new cosmos will stand in continuity with the present cosmos, but it will be utterly renewed and renovated.

Matthew 19:28 (kjv) refers to this as "the regeneration," and Acts 3:21 (nasb) speaks of the "restoration of all things." The renewed and eternal earth will be adapted to the vast moral and physical changes that the eternal state necessitates. The new heaven and new earth will conform to all that God is in a state of fixed bliss and absolute perfection. The new earth will actually be a part of heaven itself.

———

Pearl of Wisdom: *A glorious eternal future awaits you and me!*

Jesus Is Coming Soon

In the book of Revelation, Jesus made several references to His second coming, saying, "Behold, I am coming soon!" (Revelation 22:7,12,20). Almost 2000 years have passed since Jesus said this, which hardly seems soon. Scholars offer two primary suggestions of what He might have meant.

Some scholars suggest that from the human perspective it may not seem soon, but from the divine perspective, it is. According to the New Testament, we have been living in the last days since Christ's incarnation (James 5:3; Hebrews 1:2). Moreover, James 5:9 states that "the Judge is standing at the door." Romans 13:12 exhorts us that "the night is far gone; the day is at hand." Hebrews 10:25 warns against "neglecting to meet together, as is the habit of some"; instead, we should be "encouraging one another, and all the more as you see the Day drawing near." And 1 Peter 4:7 warns, "The end of all things is at hand; therefore be self-controlled and sober-minded for the sake of your prayers." These verses seem to indicate that Christ is coming soon from the divine perspective.

Other scholars suggest that perhaps Jesus meant He is coming soon from the perspective of the events described in the book of Revelation. In other words, for those who will be alive during the time of the tribulation period itself—a seven-year period of trials that culminates in the second coming (see Revelation 4–19)—Christ is coming soon.

—————

Pearl of Wisdom: *Rejoice, Christian, for your redemption draws nigh!*

Predicting the Dates of End-Time Events

We can rejoice that we appear to be living in the end times, but here are several reasons why Christians should not try to guess specific dates of end-time events:

- Those who have predicted the end have been 100 percent wrong.

- Setting dates can discourage making sound, long-term decisions.

- Unmet expectations can damage people's faith.

- If confidence in Bible prophecy wanes, it no longer motivates to holiness (Titus 2:12-14).

- Unmet expectations can lead people to believe they can't be sure of what the future holds.

- Setting dates promotes sensationalism, which is inappropriate (Mark 13:32-37).

- Setting dates can damage the cause of Christ when unbelievers mock Christians.

- Setting dates can distract Christians from pursuing righteous and holy lives.

- The times are completely in God's hands (Acts 1:7), and we don't know the details.

Pearl of Wisdom: *We should live our lives knowing the Lord may come today, but we should plan our lives as if we'll be here for our full life expectancy.*

Preterism

Partial preterists believe the resurrection of the dead and the second coming are yet future, but the other prophecies in Revelation and in Matthew 24–25 were fulfilled when Jerusalem fell to Rome in AD 70. Full preterists believe that virtually all New Testament predictions were fulfilled in the past, including those of the resurrection of the dead and the second coming.

Preterists point to Matthew 24:34, where Jesus asserted, "This generation will not pass away until all these things take place." However, Jesus likely meant that the generation alive during the tribulation will still be alive at the end of it. Or He could have been saying that the Jewish race would not pass away until God's promises to Israel were fulfilled. Either way, the verse does not support preterism.

Preterists also argue from Matthew 16:28, where Jesus said some of His followers standing there would not taste death until they saw Him coming in His kingdom. Apparently, however, Jesus had in mind His transfiguration—a preview of the glory of the kingdom—which happened one week later (Matthew 17:1-13). Supporting this view is the fact that some of the disciples standing there were no longer alive by AD 70.

Preterists also point to verses that indicate that Jesus will come quickly (Revelation 22:12,20). However, the word *quickly* often means "swiftly, speedily." So the term could simply indicate that when the predicted events first start to occur, they will progress swiftly.

———

Pearl of Wisdom: *The book of Revelation provides us with a panoramic view of history in advance.*

Biblical Prophecies—Manufactured After the Fact?

Some critics today try to argue that the biblical prophecies are not impressive because they were manufactured and inserted into the biblical text after the events that were prophesied. Such a view contradicts the facts.

Consider the book of Isaiah. Until the mid-twentieth century, our earliest manuscript copy of Isaiah was dated at AD 980. Following the discovery of the Dead Sea Scrolls in 1947, however, scholars could examine a manuscript copy of Isaiah dated at 150 BC. This manuscript is but a copy of an original document that dates back to the seventh century BC. So the specific prophecies of the coming divine Messiah recorded in Isaiah—including the facts that Jesus would be born of a virgin (7:14), be called Immanuel (7:14), be anointed by the Holy Spirit (11:2), have a ministry in Galilee (9:1-2), have a ministry of miracles (35:5-6), be silent before His accusers (53:7), be crucified with thieves (53:12), accomplish a sacrificial atonement for humankind (53:5), and then be buried in a rich man's tomb (53:9)—could not have been recorded after the fact, as some critics try to argue. These prophecies were recorded hundreds of years before the fact, and their literal fulfillment in the first century (along with hundreds of other Old Testament messianic prophecies) prove the divine inspiration of Scripture.

Pearl of Wisdom: *The evidence reveals that the biblical prophecies were written far in advance of the prophesied events.*

Death and Our Spirits

The New Testament word for *death* carries the idea of separation. At the moment of physical death, man's spirit separates from his body (2 Corinthians 5:8). This is why, when Stephen was being put to death by stoning, he prayed, "Lord Jesus, receive my spirit" (Acts 7:59). At the moment of death, "the spirit returns to God who gave it" (Ecclesiastes 12:7). Death for believers involves their spirits departing their bodies and immediately going into the presence of the Lord in heaven. Death for believers thus leads to a supremely blissful existence (Philippians 1:21-23).

For unbelievers, however, death holds grim prospects. At death, unbelievers' spirits depart from their bodies and go not to heaven but to a place of great suffering (Luke 16:19-31; 2 Peter 2:9).

Both believers and unbelievers remain as spirits, in a disembodied state, until the future resurrection of the dead. Believers' resurrection bodies will be specially suited to dwelling in heaven in the direct presence of God. The perishable will be made imperishable, and the mortal will be made immortal (1 Corinthians 15:53). Unbelievers will be resurrected too, but they will spend eternity apart from God (John 5:29).

Scripture reveals that "death is the destiny of every man; the living should take this to heart" (Ecclesiastes 7:2 NIV). People should "seek the LORD while he may be found; call upon him while he is near" (Isaiah 55:6), for "now is the day of salvation" (2 Corinthians 6:2).

———

Pearl of Wisdom: *Trusting in Christ for salvation during our short mortal years is all-important.*

Descriptions of Death

The Bible sometimes refers to death as "the way of all the earth," emphasizing its universality (1 Kings 2:1-2). Job spoke of his eventual death by saying he would "go the way from which I shall not return" (Job 16:22). Such words remind us of the permanence of passing from mortal life. Job also reflected that "man dies and is laid low; man breathes his last" (Job 14:10), pointing to cessation of life in the physical body.

The apostle Paul said, "If I am to live in the flesh, that means fruitful labor for me. Yet which I shall choose I cannot tell. I am hard pressed between the two. My desire is to depart and be with Christ, for that is far better" (Philippians 1:22-23). Paul considered departure from earthly life and into the Lord's presence something to be desired.

Paul, himself a tent maker, graphically described death as an earthly tent being destroyed (2 Corinthians 5:1). Our present bodies are temporary and flimsy abodes. They are weak, frail, and vulnerable. But a time is coming when these "habitations" will be resurrected, and our resurrection bodies will be permanent and indestructible.

Death is often described in the Bible as sleep, for the body takes on the appearance of sleep. The soul, however, does not sleep. It remains fully conscious (see Revelation 6:9-11; Luke 16:19-31).

Pearl of Wisdom: *Departing this life to be with Christ is indeed "far better."*

Fear of Death

Job aptly referred to death as the king of terrors (Job 18:14). The psalmist likewise said, "My heart is in anguish within me; the terrors of death have fallen upon me" (Psalm 55:4).

Death is the great enemy of all human beings. Death strikes down the good and the wicked, the strong and the weak. Without any respect of persons, death carries its campaign of rampage and destruction through communities and nations.

Something in each of us shrinks back from the very mention of death. After all, God created us to live. Life is natural. But when sin entered the world, the universe was invaded by death. Death is unnatural. Even the apostle Paul—a spiritual giant if there ever was one—considered death the "last enemy" to be conquered (1 Corinthians 15:26).

Except for those Christians who will be instantly transformed into a state of glory at the rapture, all Christians will eventually go through death's door (1 Thessalonians 4:13-18). As the apostle Paul said, however, death no longer has the sting it once had before we became Christians: "O death, where is your victory? O death, where is your sting?" (1 Corinthians 15:55). Because of what Christ accomplished on the cross and in His resurrection, we need never be distracted by death's ever-present threat again. Because He is risen, we too shall rise!

Pearl of Wisdom: *The Lord has taken the stinger out of death. Because of this, we need never fear death again. Trust Him!*

The Three Heavens

Words can carry different meanings in different contexts. For example, the English word *trunk* can refer to the front of an elephant, the back of a car, the bottom of a tree, the torso of a man, or a suitcase—all depending on the context. Biblical words are no different.

I make this point because Scripture refers to the ineffable and glorious dwelling place of God as the third heaven (2 Corinthians 12:2). It is elsewhere called the "heaven of heavens" and the "highest heaven" (Deuteronomy 26:15; 1 Kings 8:27,30; 2 Chronicles 2:6; Psalm 14:2; Matthew 6:9-10; 18:10; 28:2). The apostle Paul was caught up to this heaven and "heard things that cannot be told, which man may not utter" (2 Corinthians 12:4). Apparently this heavenly abode is so resplendently glorious, so ineffable, so beyond anything we have ever witnessed, Paul was prohibited to talk about it once he was back on earth.

If God's glorious and ineffable abode is the third heaven, what are the first and second heavens? Scripture gives us the answer. The first heaven contains the earth's atmosphere (Genesis 1:20,26,28; 8:2; Deuteronomy 28:12; Job 35:5; Psalm 147:8; Matthew 8:20; 13:32; 16:2-3). The second heaven reaches out into the stellar universe (Genesis 1:14-15,17; 15:5; Deuteronomy 4:19; 17:3; 28:62; Acts 2:19-20; Hebrews 11:12).

Pearl of Wisdom: *As awesome as the first and second heavens are, they dim in comparison to the third heaven, God's glorious abode.*

Today's Heaven and the Future Heaven

Theologians and Bible expositors have been careful to distinguish between the present heaven, where God now dwells and where believers go at the moment of death (2 Corinthians 5:8; Philippians 1:21-23), and the future heaven, where believers will spend all eternity (2 Peter 3:13; Revelation 21:1). Scripture reveals that God will one day create a new heavens and a new earth. The New Jerusalem, the heavenly city, will rest on this new earth (Revelation 21:10). This glorious city is where you and I will reside for all eternity (see Revelation 21–22). And this new earth will itself be a part of heaven!

Christ Himself is the Architect and Builder of this city. We read Christ's own words in John 14:2-3: "In my Father's house are many rooms. If it were not so, would I have told you that I go to prepare a place for you? And if I go and prepare a place for you, I will come again and will take you to myself, that where I am you may be also."

If you are impressed by the glory of stellar space, which Christ also created (John 1:3), hold on because "you ain't seen nothin' yet!" As the apostle Paul said, "No eye has seen, no ear has heard, no mind has conceived what God has prepared for those who love him" (1 Corinthians 2:9 NIV).

Pearl of Wisdom: *Scripture promises that for the Christian, the best truly is yet to come!*

The New Heaven and New Earth

S cripture reveals that God will one day create a new heaven and a new earth (Revelation 21:1). Many have understandably wondered which heaven (or heavens) will pass away and be made new.

The only heavens that have been negatively affected by humankind's fall are the first and second heavens—earth's atmosphere and the stellar universe (Genesis 3:17; 5:29; Romans 8:20-22). The entire physical universe is running down and decaying. But the third heaven—God's perfect and glorious dwelling place (2 Corinthians 12:2,4)—remains untouched by human sin. It needs no renewal. This heaven subsists in moral and physical perfection and undergoes no change.

So when Scripture refers to the old heaven and earth passing away, and when it speaks of a new heaven and earth (Isaiah 65:17; 66:22; 2 Peter 3:13; Revelation 21:1), it is apparently not referring to God's glorious and ineffable dwelling place but rather the first and second heavens, earth's atmosphere and stellar space. When these heavens and the earth are made new, they will be included in the third heaven. In the eternal state, believers will be in heaven while they are on the new earth, for the heavenly city—the New Jerusalem—will rest on the new earth (see Revelation 21:1-2,10). Meanwhile, Satan, demons, and unredeemed sinners will be eternally quarantined in an isolation ward that Scripture calls hell.

Pearl of Wisdom: *You and I will one day have resurrection bodies, and we will live on a resurrected earth in a resurrected universe.*

Pictures of Heaven

Each of the Bible's descriptions of heaven reveals something new and exciting about our future abode. Revelation 21, for example, describes a city of glory—the New Jerusalem—which will be the eternal dwelling place of Christians. The human mind can scarcely take in a scene of such transcendent splendor, ecstatic joy, and fellowship of sinless angels and redeemed glorified human beings. The voice of the Alpha and the Omega, the beginning and the end, utters a climactic declaration: "Behold, I am making all things new" (Revelation 21:5).

Certainly the actual splendor of heaven far exceeds anything we have yet experienced. As the apostle Paul said, "No eye has seen, no ear has heard, no mind has conceived what God has prepared for those who love him" (1 Corinthians 2:9 NIV).

Heaven is also called the "paradise of God" (Revelation 2:7). The word *paradise* literally means "garden of pleasure" or "garden of delight." Paul was once caught up to this paradise and "heard things that cannot be told, which man may not utter" (2 Corinthians 12:4).

Heaven is fittingly described as "the holy city," for no sin or unrighteousness of any kind will be there (Revelation 21:1-2). Heaven is a place "in which righteousness dwells" (2 Peter 3:13). What a perfect environment this will be to live in!

Pearl of Wisdom: *Contemplating heaven is a healthy practice, for it can fan faith into a flame.*

The Eternal Heaven—a Physical Place

Many throughout church history have thought of heaven as a kind of ethereal, spiritual dimension. The biblical evidence, however, indicates that the future heaven will be a physical place, something seemingly required by the fact that you and I will be physically resurrected from the dead (1 Corinthians 15:35-53) just as Jesus was. Recall that the resurrected Jesus said to the disciples, "See my hands and my feet, that it is I myself. Touch me, and see. For a spirit does not have flesh and bones as you see that I have" (Luke 24:39). Jesus also ate food on four different occasions to prove the physicality of His resurrection body (Luke 24:30,42-43; John 21:12-13; Acts 1:4). His body was also touched by various people (Matthew 28:9; John 20:27-28). A physical body must have a physical environment to live in.

The New Testament contains other indications that heaven will be a physical place. For example, in John 14:1-3, Jesus said the place He is preparing for us is in the Father's house and has many rooms. Such words suggest a physical place where the physically resurrected redeemed will forever live. In keeping with this, Revelation 21:9–22:5 describes heaven—more specifically, the heavenly city called "the New Jerusalem"—in terms that indicate a physical place, for the heavenly city has walls, gates, foundations, a street, river, trees, and more.

Pearl of Wisdom: *You and I will eternally live in a physical city (the New Jerusalem) on a physical new earth!*

Heaven's Location

Christians have different opinions about where heaven might be located. Some suggest that heaven is somewhere in our space-time universe—far, far away, perhaps shrouded by a cloud of God's glory. They speculate that perhaps heaven is located in the north of our universe, for Job 37:22 (NIV) reveals, "Out of the north he comes in golden splendor; God comes in awesome majesty" (see also 26:7). A supportive evidence for this view is that at the ascension, Jesus literally went up into the sky as some of His disciples watched—that is, He "was lifted up, and a cloud took him out of their sight" (Acts 1:9-11).

Other Christians suggest that perhaps heaven is located in an entirely different dimension than ours. On several occasions, Jesus seemed to enter and depart the space-time dimension when in His physical resurrection body. For example, after Jesus made a resurrection appearance to some of His followers, He "vanished from their sight" (Luke 24:31). Moreover, when some of His disciples were in a house, "although the doors were locked, Jesus came and stood among them and said, 'Peace be with you'" (John 20:26). Further, Mark 1:10, which speaks of Jesus' baptism, says, "When he came up out of the water, immediately he saw the heavens opening and the Spirit descending on him like a dove." Perhaps this points to heaven being in a different dimension.

Pearl of Wisdom: *Contemplating the mystery of heaven's location can be fascinating and inspiring.*

Time in Heaven

Is there a sense of time in heaven? The book of Revelation indicates we will sing in heaven (Revelation 5:9). How can there be songs with a beat, with lyrics that are sung, with singers transitioning from verse to chorus, with a beginning and an end, without a sense of time?

Revelation 6:9-10 speaks of Christians who will be martyred in the future tribulation period, and they ask God, "O Sovereign Lord, holy and true, how long before you will judge and avenge our blood on those who dwell on the earth?" The phrase *how long* indicates a sense of time passing in heaven.

God's people "serve him day and night" (Revelation 7:15). The opening of the seven seals (judgments) are sequential (with intervals in between), and there is "silence in heaven for about half an hour" after the opening of the seventh seal (Revelation 8:1). In Revelation 22:2 we read that the tree of life yields its fruit each month. Moreover, if those who reside in heaven rejoice whenever a sinner repents on temporal earth (Luke 15:7), this would seem to indicate a sense of moments passing in heaven, because not everyone repents at the same time.

Pearl of Wisdom: *The best conclusion is probably that the actual nature of redeemed human beings in heaven will be timeless, but they will still have the capacity to engage in acts that involve time.*

The Eternal Heaven

I am occasionally asked whether heaven will last forever. The good news is that yes, heaven will last forever!

Some theologians have suggested that heaven will last as long as God exists, and since God will last forever (He is eternal), heaven will last forever. They also suggested that since heaven is the place where the redeemed of all ages will experience eternal life, heaven itself must be eternal. In keeping with this, Titus 1:2 speaks of the "hope of eternal life, which God, who never lies, promised before the ages began." Jesus Himself promised that the righteous will go "into eternal life" (Matthew 25:46).

In the book of Revelation, John declared, "I heard every creature in heaven and on earth and under the earth and in the sea, and all that is in them, saying, 'To him who sits on the throne and to the Lamb be blessing and honor and glory and might forever and ever!'" (Revelation 5:13). If "blessing and honor and glory" are shown to God "forever and ever" by creatures in heaven, then heaven obviously must exist forever.

We might also surmise that since the Architect and Builder of the New Jerusalem (the eternal city) is none other than Christ Himself (see John 14:1-3), the city will be absolutely perfect in every way and will not be subject to decay or deterioration. In other words, it will last forever.

Pearl of Wisdom: *You and I will have eternal resurrection bodies and will enjoy eternal life in an eternal dwelling place (heaven) as we fellowship with an eternal God!*

With God in Heaven

Can anything be more sublime and more utterly satisfying for the Christian than to enjoy the sheer delight of unbroken fellowship with God and Christ and to have immediate and completely unobstructed access to the divine glory (2 Corinthians 5:6-8; Philippians 1:23)? We shall see our beloved Lord face-to-face in all His splendor and glory. We will gaze on His countenance and behold His resplendent beauty forever.

Surely our greatest joy and most exhilarating thrill will be to look upon the face of the divine Creator and fellowship with Him forever. He "who alone has immortality, who dwells in unapproachable light" (1 Timothy 6:16) shall reside intimately among His own, and "they will be his people, and God himself will be with them as their God" (Revelation 21:3).

In the afterlife, our fellowship with the Lord will no longer be intermittent, blighted by sin and defeat. Instead, it will be continuous. Sin will be utterly and forever banished from our being.

To fellowship with the Lord God is the essence of heavenly life, the fount and source of all blessing: "In your presence there is fullness of joy; at your right hand are pleasures forevermore" (Psalm 16:11). We may be confident that the crowning wonder of our experience in the eternal city will be the perpetual and endless exploration of that unutterable beauty, majesty, love, holiness, power, joy, and grace which is God Himself.

Pearl of Wisdom: *To fellowship with the Lord God is the essence of heavenly life, the fount and source of all blessing!*

An Eternal Reunion in Heaven

One of the most glorious aspects of our lives in heaven will be our reunion with Christian loved ones. The Thessalonian Christians were apparently very concerned about their Christian loved ones who had died. They expressed their concern to the apostle Paul. So in 1 Thessalonians 4:13-17, Paul deals with the "dead in Christ" and assures the Thessalonian Christians that they will indeed enjoy a reunion. And yes, believers will recognize their loved ones in the eternal state.

How do we know this is so? Besides the clear teaching of 1 Thessalonians 4 (see especially verse 18), we see in 2 Samuel 12:23 that David knew he would be reunited with his deceased son in heaven: "Now he is dead...I shall go to him, but he will not return to me." He had no doubt about recognizing him.

When Moses and Elijah—who had long passed from earthly life—appeared to Jesus on the mount of transfiguration (Matthew 17:1-8), they were recognized by all who were present. Furthermore, in Jesus' story of the rich man and Lazarus, who had both died, the rich man, Lazarus, and Abraham all recognized each other (see Luke 16:19-31). Still further, Scripture often refers to God's people at death being gathered to their people (Genesis 25:17; 35:29; 49:33), a phrase that would be meaningless if they did not recognize each other in the afterlife.

Pearl of Wisdom: *Take comfort in the fact that you will one day be reunited with your Christian loved ones!*

Babies Go Straight to Heaven
When They Die

All of us—including infants who can't believe—are born into the world lost (Luke 19:10) and perishing (John 3:16), and we all need the gift of salvation. When infants die, I believe Christ at that moment applies the benefits of His sacrificial death to them, and they go straight to heaven. Here's why I believe this.

God's purpose in salvation. God's primary purpose in saving human beings is to display His wondrous grace. Would the riches of His grace be displayed in wisdom and insight (Ephesians 1:7-8) if God sent babies to hell? Of course not.

Descriptions of hell. No biblical description of hell includes infants or little children. Nor do we read of infants or little children being judged at the great white throne (Revelation 20:11-15).

Jesus and the children. Jesus, who loved children, said, "Unless you turn and become like children, you will never enter the kingdom of heaven...Whoever receives one such child in my name receives me" (Matthew 18:3,5).

King David and his son. David certainly believed he would go to heaven and again be with his young son who died (2 Samuel 12:22-23).

The basis of the judgment of the lost. Revelation 20:11-13 reveals that the lost are judged "according to what they had done." Infants cannot be the objects of this judgment because they are not responsible for their deeds.

Pearl of Wisdom: *Christian parents who have lost a baby in death can look forward to a glorious reunion in heaven.*

Firsthand Reports of Heaven

Many today claim to have visited heaven during a so-called near-death experience. In many cases, people provide firsthand reports of what they witnessed. We should be cautious about such reports.

When Paul was caught up to the third heaven (paradise), he "heard things that cannot be told, which man may not utter" (2 Corinthians 12:4). If God forbade Paul to speak of the things he witnessed, why would God allow dozens of modern people—who are not even apostles, which Paul was—to speak of what they witnessed and inform us of things not corroborated by the Bible?

Much of what we learn about heaven is found in the book of Revelation. After John received this revelation from God, God warned that no one should add words or take away words from what is written (Revelation 22:18-19). People who claim to have been to heaven and back and who write sensational books with new revelations about heaven come perilously close to violating the spirit of this passage.

Many individuals who have had such an experience claim they encountered a Jesus who says things contrary to the Jesus of Scripture, such as that sin is not a problem, hell does not exist, and all people are welcome in heaven regardless of their religion. Such individuals have obviously encountered a counterfeit Christ (2 Corinthians 11:14-15).

Pearl of Wisdom: *Christians ought to let the Bible be a barometer of truth for all experiential claims.*

Husbands and Wives in the Afterlife

Believers will apparently no longer be married in the afterlife. Paul taught that marriage as a physical union is terminated at the death of either spouse (Romans 7:1-3; 1 Corinthians 7:39). Moreover, Jesus Himself said, "In the resurrection they neither marry nor are given in marriage, but are like angels in heaven" (Matthew 22:30).

Of course, my wife, Kerri, and I will always have been married on this earth. And in the eternal state, we will retain our memory that we were married on the old earth. Moreover, I am confident that even though we will not be physically married, we will continue to grow in an ever-deepening and loving relationship with each other.

Will our children still be our children in the afterlife? Of course they will! Your daughter will always be your daughter, and your son will always be your son. Husbands and wives will receive glorified bodies, but that does not obliterate the fact that they conceived and gave birth to children.

In the eternal state, however, we will enjoy a broader relationship in which we are all equally sons and daughters in God's eternal family. We have each become adopted into His forever family (Ephesians 1:5). And you can count on enjoying even deeper and more fulfilling relationships with your loved ones in heaven.

Pearl of Wisdom: *Christians will have all eternity to grow closer and closer and closer to their Christian loved ones!*

Heaven's Population

J esus said that "the gate is narrow and the way is hard that leads to life, and those who find it are few" (Matthew 7:14). But this Scripture passage may deal primarily with the immediate and local response to Jesus' message in New Testament times, not to people throughout human history. If this view is correct, then Matthew 7:14 should not be used as a gauge for how many people make it into heaven.

Some suggest that the accumulative total of infants and children before the age of accountability who have died since the time of Adam and Eve must represent a significant portion of those who make it into heaven. Moreover, assuming that life begins at conception—and aborted and miscarried babies go to heaven too—this fact alone would indicate that quite a few people will end up in heaven!

Still further, a significant percentage of all the people who have ever lived is alive today. If a significant revival broke out prior to the second coming of Christ, the number of humans who end up in heaven would be greatly escalated.

Pearl of Wisdom: *Our all-loving God certainly desires that all be saved (2 Peter 3:9; 1 Timothy 2:4), although Scripture is clear that not all will be (see Revelation 21:8). God offers salvation to all, but not all accept His invitation.*

Food in Heaven

Some Christians have claimed that we will not eat food in heaven because Romans 14:17 states that "the kingdom of God is not a matter of eating and drinking but of righteousness and peace and joy in the Holy Spirit." But this verse has nothing to do with the afterlife or heaven. Paul was simply teaching that we should be cautious not to cause other Christians to stumble by what we eat and drink while we are on earth.

Jesus Himself ate physical food four times after His resurrection from the dead (Luke 24:30,42-43; John 21:12-13; Acts 1:4). Our resurrection bodies will be like His (Philippians 3:21; 1 John 3:2), so we too will be able to eat food in our resurrection bodies. This seems to be confirmed in Revelation 22:1-2, where we read of "the tree of life, bearing twelve crops of fruit, yielding its fruit every month." However, we will eat only for enjoyment, not for sustenance, for our resurrection bodies will not need sustenance.

Some suggest that we may be vegetarians in the afterlife. After all, animal death did not occur until after humankind's fall and the subsequence curse (Genesis 3). The fall and the curse will not exist in heaven, so animals may no longer be eaten.

Pearl of Wisdom: *Apparently we will never get fat by what we eat in heaven, and we will never have to diet. Awesome!*

Our Resurrection Bodies

This is important, for Scripture reveals that God dwells in "unapproachable light" (1 Timothy 6:16; see also Psalm 104:2). So brilliant and glorious is this light that without a renewed body, no mortal can survive in it.

On more than one occasion in Scripture, a believer catches a brief glimpse of God's glory, and the result is always the same: He falls to his knees as if about to die. Such an unveiled view of God is impossible for mortal humans.

For example, the apostle John saw Christ in His glory and "fell at his feet as though dead" (Revelation 1:17). Likewise, when Abraham beheld the Almighty, he "fell on his face" (Genesis 17:3). When Manoah and his wife saw a manifestation of the Lord, they "fell on their faces to the ground" (Judges 13:20). Ezekiel, upon seeing the glory of God, admits, "I fell on my face" (Ezekiel 3:23; 43:3; 44:4).

Scripture tells us that "this perishable body must put on the imperishable, and this mortal body must put on immortality" (1 Corinthians 15:53). Only then will we be able to dwell in God's presence face-to-face (Revelation 21:1-3). Just as the caterpillar has to be changed into the butterfly in order to inherit the air, so we have to be changed in order to inherit heaven.

Pearl of Wisdom: *Are you ready for the perishable to become imperishable and the mortal to become immortal?*

Clothes in Heaven

Will we wear clothes in heaven? The question probably wouldn't come up at all except for the fact that when God first created Adam and Eve, He created them naked (Genesis 2:25), and they had no shame. Only after they sinned did they feel shame and start wearing clothes (3:7). For this reason, some wonder whether we will wear clothes in our sinless state in heaven.

Personally, I think so—and I base my opinion largely on the book of Revelation. Revelation 1:13, speaking of the glorified Christ, tells us that He was "clothed with a long robe and with a golden sash around his chest." Revelation 3:5, speaking of members of the church in Sardis, tells us that "the one who conquers will be clothed thus in white garments." The martyrs of Revelation 6:11 "were each given a white robe." Revelation 7:9 speaks of a multitude of redeemed people in heaven who are "clothed in white robes." When Christ leaves heaven and comes again at the second coming, He will be "clothed in a robe dipped in blood" (Revelation 19:13). Moreover, in the transfiguration account in Matthew 17, Moses and Elijah appeared from heaven and spoke with Jesus about His coming departure. I can't imagine that they suddenly appeared stark naked, right in front of the disciples. Verses such as these lead me to believe that all of us will be dressed in the afterlife—with white robes being the fashionable attire of the day.

Pearl of Wisdom: *The scriptural evidence indicates that both Christ and the redeemed will be dressed in the afterlife.*

Seeing Earth from Heaven

In Hebrews 12:1 we read, "Since we are surrounded by so great a cloud of witnesses, let us also lay aside every weight, and sin which clings so closely, and let us run with endurance the race that is set before us." Some conclude from this that we are being watched from heaven, with folks looking over heaven's balcony to observe our behavior. Here is some support for this idea.

Samuel (1 Samuel 28:16-18), Moses and Elijah (Luke 9:31), and the Christian martyrs (Revelation 6:9-10) seemed aware of circumstances on earth after they died. Angels in heaven also are aware of events on earth (1 Corinthians 4:9).

On the other hand, Samuel may have been "in the know" because he (unlike us) was a prophet of God, or perhaps God simply informed him of things before he appeared to Saul. The same could be true regarding Moses and Elijah. The Christian martyrs may also have been informed of circumstances on earth. Angels' experience is different from ours, for many of them are carrying out assignments on earth. Finally, how could Christians in heaven have no more mourning or tears if they were always looking at earth?

Pearl of Wisdom: *The main idea of Hebrews 12:1 is apparently that because we have been preceded by superheroes of the faith (mentioned in Hebrews 11), we should seek to mimic their behavior, following their lead in godly behavior.*

Not in Heaven

Here is a list of things that will not be in heaven:

- Heaven will not contain a temple where people meet with God (Revelation 21:22). Scripture metaphorically indicates that God Himself is the temple in heaven.

- Heaven will have no sea (Revelation 21:1) to remind people of the flood of Noah's time or represent a great gulf of separation between loved ones. A sealess heaven would mean no more exile or separation.

- Death will not exist in heaven (Revelation 21:4). The "last enemy" will be forever gone. No more funerals. Only life, life, and more life (1 Corinthians 15:54-55)!

- No one will suffer pain in heaven—physical, emotional, spiritual, or any other kind (Revelation 21:4).

- No one will experience crying or mourning or tears in heaven (Revelation 21:4). We will know only endless joy, bliss, and serenity.

- The darkness of night will never fall on heaven (Revelation 22:5). We will no longer have mortal bodies that need recuperation through sleep.

- The curse and all corruption will be done away with in heaven (Revelation 22:3). All will be perfect.

- Satanic opposition will not exist in heaven (Revelation 20:10). Satan will be forever bound, never again free to harass the saints of the living God.

Pearl of Wisdom: *We can be glad that certain things will not be in heaven!*

Animals in Heaven?

Will animals and our earthly pets be in heaven? That's a tough question. I know how emotionally loaded this issue is. To be frank, some theologians seem quite sure that our pets will not be in heaven. Others have questioned that thinking.

Romans 8:21 (NKJV) may open the door for us to believe that our pets will be in heaven: "The creation itself will be set free from its bondage to corruption and obtain the freedom of the glory of the children of God." Since animals (even dead animals) are part of creation, perhaps creation's freedom from its bondage to corruption includes a reviving and restoration of the animals.

God certainly went to great effort to save some animals from the worldwide flood (Genesis 6:19-20). Moreover, Psalm 148:10-13 refers to all of creation rendering praise to God, including the animal kingdom: "Beasts and all livestock, creeping things and flying birds!...Let them praise the name of the LORD." Psalm 150:6 likewise instructs, "Let everything that has breath praise the LORD." This would certainly include animals. Besides, Elijah was taken up into heaven in a chariot pulled by horses (2 Kings 2:11), and heaven's army rides on horses (Revelation 19:11-14), so animals are apparently already a part of heavenly existence.

Pearl of Wisdom: *It is always possible that God's redemption of the creation will include your beloved pets.*

Joy in Heaven

How can believers be joyful in heaven, knowing that people (perhaps even acquaintances) are suffering in hell? On this side of eternity, we do not have all the wisdom and insight we need to fully answer this question. But some scriptural considerations can help us keep this issue in perspective.

First, God Himself has promised that He will take away all pain and remove all our tears (Revelation 21:4). The abolishment of mourning is in His sovereign hands. Some theologians suggest God may purge the memories of the saints in heaven so they do not remember those who are now in hell. In Isaiah 65:17-19, God affirms: "Behold, I create new heavens and a new earth, and the former things shall not be remembered or come into mind." This memory purge will apparently be selective, for our good memories will still be retained.

Second, all of us in heaven will be aware of the full justice of God's decisions. We will clearly see that those who are in hell are there precisely because they rejected God's only provision for escaping hell.

Third, we will recognize that hell has degrees of punishment, just as heaven has degrees of reward. God is perfectly wise and just. He knows what He is doing! You and I can rest with quiet assurance in God's wisdom and justice.

Pearl of Wisdom: *The reality of hell will not dampen heavenly joy in the slightest.*

Hell Is Real

Hell is a real place. But hell was not part of God's original creation, which He called "good" (Genesis 1:31). Hell was created later to accommodate the banishment of Satan and his fallen angels who rebelled against God (Matthew 25:41). Humans who reject Christ will join Satan and his fallen angels in this infernal place of suffering.

The Scriptures use a variety of words to describe the horrors of hell. It is designated the lake of fire, where the wicked dead will be tormented day and night forever (Revelation 19:20). Jesus often referred to this place as "eternal fire" and "fiery furnace" (Matthew 25:41). "In that place there will be weeping and gnashing of teeth" (Matthew 13:42). This weeping will be caused by the environment, the company, remorse and guilt, and eternal shame.

What is the fire of hell? Some believe it is literal. Others believe fire is a metaphorical way of expressing the great wrath of God. Scripture tells us, "The LORD your God is a consuming fire" (Deuteronomy 4:24). "His wrath is poured out like fire" (Nahum 1:6). How awful is the fiery wrath of God!

The greatest pain suffered by those in hell is that they are forever excluded from the presence of God. If ecstatic joy is found in the presence of God (Psalm 16:11), then utter dismay is found in the eternal absence of His presence.

Pearl of Wisdom: *Hell will be as horrible as heaven will be wonderful.*

Endless Punishment for the Wicked

Several lines of evidence indicate that the lost will suffer everlasting conscious torment.

- The rich man who died was in conscious torment (Luke 16:22-28).

- Jesus said people in hell weep and gnash their teeth (Matthew 8:12; 22:13; 24:51; 25:30).

- Hell is of the same duration as heaven, namely, "everlasting" (Matthew 25:41).

- Everlasting punishment requires that the people are everlasting (2 Thessalonians 1:9). "Endless annihilation" is an oxymoron.

- The beast and the false prophet were thrown alive into the lake of fire at the beginning of the thousand years (Revelation 19:20), and they were still there, conscious and alive, after the thousand years passed (20:10).

- The devil, the beast, and the false prophet will be "tormented day and night forever and ever" (Revelation 20:10). This must mean they will be conscious forever and ever.

- There are no degrees of annihilation. But Scripture reveals that there will be degrees of punishment and suffering among the lost (see Matthew 10:15; 11:21-24; 16:27; Luke 12:47-48; John 15:22; Hebrews 10:29; Revelation 20:11-15; 22:12).

Pearl of Wisdom: *The Bible clearly teaches the eternal conscious punishment of the wicked.*

Hell and Our Loving God

Some people claim that a loving God would not send people to hell. They thus refuse to believe in God. Others choose to believe in God but reject belief in hell.

Of course, God does not want to send anyone to hell. God is characterized by love (John 4:24), and He loves every human being (John 3:16). He is "not wishing that any should perish, but that all should reach repentance" (2 Peter 3:9). Scripture consistently portrays God as pleading with people to turn from their sins and turn to Him for salvation.

The fact that God wants people to be saved is precisely why He sent Jesus to pay the penalty for our sins at the cross (John 3:16-17). Unfortunately, not all people are willing to accept the payment of Jesus' death on their behalf. God therefore allows them to experience the results of their own choice— an eternity in hell (see Luke 16:19-31).

C.S. Lewis was right when he said that in the end there are two groups of people. One group of people says to God, "Thy will be done." These people have placed their faith in Jesus Christ and will live forever with God in heaven. The second group of people are those to whom God says, sadly, "*Thy will be done!*" These people reject Jesus Christ and will thus spend eternity apart from Him. God does not force anyone to be saved.

Pearl of Wisdom: *God offers salvation to all, but He forces salvation on none!*

"You fool!"

In Matthew 5:22 Jesus sternly warned, "I say to you that everyone who is angry with his brother will be liable to judgment; whoever insults his brother will be liable to the council; and whoever says, 'You fool!' will be liable to the hell of fire." This verse is found in a discourse in which Jesus is teaching against murder (Matthew 5:22-26). Jesus declared that just as a murderer is guilty, so also anyone who gets angry and calls another person a fool is guilty (verse 22).

The Pharisees taught that murder involved only the external act of taking someone else's life. But Jesus challenged the Pharisees' understanding by pointing out that not only the external act but also the internal attitude brings guilt. More specifically, people who say, "You fool" to others demonstrate within their hearts the anger that can lead to murder. People with such anger are obviously sinners on a path that leads to hell—and will actually end up in hell if they do not turn to Christ for salvation.

Jesus then discusses the law of reconciliation. Wrong inner attitudes must be made right. Anger must be dismissed and replaced with forgiveness (Matthew 5:23-26). Words of hurt ("you fool") must be replaced with words of forgiveness. This is the path Christ calls Christians to.

Pearl of Wisdom: *Remaining bitter at someone only hurts one person: you. Better to forgive!*

The Judgment Seat of Christ

Christians will one day stand before the judgment seat of Christ (Romans 14:8-10). At that time, Christ will examine the deeds they performed while in their earthly bodies (Ephesians 6:7-8). He will also weigh their personal motives, the intents of their hearts, and the words they have spoken (Jeremiah 17:10; 1 Corinthians 4:5).

The idea of a judgment seat relates to the athletic games of Paul's day. When races and games concluded, a dignitary took his seat on an elevated throne in the arena, and one by one the winning athletes would come forward to receive a reward. Similarly, Christians will stand before Christ the Judge and receive (or lose) rewards. These rewards are called *crowns* (Revelation 2:10).

This judgment has nothing to do with whether Christians will remain saved. Those who have truly placed faith in Christ are saved, and nothing threatens that (John 10:28-30; Romans 8:29-39; Ephesians 4:30). This judgment rather has to do with the reception or loss of rewards (1 Corinthians 3:1-10).

Some Christians at the judgment may have a sense of deprivation and suffer some degree of forfeiture and shame (1 Corinthians 3:15; 1 John 2:28). Indeed, certain rewards may be forfeited that otherwise might have been received. Second John 8 understandably warns, "Watch yourselves, so that you may not lose what we have worked for, but may win a full reward."

Pearl of Wisdom: *The fact that we will face the judgment seat of Christ ought to be an incentive to holy living.*

The Great White Throne

Unlike Christians, whose judgment deals only with rewards and loss of rewards, unbelievers face a horrific judgment that leads to the lake of fire (Matthew 25:41; Revelation 21:8). Unbelievers face this judgment at the great white throne (Revelation 20:11-15). Christ is the divine Judge, and those who are judged are the unsaved dead of all time. The judgment takes place at the end of the millennial kingdom, Christ's 1000-year reign on the earth (Revelation 20:1-3).

Those who face Christ at this judgment will be judged on the basis of their works: "The dead were judged by what was written in the books, according to what they had done. And the sea gave up the dead who were in it, Death and Hades gave up the dead who were in them, and they were judged, each one of them, according to what they had done" (Revelation 20:12-13).

The important thing to understand is that they actually get to this judgment because they are already unsaved. This judgment will not separate believers from unbelievers, for all who will experience it will have already made the choice during their lifetimes to reject the God of the Bible. Once they are before the divine Judge, they are judged according to their works not only to justify their condemnation but to determine the degree to which each person should be punished throughout all eternity (see Luke 12:47-48).

Pearl of Wisdom: *If you have not yet trusted in Christ for salvation, what is holding you back?*

Purgatory

Some believe that Christians who are not perfectly cleansed and are still tainted with the guilt of venial sins at death do not go to heaven but rather go to purgatory, where they allegedly go through a process of cleansing, or purging. This doctrine is unbiblical.

We are cleansed not by some alleged fire of purgatory but by the blood of Christ (Hebrews 9:14). Jesus Himself "is the propitiation for our sins" (1 John 2:2). We are made righteous solely through Jesus' work on the cross (2 Corinthians 5:21). Paul spoke of his life this way: "not having a righteousness of my own that comes from the law, but that which comes through faith in Christ, the righteousness from God that depends on faith" (Philippians 3:7-9). Through this wonderful work of Christ on the cross, believers are blameless and therefore need no purgatory (Jude 1:24).

When Jesus died on the cross, He said, "It is finished" (John 19:30). Jesus completed the work of redemption at the cross. In His high priestly prayer to the Father, Jesus said, "I glorified you on earth, having accomplished the work that you gave me to do" (John 17:4). Hebrews 10:14 declares, "By a single offering he has perfected for all time those who are being sanctified." First John 1:7 says, "The blood of Jesus his Son cleanses us from all sin." Romans 8:1 says, "There is therefore now no condemnation for those who are in Christ Jesus."

Pearl of Wisdom: *By virtue of what Christ has accomplished for us at the cross, the doctrine of purgatory is impossible.*

God Is Holy—We Should Be Holy Too

The word *holy* comes from the Greek word *hagios*, which literally means "set apart" or "separated." It refers to being set apart from sin and all that is unclean.

God is the absolutely holy one of the universe. His holiness means not only that He is entirely separate from all evil but also that He is absolutely righteous (Leviticus 19:2). He is majestic in holiness (Exodus 15:11). He is pure in every way. He is separate from all that is morally imperfect (see Exodus 15:11; 1 Samuel 2:2; Psalm 99:9; 111:9; Isaiah 6:3; Revelation 15:4). He cannot be tempted by evil (James 1:13). His very name is holy (Psalm 99:3; Isaiah 57:15). No wonder the angels proclaim, "holy, holy, holy" (Isaiah 6:3).

God desires His children, who are adopted into His family by faith in Christ, to take on the family likeness of holiness. We read in 1 Peter 1:15, "As he who called you is holy, you also be holy in all your conduct." We are called to serve God "in holiness and righteousness before him all our days" (Luke 1:75). In 1 Thessalonians 3:13 (NIV), Paul exhorts, "May he strengthen your hearts so that you will be blameless and holy in the presence of our God and Father when our Lord Jesus comes with all his holy ones."

Pearl of Wisdom: *Let's all shine as holy lights in our community so that people notice our behavior as Christians.*

Three Aspects of Sanctification

The word *sanctification* is rooted in the Greek word *hagiasmos*, which means "to set apart." The word's etymology shows that it indicates a twofold separation: separation *from* sin and separation *to* a life of obedience to God.

Sanctification has three aspects. The first is positional sanctification, which becomes a reality for the believing sinner from the moment of conversion (1 Corinthians 6:11; Hebrews 10:10,14,29). The believer is positionally set apart from sin. This position bears no relationship to the believer's daily life. It depends only on his or her union with and position in Christ (Romans 1:7; 1 Corinthians 1:2; 2 Corinthians 1:1).

The second aspect is progressive or experiential sanctification, which has to do with the believer's daily growth in grace, becoming in practice more and more set apart for God's use. This comes about by daily yielding to God and separating from sin (1 Peter 1:16). This experiential sanctification increases as believers dedicate their lives to God and are nourished by God's Word.

The third aspect is ultimate sanctification, which is attained only when we are fully and completely set apart from sin and to God in heaven (following death). Believers will be "like him" (1 John 3:2), and conformed to His image (Romans 8:29). The church will be guiltless before the presence of His glory (1 Corinthians 1:8). His bride will be free from every spot or wrinkle (Ephesians 5:27).

Pearl of Wisdom: *Once we're in the family of God, we begin to take on the family likeness—holiness!*

Abide in Christ and Bear Fruit

In John 15:2, Jesus teaches about the fruitfulness of those who follow Him: "Every branch in me that does not bear fruit he [the Father] takes away, and every branch that does bear fruit he prunes, that it may bear more fruit." Christian scholars interpret this verse variously.

Some believe it refers to lopping off the branch and throwing it away. Seen in this light, the phrase could refer to the physical death of fruitless Christians. This would be the ultimate form of divine discipline for a believer engaged in persistent and unrepentant sin (1 John 5:16; 1 Corinthians 11:30).

Others interpret the verse as a metaphorical way of describing less drastic forms of God's discipline—that is, God disciplines believers in the sense of lopping off all that is bad in their lives so that they bear more spiritual fruit.

Still others interpret the verse to mean that not all who claim to be followers of Jesus Christ are in fact true believers—a reality that soon reveals itself by a complete lack of spiritual fruit. In such a case, this branch is truly dead and can only be lopped off, much as Judas was.

Still others interpret the verse in terms of how gardeners in biblical days often lifted vines off the ground and propped them up on sticks so that they would bear more fruit. Seen in this light, John 15:2 may be saying that the Father does whatever is necessary in each Christian's life to ensure maximum production of fruit.

Pearl of Wisdom: *Let's all seek to be fruit-bearing Christians.*

Take Up Your Cross

In Mark 8:34, Jesus said to a group of followers, "If anyone would come after me, let him deny himself and take up his cross and follow me." Jesus' statement would certainly have made sense to His first-century hearers because the cross was a common tool of execution. Roman executioners required condemned criminals to carry their own crosses to the places of execution (John 19:17).

Jesus is calling for a total commitment. Here is a paraphrase: "If you really want to follow me, do not do so in word only, but put your life on the line and follow me on the path of the cross—a path that will involve sacrifice, suffering, and possibly even death."

Becoming saved is only the beginning of following Christ as a disciple. Scripture is clear that we become saved by faith alone in Jesus Christ (see John 5:24; 11:25; 12:46). A life of discipleship, however, goes beyond the initial conversion experience and calls for a life of sacrifice and commitment. The disciple is to deny himself. He must turn his back on selfish interests. He is no longer to live his life with self on the throne of his heart. Rather, Christ must reign supreme.

Pearl of Wisdom: *The original Greek of this verse contains a present imperative construction—the present tense indicates continuous action, and the imperative indicates a command. Jesus commands us to perpetually and unceasingly follow Him, day in and day out.*

David: Our Example for Faith in God

The object of our faith is not our own abilities. The object of our faith is our all-powerful God.

Consider the story of David and Goliath. David appeared to have no earthly chance of conquering the mighty giant Goliath, who had been arrogantly defying the armies of Israel. But David, looking at the challenge through the eye of faith, could perceive the unseen divine forces that were fighting on his side.

Saul—who was blind to all of this—warned David, "You are not able to go against this Philistine to fight with him, for you are but a youth, and he has been a man of war from his youth" (1 Samuel 17:33).

But David asserted, "The LORD who delivered me from the paw of the lion and from the paw of the bear will deliver me from the hand of this Philistine" (1 Samuel 17:37).

When David came face-to-face with the giant warrior, he declared, "This day the LORD will deliver you into my hand, and I will strike you down and cut off your head...The battle is the LORD's, and he will give you into our hand" (1 Samuel 17:46-47).

The rest is history. Goliath lost the fight before it even began. Why? Because the object of David's faith was a mighty God (see Jeremiah 32:27).

Pearl of Wisdom: *The eye of faith does not focus on human weakness and inability. The eye of faith is focused solely on the Deliverer—the Lord Himself.*

Conditioning Our Faith Muscles

Faith is like a muscle. A muscle has to be repeatedly stretched to its limit of endurance in order to build more strength. Without increased stress in training, the muscle simply will not grow.

In the same way, faith must be repeatedly tested to the limit of its endurance in order to expand and develop. God thus allows His children to go through trying experiences so they can develop their faith muscles (1 Peter 1:7).

This principle is illustrated in the book of Exodus. Following Israel's deliverance from Egypt, God first led them to Marah, a place where they would have to trust God to heal the water to make it drinkable. Only later did God lead them to Elim, a gorgeous oasis with plenty of good water (Exodus 15:22-27). God could have bypassed Marah altogether and brought them directly to Elim if He had wanted to. But, as is characteristic of God, He purposefully led them through the route that would yield maximum conditioning of their faith muscles. God does the same thing with us.

Of course, when those tough circumstances hit, we need to dive deep into the Word of God. For without a doubt, the Word of God can strengthen believers' faith during trials. Paul tells us that "faith comes from hearing, and hearing through the word of Christ" (Romans 10:17).

———

Pearl of Wisdom: *If someone should ask, "How can I increase my faith?" the answer is this: Saturate your mind with God's Word.*

Wisdom in the Proverbs

S olomon provides wisdom on many key issues in life. Look up some of the following verses in the book of Proverbs and feast on Solomon's words on a variety of life issues:

- Your relationship with God—2:7-8; 3:5-6; 10:3,22,27; 14:26,31; 16:2,7; 17:3,5; 19:23; 20:27; 22:2; 28:25; 29:25.

- How you should respond to people who treat you wrongly—20:22; 24:17-18; 25:21-22.

- Your family—10:5; 13:24; 14:26; 18:22; 19:14,18; 20:7; 22:6,15; 23:13-14; 27:15-16; 28:7; 30:17; 31:10-31.

- Your friends—3:27-28; 11:13; 12:26; 17:9,14,17; 18:24; 19:11; 20:3; 22:11; 25:17; 27:9-10.

- People to avoid—15:18; 16:28; 18:1-2; 20:19; 22:24-25; 23:6-8; 25:19-20; 26:18-19,21.

- Your sexual purity—5:3,7-14; 6:25-26,30-35; 7:6-27.

- Your need for humility—3:7; 16:18; 18:12; 22:4; 25:27; 26:12; 27:2.

- Your work—6:6-9; 10:26; 15:19; 20:4; 21:25; 22:13; 24:30-34; 26:16.

- Your speech—10:19; 12:25; 16:24; 17:9,27; 18:8,13; 24:26; 25:11; 28:23; 29:5; 31:8-9.

- Your money—8:18,21; 10:4,22; 11:1,4,24-25; 13:11; 14:23,31; 19:17; 20:13,17; 21:5,17; 22:7,9,26-27; 23:21; 28:19,22,25,27.

———

Pearl of Wisdom: *Take it from me: Live wisely and save yourself a lot of grief!*

Recovery and Scripture

For those involved in recovery, these four biblical steps are key:

1. Become biblically literate. Biblical doctrine enables us to develop a realistic worldview, without which we are doomed to ineffectual living (Matthew 22:23-33; Romans 12:3; 2 Timothy 4:3-4). Doctrine can also protect us from false beliefs that can lead to destructive behavior (1 Timothy 4:1-6; 2 Timothy 2:18; Titus 1:11).

2. Understand humanity's sin nature. Recovery experts speak of getting rid of character defects. However, the entire old self is defective and depraved (2 Corinthians 4:4; Ephesians 4:18; Romans 1:18–3:20) and must be dealt with.

3. Recognize the three enemies of the Christian. They all have some bearing on human behavior.

   - the world (1 John 2:16)

   - the flesh (Galatians 5:20-21)

   - the devil, who would tempt us (1 Corinthians 7:5), deceive us (2 Corinthians 11:14), afflict us (2 Corinthians 12:7), and hinder us (1 Thessalonians 2:18)

4. Depend on the Holy Spirit. Self-control is the fruit of the Holy Spirit (Galatians 5:22). As we walk in the Spirit (verse 25), the fruit will grow in our lives.

Pearl of Wisdom: *If you want to experience true recovery, base your life on biblical principles.*

Prayer: Communicating with God

These are the key components of prayer:

Thanksgiving. In prayer we ought always to give thanks to God for everything we have (Ephesians 5:20; Colossians 3:15). We should "enter his gates with thanksgiving" (Psalm 100:4).

Praise. Like David, we should always have praise for God on our lips (Psalm 34:1). We should praise God in the depths of our heart (Psalm 103:1-5,20-22) and "continually offer up a sacrifice of praise" (Hebrews 13:15).

Worship. Like the psalmist of old, we should bow down in worship before the Lord our Maker (Psalm 95:6). We are to "worship him who made heaven and earth, the sea and the springs of water" (Revelation 14:7). We should worship Him "with reverence and awe" (Hebrews 12:28) and worship Him alone (Exodus 20:3-5; Deuteronomy 5:7).

Confession. Confession in prayer is wise, for "whoever conceals his transgressions will not prosper, but he who confesses and forsakes them will obtain mercy" (Proverbs 28:13). We are promised that "if we confess our sins, he is faithful and just to forgive us our sins and to cleanse us from all unrighteousness" (1 John 1:9).

Requests. Certainly we can also go to God for specific requests. The apostle Paul wrote, "Do not be anxious about anything, but in everything by prayer and supplication with thanksgiving let your requests be made known to God. And the peace of God, which surpasses all understanding, will guard your hearts and your minds in Christ Jesus" (Philippians 4:6-7).

Pearl of Wisdom: *What an awesome privilege we have to pray to the God of the universe!*

Praying Effectively

H ere are some key Scriptural insights about effective prayer:

- All our prayers are subject to the sovereign will of God (1 John 5:14).

- We should pray continually, not occasionally (1 Thessalonians 5:17).

- Sin is a hindrance to answered prayer (Psalm 66:18).

- Living righteously is a great benefit to prayer being answered (Proverbs 15:29).

- The Lord's Prayer in Matthew 6:9-13 is a good model. It includes praise (verse 9), personal requests (verses 11-13), and an affirmation of God's will (verse 10).

- We should be persistent. "Keep on asking and it will be given; keep on seeking and you will find; keep on knocking and the door will be opened" (Matthew 7:7-8, literal translation).

- We should pray with faith in God and believe that we have received what we have asked for. If our request is within God's will, He will grant it (Mark 11:22-24).

- We pray in Jesus' name (John 14:13-14). He is the bridge between humanity and God.

- Unanswered prayer calls for trust. God has a reason for the delay. You can count on it.

Pearl of Wisdom: *Our spiritual health will be in direct proportion to the amount of time we spend in prayer.*

The Many Benefits of Prayer

Prayer is not just a dry religious exercise. Rather, it involves communicating with the living God of the universe (Matthew 7:7-8). The Bible reveals many benefits of prayer. It can...

- reveal God's purposes for us (Ephesians 1:18-19)

- help us understand God's will for our lives (Colossians 1:9-12)

- increase our love for other people, which is vital in the church (1 Thessalonians 3:10-13)

- encourage and strengthen us—especially in tough times (2 Thessalonians 2:16-17)

- keep us from harm and pain (1 Chronicles 4:10)

- facilitate deliverance from our troubles (Psalm 34:15-22)

- protect us from lies and falsehood (Proverbs 30:7-9)

- lead to provision of our daily food (Matthew 6:11)

- help us to live righteously, in obedience to God (1 Thessalonians 5:23)

- lead to physical healing (James 5:14-15)

The whole of Scripture affirms that the Father readily responds to the needs of His children—even more so than an earthly father responds to the needs of his children (Matthew 7:9-11). Just as an earthly father finds delight in satisfying the needs of his children, so our heavenly Father delights to give us the things we need.

Pearl of Wisdom: *In view of the incredible benefits of prayer, it's a no-brainer that we should pray without ceasing (1 Thessalonians 5:17)!*

God Delights to Answer Our Prayers

Luke 11:5-10 records Jesus' parable about prayer in which a person knocked on a friend's door at midnight in need of three loaves of bread. The one inside answered, "Do not bother me; the door is now shut, and my children are with me in bed. I cannot get up and give you anything" (verse 7).

This was likely a one-room house—meaning that if the person got up in the night, he would probably wake the children. Though friendship alone was not enough to move the person inside to arise and provide bread, the boldness expressed in knocking on the door at midnight and his continued persistence in doing so (verse 8) was enough to finally yield the desired result. Some thus conclude that Jesus is implying that God is resistant to answering our prayers. But that is not the intent of His words.

The whole of Scripture affirms that the Father responds to the needs of His children as readily as an earthly father responds to the needs of his children (Matthew 7:9-11). The primary purpose of the parable was to teach Christ's followers that we need to be persistent in prayer precisely because God longs to give good gifts to us.

We see this persistence stressed in verses 9 and 10, which follow the parable. Jesus instructed, "Ask and it will be given to you." The word *ask* is a present tense, indicating continuous action: "Keep on asking."

Pearl of Wisdom: *Let's be persistent in prayer!*

Short Prayers

J esus taught His followers, "When you pray, do not heap up empty phrases as the Gentiles do, for they think that they will be heard for their many words" (Matthew 6:7). These words of Jesus were aimed straight at the Pharisees. These individuals always prayed conspicuously—making a public show of their prayers. They also made their prayers excessively long, a practice picked up from the pagans, who engaged in endless repetition and incantation.

We see such endless babbling in 1 Kings 18:26: They "called upon the name of Baal from morning until noon, saying, 'O Baal, answer us!' But there was no voice, and no one answered." The Pharisees evidently believed that endless repetition of specific requests endeared the petitioner to God, so God would be obligated to answer. They used prayer as a lengthy formula or technique to manipulate God into action.

The point of Jesus' instruction is not that we should necessarily utter short prayers before God (see Matthew 26:44; Luke 6:12; 18:1)—although short prayers are just fine if that is all you have time for or if that meets your particular need at the moment. The point of Jesus' instruction is that we should not engage in endless babbling, repeating the same request over and over again within the confines of a single prayer, as if that would force God's hand to answer.

Pearl of Wisdom: *Long and short prayers are perfectly acceptable. But don't engage in endless repetition of specific requests, thinking that will force God to act.*

Angels and Answered Prayer

God most often answers our prayers directly, without any involvement of the angels (for example, see 1 Chronicles 5:20; 1 Peter 3:12). Nevertheless, God may sometimes choose to use angels when He answers our prayers.

In Acts 12, we find Peter wrongfully imprisoned. While Peter was in prison, "prayer for him was made to God by the church." Suddenly an angel appeared in Peter's prison cell and helped him escape. It's fascinating to ponder that when we pray to God, He may occasionally dispatch an angel to take care of our request.

This brings me to issue a warning. Just as angels are sometimes dispatched by God to take care of our requests, so demons—fallen angels—sometimes seek to thwart the angels God uses in the process of answering a particular prayer. This happened when the prophet Daniel prayed. According to Daniel 10:13, God sent an angel to take care of Daniel's prayer request, but he was detained by a more powerful fallen angel. Only when the archangel Michael showed up to render aid was the lesser angel freed to carry out his task.

Pearl of Wisdom: *We must be fervent in our prayers and trust that God is listening even when His answer seems to be delayed.*

Contemplative Prayer

Perhaps the most significant manifestation of mysticism in the modern church is contemplative prayer, which draws very heavily from Buddhism and Hinduism. In this form of mystical prayer, one becomes deeply quiet, empties the mind (as in Eastern meditation), falls into an altered state of consciousness, and goes into his center, where he supposedly merges with the divine. Rational thought is completely transcended.

To help induce a mystical state, proponents use breathing exercises (much like Taoists) and a mantra (or sacred word, such as *ma-ra-na-tha*), which is repeated over and over again to aid in deep meditation. Apparently, Christian mystics believe that simply because they utilize a Christian-sounding mantra makes the practice itself a Christian practice—a dangerously wrong assumption.

Amazingly, many who practice contemplative prayer cite Psalm 62:5 in support of the practice: "For God alone, O my soul, wait in silence, for my hope is from him." However, this verse has nothing to do with prayer or contemplation but rather simply encourages believers to wait without distraction in eager expectation for God to act in deliverance.

Another verse taken out of context is Psalm 46:10 (KJV): "Be still, and know that I am God." The act of being still, however, has nothing to do with prayer or contemplation, but simply indicates that one should slow down and trust God rather than get in a fuss over tough circumstances.

Pearl of Wisdom: *Beware of the Scripture-twisting of Christian mystics!*

A Top-Down Perspective

As we close our journey together, I want to exhort you to maintain a top-down perspective. By this I mean that during our earthly pilgrimage toward the heavenly country (Hebrews 11:16), we ought to view everything—including our lives, our circumstances, our trials, and our relationships—from God's eternal vantage point. Let's keep God and His glorious kingdom constantly before our eyes (Matthew 6:33), allowing our daily anxieties, emotional hurts, and earthly tragedies to fall on the shoulders of our divine Shepherd (Psalm 23; John 10).

In Colossians 3:1-2 we read, "If then you have been raised with Christ, seek the things that are above, where Christ is, seated at the right hand of God. Set your minds on things that are above, not on things that are on earth." The original Greek of this passage is intense: "Diligently, actively, single-mindedly pursue the things above." This speaks of focused attention. The verse also utilizes a present tense: "Perpetually keep on seeking the things above…Make it an ongoing process." Strong words! I love this passage, and I can tell you that putting the passage into practice on a daily basis can make all the difference in our level of spiritual joy as we sojourn on this temporal earth.

Pearl of Wisdom: *Setting our minds on things above makes good sense. After all, the earth is temporal. It is passing away. Heaven is eternal, and it lasts forever. Why set our minds on that which is fleeting (earth)?*

Postscript: Keep On Learning

Here we are on the final day of our one-year journey together. I'd like to close by challenging you to keep on learning about the Bible, Christian doctrine, Christian ethics, and more. Be a perpetual student, and remember...

- Knowledge is better than wealth (Ecclesiastes 7:12). What a motivation to keep learning!

- The Holy Spirit, our teacher (John 14:26), illumines us so we understand spiritual things.

- Knowledge can lead to pride (1 Corinthians 8:1). Remain humble in your studies.

- Pray for wisdom (James 1:5). Solomon did, and God answered (1 Kings 4:29)!

- Learn from life's circumstances (see Psalm 78:1-8). This will help make you wise. When you make a mistake, learn a lesson.

- Learn more and more about God and His ways (see Deuteronomy 4:10; 11:19; Proverbs 22:6) by spending time daily in God's Word. As you study, also pray, "Open my eyes that I may see wonderful things in your law" (Psalm 119:18 NIV).

- Let your life be changed by what you learn. Be a doer of the Word and not just a hearer (James 1:22).

Pearl of Wisdom: *The more you learn, the better decisions you will make throughout life!*

Index by Day

Choose from this sampling of my books, which go into much greater detail on some of the topics we have covered in this book.

Angels Among Us

Answering the Objections of Atheists, Agnostics, and Skeptics

Commonly Misunderstood Bible Verses

The Complete Guide to Bible Translations

Conviction Without Compromise (with Norman Geisler)

Find It Quick Handbook on Cults and New Religions

Northern Storm Rising

The Truth Behind Ghosts, Mediums, and Psychic Phenomena

What Does the Bible Say About...?

The Wonder of Heaven